IN MY OWN WORDS

SEÁN QUINN

Published by
Red Stripe Press
an imprint of
Orpen Press
Upper Floor, Unit B3
Hume Centre
Hume Avenue
Park West Industrial Estate
Dublin 12
Ireland

email: info@orpenpress.com

www.redstripepress.com

© Seán Quinn, 2023

Paperback ISBN 978-1-78605-191-2
ePub ISBN 978-1-78605-192-9

Printed in the EU

IN MY OWN WORDS

To all the staff who worked so loyally for the Quinn Group over many years, in particular those who died during their time with the company

Contents

Acknowledgements

In writing this book, I feel that a weight has been lifted off my shoulders, as I finally share my story. It has also helped me to examine again my own life, and here I want to acknowledge the many people who have played a part in my story.

I believe that I have lived a good life, from humble beginnings, and in the early years, while our sporting achievements may not have been huge nationally, I felt that they were significant locally. I was also captain of the team that transformed the Fermanagh–Cavan border region between 1973 and 2000, with developing quarries, factories, windfarms, hotels, offices, and houses covering more than 2,000 acres, which has multiplied the population in our area. I would like to record my appreciation to the approximately ninety farmers who sold me land in order to develop our businesses over nearly four decades.

Even though the businesses are gone from our ownership, no new investment has been made since 2008, and all profits are leaving the country, the businesses that are there are still of a very high quality and will last the test of time for future employment. Two of the factories – the glass factory and autoclave block factory, which we built in the 1990s – are still the only ones of their kind on the island of Ireland. I give my sincere thanks to all of our customers in the various businesses we owned over the forty-year period for their loyal and unstinting support, especially to those who assisted us financially, hoping that justice would be done. I also have taken great heart from the many letters and contacts of support I've had from those customers over the past twelve years.

Despite what has happened and what been said over the past fifteen years, I don't think there are or were many people who believed that a glass factory, a cement factory, and a 220-bedroom hotel along the Cavan–Fermanagh border would be successful at a time when the banks needed €50 billion and the Irish government needed €100 billion just to survive during the crash.

Of course, it all comes back to the thousands of staff who helped me to achieve what may have appeared unachievable. Many have passed away over the years, and I particularly think of those who died while employed by the company. I believe that the team we put together in the 1970s, 1980s and 1990s was an outstanding team, and I don't believe that any group of employees in the country ever had such an significant effect on a rural part of Ireland as the group I was captain of. I would like to thank each and every one of them for playing their part in that achievement.

I would like to thank my wife, Patricia, and my children, Colette, Ciara, Seán Jnr, Aoife, and Brenda, for their loyalty and support over the years. I'd like to thank my brother, Peter, and my two sisters, Miriam and Bernadette, for their love and support for more than seventy years; in particular, thank you to Bernadette for all her work in helping to write the book. A special word of thanks to members of the family, both young and not so young, who were able to read my writing over the past twelve months and make sense of what I was trying to say. They had great patience with me, and they know who they are.

I would like to express a sincere word of gratitude to Christopher McGettigan, a man who was born and reared in West Belfast, and who is now representing myself and a number of other people who have had dealings with the Quinn/Mannok management team. Money is not Chris's motivation in life; justice is. He is one in a million, and I will be forever indebted to him.

Another special word of thanks to Eileen O'Brien, Michael Brennan, and Gerry Kelly from Red Stripe Press for their invaluable assistance and support in helping a lad who knew nothing about writing a book to get this book edited and published.

I would like to pay a particular word of thanks to all the people who have supported me so diligently and steadfastly over the past twelve or fifteen years, on a weekly, and sometimes daily, basis. Their friendship and encouragement will never be forgotten.

xi

"A lie doesn't become the truth, wrong doesn't become right, and evil doesn't become good, just because it is accepted by a majority."

– Booker T. Washington, 1856–1915; advisor to a number of US presidents and a leader in the African-American community. The first Black person on a US postage stamp

Preface

I am writing this book to give an overview of my life, particularly the past twenty years, as I believe I owe it to my family, my staff, my community, and all those who have supported me over those difficult years.

I feel that a weight has been lifted off my shoulders after finishing this book, as I was never used to this type of work. I found it harder than managing the Quinn businesses from 1973, when we had eight people working for us, to 2010, when we had eight thousand working for us. I had thirty-eight years of learning experience along the way for that; I only had one year to learn how to write a book, and this was made more difficult when the Gardaí confiscated a lot of information I had gathered up to assist me.

The relief that I am currently feeling is caused by the fact that for the past fifteen years, even those who were sympathetic towards me and my family didn't have our side of the story. Now, in my seventies, I can fade into the shadows, knowing that my story is out there.

There are many who have supported me 100 per cent, even in recent years, and there are many who have had doubts about me in recent years, based on the narrative that has been portrayed, and I can understand that. The third group, who believe, or want to believe, everything negative that has been said against me, I'm not attempting to change their view, but maybe those who have been criticised and ridiculed for supporting me might get some comfort that their view all along was close to the mark.

It never crossed my mind to write a book, in all the years my name has been in the public domain, until the continuous character assassination of me and my family over the past fifteen years, culminating in the disgraceful insinuations made by some that I may have had some involvement in Kevin Lunney's abduction. It would have been remiss of me, now in my seventies, not to put the record straight.

The narrative that has been commonly used is that I was to blame for everything, and I certainly accept that I am not blameless. While there are hundreds of points made in this book that differ from the narrative over the past fifteen years, I would ask the reader to consider if the course of justice might have been perverted by a number of companies and individuals.

My view was well known all along. What I stated in court to Judge Dunne was what I felt – that the Quinn Group was put into receivership to cover up a bigger issue: the share support that was provided by Anglo to cover up the CFD losses. They didn't want me or anyone else to tell the truth, and they didn't want our main case to be heard. I felt then and I feel now that the Irish people deserve to know the truth about what happened in relation to the CFDs, and about the attempted cover-up.

Minutes before I was taken to prison, I told journalists: "The whole thing is a charade. ... Anglo took all of my money, they took my companies, they took my reputation and they put me in jail. Yet that have proved nothing, they haven't proved that this money is owed, they haven't proved they had a right to put in a receiver, they haven't proved that they loaned any money to the assets in Russia, Ukraine, or India." Even now, eleven years later, I am still of the belief that my statements to Judge Dunne and to the journalists were accurate.

What I can say is that from when I founded my business in April 1973 to the day I was ousted as chairman in April 2010, I never lied to or misled a Garda, solicitor, auditor, banker, board member, or any of the thousands of staff who worked for me during that period. Nor did I ever ask anyone to lie on my behalf. Furthermore, I did not have any hand, act, or part in Kevin Lunney's abduction, either arranging or paying for it. As I stated publicly at the time, it was a barbaric act to perpetrate on a man travelling home from work.

Cast of Characters

Seán Quinn (born 3 September 1946)
Patricia Quinn (born 7 November 1952); *Married 12 October 1974*

Family

My parents: Hugh (born 5 May 1902) and Mary Quinn (born 4 April 1913); married on 16 January 1935
My brother Peter (born 1943); *married Mary Clarke, 1972*
His son, my nephew Petey (born 13 April 1977)
My sister Miriam (born 1945); *married Tom McMahon, 1972*
My sister Bernadette (Bernie) (born 1949); *married Brian Maguire, 1974*

Our children

Colette, Ciara, Seán Junior, Aoife and Brenda

Quinn Group executives

John Lee, *Quinn Group Operations Director, began working in the company in 1973, and was my right-hand man for decades*
Con Dolan, *Quinn Group's first accountant*

David Mackey, *Chief executive from 1989 to 1999*

Liam McCaffrey, *Chief executive from 1999 until the appointment of the share receiver*

Dara O'Reilly, *Finance director from 2002 until the appointment of the share receiver*

Kevin Lunney, *Head of property investments*

National relevant figures

Seán FitzPatrick, *Chairman of Anglo Irish Bank*

David Drumm, *Chief executive of Anglo Irish Bank*

Michael O'Sullivan, *the Anglo Irish manager in charge of our account*

Brian Cowen, *Taoiseach 2008–2011*

Ray O'Rourke, *international businessman*

Paul Gallagher, *Attorney General of Ireland during the banking crisis of 2007–2011, the barrister who defended Anglo Irish against my numerous legal actions from 2011 to 2019, and Attorney General again from 2020 to 2022*

Kevin Cardiff, *Head of Ireland's Department of Finance*

Ann Nolan, *Senior executive, Department of Finance*

John Hurley, *Governor, Central Bank of Ireland*

Patrick Neary, *Regulator, Central Bank of Ireland (later succeeded by Matthew Elderfield)*

Matthew Elderfield, *Regulator, Central Bank of Ireland 2010–2013. Recruited from Bermuda but formerly of the United Kingdom's Financial Services Authority*

Pat Brady, *Responsible for regulation of Quinn Insurance Limited in the Office of the Financial Regulator*

Moore Stephens, *international financial advisors*

PriceWaterhouseCoopers (PwC), *Quinn Group's auditor*

Eversheds Solicitors, *Quinn family solicitors*

Michael Ryan, *Quinn family solicitor*

Mason, Hayes and Curran, *Quinn family solicitors*

Ernst and Young (EY), *Anglo Irish Bank's auditors, and now auditors of Mannok*

Alan Dukes, *New public interest chairman of Anglo Irish Bank from December 2008 (former leader of Fine Gael)*

Mike Aynsley, *New chief executive of Anglo Irish Bank (recruited from Australia)*

Richard Woodhouse, *Head of Asset Management, Anglo Irish Bank*

John Bowe, *Head of Capital Markets, Anglo Irish Bank*

Murdoch McKillop, *Consultant for Quinn Group's international banks*

Kieran Wallace, *From KPMG; receiver appointed for both Anglo Irish Bank and Quinn Group*

McCann Fitzgerald, *Anglo Irish Bank's lead solicitors against the Quinn family*

1

On 3 September 1946, a baby boy was born at home in Gortmullen to Mary and Hugh Quinn. According to the local midwife, I weighed more than 11 lbs, but my mother believed that I was only 10 lbs. So even my arrival divided opinion: something that has dogged me on many occasions in the intervening 76 years.

Both my parents came from farming families in County Fermanagh, from neighbouring farms in the townlands of Gortaree and Gortmullen, about a mile from the border with the Irish republic. Both families were small by Irish standards. I had only two aunts, one on each side of the family, and both of them lived within half a mile of us.

Neither my father nor my two grandfathers went to school for too long. Thankfully there was not much paperwork for farmers in those days. My father, Hugh Quinn, was born at home in Gortmullen in 1902, the son of Peter and Maria Quinn. They had farmed there for generations. My father had one sister, Cissie, who died in 1951, and my mother had one sister, Eileen, who died in 1989. I never had an uncle. Mum was very clever at school and her teacher wanted her to go to secondary level but she didn't want to leave home.

My parents married in Teemore Catholic Church on 16 January 1935. Dad was 33, but Mum was only 22, so more than a decade younger than him. Legend has it that my father was caught drinking poitín (Irish moonshine) with his prospective father-in-law Arthur just before the wedding, and they were both fined for doing so. Home-brewing liquor was unlawful in the border counties, but very common at the time.

I was the third of Hugh and Mary's four children: my brother, Peter (born on 22 November 1943), my sister Miriam (born 25 March 1945), me, and my younger sister, Bernadette (born 24 February 1949). My memories of my very early years are non-existent. Reputedly I was independent, active and a bit wild as a toddler. My teachers later described me as likeable, but hard to manage.

Home was a single-storey, three-roomed thatched farmhouse along the main Derrylin–Ballyconnell road, and known simply as "Quinns of Mountain Road". The house was a well-known landmark, even then, because in front of it was a long stone bridge, about 500 yards long. It was on that bridge that my father sat on a Sunday evening, and many passers-by – on their way to Ballyconnell for a drink, or to go to the Star ballroom, or to buy (or smuggle) cigarettes or tobacco – would stop for a chat. The primary means of travel was, of course, by bicycle, and an excuse for a rest was welcome. There were only three or four cars locally – owned by the local priest, rector and headmaster, and a taxi, or hackney car as it was called in those days.

We often used the road outside our home as our playground as children. My first memories are of playing on that road, and two occasions in particular stand out. Once, aged three or four, I ran out in front of the rector's car and he was forced to crash, while on another occasion, Ted Maguire, a local businessman, managed to avoid hitting me. Somewhat shaken, he reported the incident to my mother. She was really appreciative of Ted, but not so much of me! Ted was a sand and gravel merchant, who was later killed when a slip of gravel engulfed him. I, coincidentally, became involved in a similar sand and gravel business in later life.

In the early 1950s, many Irish farmers made only £1 a week profit. My father did better than that; in the early days he owned 23 acres of land, where he raised his dairy cows. The land had been in Quinn family hands for several generations, at least as far back as the Famine of the 1840s.

In 1950 Dad bought a second, 75-acre farm, three times bigger than the one he inherited, five miles from our home, outside Ballyconnell, across the border in the Republic of Ireland. He paid £2,000 for it – none of it borrowed. Not many farmers had that kind of cash in those days. It is easily seen how thrifty and hardworking my parents were and how they increased their wealth gradually over the years, saving every penny possible. They certainly were not big spenders and while both of them took a drink, they seldom did so. They kept one sow and raised the pigs for sale, sometimes killing one for food, although Dad didn't eat pork. They reared their own fowl also so their protein intake was practically free to them.

Our lifestyle started to improve once they had bought the second farm. In the late 1950s my parents lived temporarily in a byre (cowshed) while our old, thatched farmhouse was rebuilt. The new house was two storeys, with a slate roof and several more bedrooms. It didn't have a bathroom, or even an indoor toilet: my parents simply did not feel the need for such luxuries. Everyone washed in a tin bath in front of the fire every Saturday night. Lighting was initially by a tilly oil lamp and later by gas. Only in the mid-1960s did the house get electricity and an indoor loo.

Before buying the second farm my father had ten to twelve dairy cows. After the purchase of Cranaghan he usually had more than 50 cattle. He and my mother milked the cows, reared pigs, kept hens and geese for Christmas, and grew their own potatoes, vegetables, rhubarb, blackcurrants, apples, and even cherries. On top of money for eggs and vegetables, my parents would get a monthly 'milk cheque' from the local creamery for the milk that the cows produced. My father worked hard, but he also supplemented his farming income with a bit of smuggling of cattle, pigs, flour, tea and sugar. Dry foodstuff was often rationed after the war and there was a lucrative business in smuggling.

The 'egg money' from our chickens paid for the few groceries that we needed, from a travelling shop that called on us weekly. My mother was always pleased if she had some change left over once she bought the tea, sugar, and other goods that couldn't be grown or made at home. The change paid for the tobacco for my father's pipe, and other items such as clothes, shoes and household items. However, no one ever went hungry, and no visitor ever left our house without at least a cup of tea, bread and jam. Many of our friends loved the homemade jams that Mam provided.

My father survived many heart attacks before he eventually succumbed to a fatal one in 1967. But throughout his life he continued to work very hard. It was manual work, but Dad was a tall, strong man. At a 'meitheal', where neighbouring farmers joined together for big jobs like reaping the corn, he was generally regarded as the strongest man there.

As children, we were all expected to help on the farm, and we did. We all learned to milk at six or seven years of age. With a little stool and milk pail, we each started with the quietest cow and worked our way up. The milk was then carried in buckets to the nearby river to cool before being put into milk tanks, ready to be collected by the milkman in his lorry the following morning. Each of us learned to attend to a sow giving birth, and to break the teeth of the piglets immediately. We helped with the hay and the turf, and all the other activities on the farm.

I never really liked farm work, but I enjoyed the easy, relaxed companionship between my father and the various workmen who helped him. I joined them whenever I could. It was better than school! Mum valued education and she wouldn't let me miss a day. But Dad had given up school at the age of seven, after the death of his own father, and he and his mother had farmed the 23 acres ever since. School had been completely unimportant to him, and life was his great educator. I learned much from him, and I inherited his philosophy. He was not a very healthy man, but he kept his health problems to himself and never shared them with us. Neither did Mum, except when they were too serious to be hidden.

I was an adventurous rascal as a child. Once, when I was about four years old, I disappeared, and my parents went out looking for me. They eventually arrived at Pa Donohoe's house, a mile or so up the mountain, to ask if he had seen me. Pa was an elderly man, living on his own, who had played in goal for Teemore for many years. Pa told them, "There's a cub in here; that must be him." They came into the kitchen and found me eating an egg at Pa's table; I had certainly made myself at home. In later years I bought Pa's farm, which contained valuable reserves of sand and gravel; the remainder I planted with trees.

When I bought the farm, people were a lot more honourable than they are today, and I made a simple arrangement with the then-owner, Pa's nephew Pearse Martin. We had a handwritten note, I paid him £35,000, and we started using his land immediately, before the transaction was effective.

My first memory of roguish behaviour was when, at age six or seven, I kicked a stone at a window at home and it landed beside the live-in workman shaving at a basin. In later years, my sister Miriam and I robbed our neighbour Eddie Kells' orchard when we thought he was away. When we saw him at his door with his shotgun, Miriam jumped over a hedge. I jumped on top of her and I could have broken her back. Thankfully, she was fine, and it wasn't our last visit to Kells' orchard! Other little misdemeanours followed, but I enjoyed my childhood. I was the envy of my siblings with the godparents that I had. Margaret Curry, a cousin of my father's who lived in America, sent me dollars every year for my birthday, and my mother saved them all until I eventually went to Chicago in 1966 to visit our relatives. My godfather was my first cousin Joe, who spoiled us all with treats, and he gave me my first half-crown, and later my first 10-shilling note. When Joe was older and unable to look after his farm the way he would like, I was delighted to be able to help him by providing fodder and fencing his land. When I was growing up, Joe was my hero, and in Joe's final years, I was his hero.

I joined Peter and Miriam at Garvary primary school, about two miles from home, at the age of four. My first teacher was a lovely lady, Miss Mary B. Cassidy, and she was a patient, gentle and hardworking teacher who cycled to school daily with her lunch and flask of tea, as was customary. She taught me reading, writing, numbers and singing. Though I was naturally left-handed, she insisted that I wrote with my right hand, as I believe was common practice at the time. Anyone who has ever seen my current scrawl would know that it was a mistake, and I am now an ambidextrous scribbler, who has neither the ability nor patience to write properly.

Miss Cassidy, a devout Catholic, prepared us conscientiously for our first confession and first communion, with the assistance of Father Galligan, one of the few car owners in the parish. He was very fond of children, and we were allowed an extra few minutes of breaktime when he came into school. My second teacher was Mrs Elizabeth Dunne, who was also a devoted teacher. While I caused her much trouble with mischief, she always stated that I was one of her favourite pupils. In my lifetime I have had dealings with two ladies with the name Elizabeth Dunne: the first one was my teacher, of whom I was very fond, and the second one was the judge who sent me to jail for contempt of court in 2012. I wasn't quite as fond of her!

I enjoyed my schooldays because there was great camaraderie. There was no bullying, and we were all innocent country children. A gang of us walked to school together: pupils from Gortahurk to Umera, all down the same road. In the summer months we went to school in our bare feet, which was only a problem when we wanted to play football. I found most of the subjects very boring at school, but I enjoyed the craic with all my neighbours and fellow pupils. I formed good relationships with several other boys in my classroom and we all amused each other and the class. Our teacher, while stern, accepted that she would never make an academic success out of me, like my brother, Peter, but as long as we didn't disrupt her class and did odd jobs for her, she tolerated us. We had to clean the toilets, which were wooden structures with holes in the ground. It was convenient for her to have a few lads who were willing to carry water and wash them out occasionally. I preferred that to studying.

Although I was seen as very good at mental arithmetic, I found painting and other such subjects boring and useless. I was reminded of a story of the time, one summer's day, when we were given sheets of paper and told to paint a picture of the men cutting the hay. I duly painted half the page blue for the sky, and the other half green for the meadow. I then turned over the page and folded my arms. Mrs Dunne came over to examine my master-piece. "Where are the men?" she asked. "They went home because the grass is not ready for saving, it's still green", I replied. She couldn't control her smile.

Shortly afterwards, there was a knock at the classroom door. My father respectfully asked, "Could I have Seán out for the afternoon to help with the hay?"

"You certainly can, Hugh, and I hope he does more for you than he is doing for me", Mrs Dunne replied. I was free for that day!

My favourite days at school were the ones when our teacher took us to Johnny Curry's field to play football. I was big and strong, and I loved the opportunity to practise my skills. We also played skittles in the school yard, and I once hit a fellow pupil, Hughie Brough, with a skittle and marked him below the eye, where a slight scar remains to this day. He and I talked about the incident recently following his brother Jack's funeral. Jack was my first employee; a very loyal and hardworking man he was!

For a time, the travelling shop would only buy our large eggs, and I used to take the small ones up to Ballyconnell to sell to Magee's or Crowe's grocers' shops, getting the same price for the small eggs as my mother received for the big ones in the North. I remember one day Billy O'Neill, the Garda sergeant in Ballyconnell at the time, stopped me on my bicycle and asked me what I had in the bag. I'm not sure what I told him, but he just smiled and told me to go ahead. At the time, some goods were cheaper in the North and others were cheaper in the South. Sixty years later, nothing has changed, and while the majority of goods are cheaper in the North, Northern people from the border area go south for their petrol and diesel.

In my early twenties, I got to know Billy very well, as he and the local chemist, Eugene O'Reilly, asked me and Brian McCaffrey to play football for Ballyconnell, which was against the rules, as it was a different county. We wouldn't get away with it today! When our wonderful local priest, Father Dessie O'Dowd, found out, he gave Eugene a fairly sharp rebuke for encouraging players to break the rules. I remember going with Brian to a match in Bailieborough, and Brian saying to me "I'll go for everything around midfield, and I'll either catch it or break it to you, and you stick it over the bar." Brian had a real stormer of a game on the day, and the arrangement worked. As the game progressed, I felt I needed more of the action and went into midfield to catch a ball, but someone landed on my chest and knocked me to the ground. Brian pulled me up off the ground, and said "What the fuck did I tell you on the way up?" Billy, Eugene, Brian, and Fr O'Dowd were all real gentlemen, and sadly they have all passed away since.

My childhood was very carefree, and we had good neighbours, friends, and relations. I created a social life with them, and my Gaelic football colleagues. As a family we played dominoes, snakes and ladders, and cards. We used to play for pennies, or maybe 3d if we had it. Twenty-five was our favourite card game, and both my parents were very good at it. There were local men who went on their céilí most nights, and there were houses that were known as céilí-ing houses. My father never went céilí-ing as ours was a céilí-ing house, and every night we received 'céilí-ers'. They joined in our games, and they taught us a lot too. We had one man, Phil Bannon, who called every night for some time. He always went home early, but others stayed 'till bedtime': anytime between 9 p.m. and midnight. They all shared in every aspect of our lives. Phil and I used to go fishing in a lake about five miles away. One evening, we caught a few fish. When we arrived home, we were to divide the catch, but there was none – they had obviously slipped off the bicycle carrier. What a disappointment!

One principle ingrained in all of us was that we should never fall out with a neighbour. 'Love thy neighbour' was always practised. County Fermanagh has always been one of the most mixed of the six counties of Northern Ireland. The population is split almost exactly 50 per cent Roman Catholic and 50 per cent Protestant. At the time, Catholics got less than 20 per cent of the council houses available, but in our area cross-community relationships were good and the Protestant and Catholic communities generally got on with each other. Both Protestant and Catholic neighbours were treated with respect – a principle that I have tried to maintain throughout my life.

My parents were devout Catholics, and religious people. They did not impose their religion on others, but they lived religiously themselves. Mum liked to go on pilgrimage to Knock, Ireland's Marian shrine, as often as possible, and she went to Lourdes a few times. We all went to Sunday Mass and evening devotions in the horse and trap, but the latter was mostly a social outing, with neighbours walking together and chatting, while some cycled or went by horse and trap. As children, we didn't have many social outings apart from going to school and the chapel. We were taught to have great respect for priests, and many of them visited our home regularly and still do.

We didn't say the Rosary every night, apart from during Lent or the months of May or November. It often ended with laughter, too often for my mother's liking, but Dad usually joined in the laughter. Inevitably, someone made a mistake, missed a Hail Mary or something, which only seemed funny when we were supposed to be praying. If a céilí-er came in after we had started, he or she knelt and joined us.

Travelling the three miles to a weekday Mass in Teemore was generally unheard of, but Sunday Mass or holy days of obligation were never missed. In those faraway days, the congregation didn't receive Holy Communion weekly: normally only once a month, on the Sunday after going to confession. Dad always stayed at the back of the chapel. As children, we thought that was because he wanted to chat to the neighbours, but later we realised that as an epileptic, he didn't want to be too far up the aisle. One Sunday, he came from the back of the church to receive Holy Communion, but the priest had turned back to face the altar and didn't see him, much to his embarrassment, so Dad returned to his seat. The next morning, Monday, he cycled to Mass at 8.30 a.m., which was generally unheard of for him, because he had to receive communion.

In the 1950s and 1960s there was a Mission every four years or so, with visiting priests speaking, and one night, while my mother and siblings were at the Mission, my father and I stayed at home to do the milking. After the milking was complete, a neighbour named Benny McCaffrey arrived for a chat with my father. At the time, we were building our new house and it didn't have an internal stairwell yet, so my father used a builder's ladder to show Benny the house's upper floor. After they had gone up I removed the ladder so they couldn't get back down, and when my father started shouting at me to bring the ladder back I became a bit scared and I hid, for fear of what my father would do to me when he caught me. He and Benny had to stay upstairs until my mother came home. As it turned out, I got away with it, but I got a severe warning to never play the same trick again. Benny, to his credit, tried to help me out, saying that he had three boys at home who would have done the very same thing. One of his sons was Brian, whom I referred to earlier, and was probably the best midfielder that Teemore ever produced.

* * * *

At the age of eleven, my mother and my teacher assumed that I would do the transfer test and proceed to a grammar school, as Peter and Miriam had. I had other ideas. On the day of the examination, dressed in my new blue suit and short trousers, I was sent off to school as usual, but I hid in the whin (gorse) bushes, in a place called Matthews Moor, missed the bus, and missed the test. My mother was not pleased, but I think my father didn't mind. He wanted a farmer to carry on the family tradition, and my future was already determined. A number of my age group left school at the age of eleven so our class became quite small but in our last few years at school Mrs Dunne continued following a more advanced curriculum and we left proficient in numbers and general knowledge. She allowed us to play extra football, and was always pleased with the respect we showed her. If we misbehaved, she slapped us and almost seemed relieved that we held out our hands with no resistance. Even though we didn't put two and two together at the time, she had a tremendous interest in Gaelic football. She was married to Jim Dunne, one of Teemore's favourite sons, who also played for Fermanagh, and who eventually became the Fermanagh county chairman.

Having left school, I learned quite a bit in the next few years, working alongside my father and a workman, Jim Coleman, who passed away recently, and who also played for Teemore Shamrocks. They were both very methodical, and I was always running errands for them. On one of my frequent visits to the border shop grocery and tobacconist for two ounces of tobacco for my father, the Northern Customs stopped me and confiscated it.

The Grand National was the only race my parents or anyone I knew put a bet on. Once, Dad and Jim sent me to Ballyconnell to put a bet on a horse called Mr What. They gave me a half-crown to put on 'each way'. It was an expression that meant nothing to me at the time, so I put the money on the horse without saying 'each way'. Luckily for me, the horse won, and my stupidity reaped rewards.

I had a few accidents in my early teens. I remember an annual 'Donkey Derby' competition at Clabby, a village northeast of Enniskillen, which was always advertised in the *Fermanagh Herald*. I decided to enter the derby one year. When I was about eleven I borrowed a donkey from Thomas Quinn, a first cousin of my father's, and practised riding it around the football field every evening. I was enthusiastically supported by our neighbours until I ended up in Enniskillen hospital with a broken arm. My arm was put in plaster of Paris, and to this day I can't fully straighten it, despite Mum's best efforts to force me to stretch it up the wall every night. That was the end of my dreams as a donkey derby winner on Teemore Hero.

We had a shed with two doors at home, and I could kick the ball over the shed from the yard at the back. When I was twelve, I used to challenge myself by kicking it over and running through the shed to catch it on the front side before it hit the ground. I practised that for a long time, but as I was growing taller I ended up hitting my head off the architrave and knocking myself out. As my parents had been telling me for a long time that what I was doing was dangerous, I was afraid to tell them. The end of another challenge!

At the end of the 1950s and in the early 1960s, there was an IRA bombing campaign in the border areas. The main targets were bridges, and the small one close to our house, known as Hanty's Bridge, was blown up and the road made impassable (coincidentally, when my sister Miriam began to teach in Armagh in the late 1960s, she met a man socially who claimed to have been involved in blowing up the bridges). Because of these attacks, many roads across the border were spiked. Cross-border travel became more and more difficult, and direct access from our home to Ballyconnell, the small town just across the border, or the second farm that my father owned only three miles away, was only possible by foot or bicycle.

Some years later, in the 1970s, a neighbour, Freddie Hicks, asked me if I had seen his creamery tanks. He had left them by the road for the milk to be taken away by the milk man, but when he came down in the evening to collect them, one was missing. We couldn't understand what had happened, as nobody had ever heard of anyone stealing a neighbour's milk tanks. Sometime later I heard on the news that an IRA bomb had exploded in a milk tank at Roslea, about 25 miles away, and the mystery of Freddie's tanks was solved.

As the early rumblings of the Troubles began, and life became less and less innocent, Gaelic football was my saviour. There was a very clear sectarian divide between soccer and Gaelic football in those days. A friend of mine, Raymond Flack, was once banned from playing Gaelic football by the GAA simply because he had once played soccer, which was deemed to be a Protestant sport. As a result, no soccer was ever played at Croke Park, the main Gaelic football stadium in Dublin, until 2007. In the 1960s there was very little rugby or soccer played in rural Ireland, or in Catholic parts of the six counties of Northern Ireland, only Gaelic football. Only once cars became commonplace from the 1970s onwards, allowing people to travel further for sports fixtures, did other sports start to flourish.

Gaelic football was, and still is, an entirely amateur sport: none of its players are paid. I played for Teemore Shamrocks for a decade and a half, and for County Fermanagh from my late teens to my late twenties. Our house was just across the road from the football field used by Teemore Shamrocks. Most of the footballers came into our house and collected the ball from under the stairs – there were no club rooms, and since our house was beside the field, whoever arrived first for practice collected the ball. The team members were at ease as if they were part of our family. Mum could go upstairs and watch the whole game from there if she was interested. The players parked on the street and down at the sheds, and sometimes they came in for a cup of tea after the game to discuss it and plan tactics for next game.

Teemore had a strong Gaelic football tradition, as the Shamrocks had won more senior championships than any other team in Fermanagh. My brother, Peter, had a great interest in football and from childhood he used to spend a lot of time kicking stones up in the field behind the house and doing a Michael O'Hehir, a national hero for his excellent commentaries, mainly on GAA, but also on other sports, including the Grand National. Peter once kicked a stone through the kitchen window as my father sat at the end of the table having his tea.

I was also very interested in football from an early age, and I played it practically every evening. I remember going to a match as a spectator, with my wellingtons on, at the age of thirteen or fourteen, and as Teemore didn't have the full complement of players I was asked to stay in goal. As I let in two soft goals early on, and another player who had arrived late took my place, my stint in goal only lasted 15 or 20 minutes. However, by the age of sixteen I was a permanent Teemore team member, and at the same time I was playing as a minor and we won two county minor championships. I also played for Fermanagh minors, and later for the county's under-21 and senior sides. Our footballing success with Fermanagh was limited, but I had the privilege of playing at Croke Park on two occasions, once in the Corn na Cisce cup, a tournament to commemorate the victims of Bloody Sunday 1920, who were shot in Croke Park. We were fortunate to beat Dublin in that particular game in 1972. Shortly afterwards that Dublin team was managed by the late great Kevin Heffernan, who has proven himself as a great footballer and manager, and who went on to lead Dublin to a number of All-Irelands. We lost our other game in Croke Park, which was against Tipperary, who were led by the famous hurler Babs Keating, who wasn't too shabby at football either!

I remember going to my first county final in Irvinestown in the early 1960s, to watch Devenish play Newtownbutler. I was in awe of the teams marching around the pitch, and the general excitement of the game. As Teemore had a weak team at that time, I never thought I would be playing and winning a senior championship on that same pitch in that same decade, and winning our first senior championship in 1969, after 35 years.

In my early twenties, I was playing football seven nights a week on the local pitch. The pitch only had a maximum of two inches of soil on it; in places there was no soil at all, and we were really running on gravel. My left knee became very sore and I had to stop playing for a couple of weeks. My mother took me to see the doctor, who sent me off for an x-ray. It was then decided that I should go to Musgrave Park Hospital in Belfast for an operation on my knee. I was prepared the evening before, with my leg shaved, and the next morning the surgeon came to my bedside to talk to me before he operated. He asked me to walk up and down a corridor, and having felt my knee, he advised me to go home and rest the knee for a month, as he said it was getting too much strain and I was still growing. He said that if it didn't heal after a month or so, I should come back, and he would operate. Thankfully, in the sixty years since I have never had any other problems with my left knee. Wasn't that great advice?

In 1964, while I was still a minor, we lost the intermediate championship final against Irvinestown. Our really big day came five years later in 1969, when we won the senior championship for the first time in 35 years. The previous Teemore win was in the 1930s. I still remember the team who started that match: James Cassidy, Jim Owens, Benny Fitzpatrick, Paddy Reilly, Peter Reilly, Pete Fitzpatrick, Gussie Fitzpatrick, Brian McCaffrey, Seán Reilly, Pat Fitzpatrick, Peter Quinn, Peter Hegarty, Brendan Reilly, Seán Quinn – and Benny Murphy.

Peter was the captain of Teemore, aged 25 at the time, and I was 22. After he picked up the cup he made a speech in Irish, which was very uncommon for a county final speech, especially in the North and never in a Fermanagh speech in those days. While I speak no Irish at all, Peter is fluent in it. I believe that speech, at the age of 25, prompted many to regard him as a potential administrator of some merit.

Unlike me, Peter had stayed on at school. Because he had passed his 11-plus he had moved on from Garvary, where I finished my schooldays, to St Michael's Grammar School in Enniskillen. He then did an Arts degree at Queen's University Belfast, followed by a business degree, and he won the Charlie Harvey Award for best student. Later on, he lectured in business management for a while, both at Queen's and Dublin Institute of Business Management, and then the University of Manchester, before working internationally delivering lectures and seminars on business and consultancy. As well as being a fine Gaelic football player, Peter later became a football manager and administrator, rising to become president of the GAA. In the meantime, Peter travelled home every weekend for a while after graduating from Queen's, and we continued to play together for Teemore. I was always considered to be the better player, but Peter didn't always agree with that. He has always boasted about scoring the winning point in the very important 1969 final! Indeed, he scored winning points in many games throughout his career.

* * * *

The 1960s launched Brendan Reilly's outstanding career. Brendan was the most outstanding player on our team and was one of the best pound-for-pound players I have ever seen. He went on to win nine senior championships, over four decades: the 1960s, 1970s, 1980s and 1990s. The first five senior championships were with Teemore, and without him we might not have won any of them. The other four were with Navan O'Mahony's as a wing half-back, at a time when Meath were usually winning All-Ireland senior championships. There weren't many boys approaching 40 years of age, then or now, who were able to play as a wing half-back and win senior championship matches in Meath. Brendan had three brothers – Seán, Paddy, and Gerry. They, together with the four Fitzpatrick brothers, Petie, Pat, Gussie, and Benny, were the backbone of the Teemore Shamrocks from the 1960s into the 1980s.

When Brendan started off working in Tara Mines in Navan, he always came home at weekends and holidays in the early 1970s. He used to help me out delivering sand and gravel, and after work one night we went with two loads of stones to a building site belonging to Pat McCorry in Kiltyclogher, County Leitrim. When we tipped up the stones, one of us moved his lorry out without letting the tipper down and we brought down some telegraph wires. We got out of town as quickly as we could, and thankfully we never heard another word about it. The dispute about who was responsible still rages on!

While playing for Teemore, I was lucky enough to be on the side that won senior championships in 1969, 1971, 1974 and 1975. During that period, it was customary in Fermanagh to nominate the captain of the county team for the following year from the winning championship team, and I was privileged to have that honour. I also later managed the Teemore team from 1980 to 1983 and we won a senior championship in 1983, with the assistance of Fr Maguire, who had moved to a different parish a few years earlier, but was still a hero in Teemore after managing the team to four senior championships between 1969 and 1975. When he returned to help me, we won the 1983 championship; without him that would not have happened, as many of the team had become a bit long in the tooth. I managed the team again for a further three years in the 1990s, with much less success.

Everyone on the team bonded very well, and we remained lifelong friends. We were helped by two wonderfully patient priests, who worked tirelessly for the club, and local young people generally: Father Dessie O'Dowd and Father John Maguire, both now deceased, but Teemore people are still very grateful to them. Playing Gaelic football was very character-building for me as a young man. Any arguments were forgotten as soon as the game was over. Once, when playing against Tempo, things became a bit fractious between myself and Tempo's Dessie Campbell. He was bigger and stronger than I was, and gave me a good thump, and I retaliated verbally. The following Sunday, both of us were playing for Fermanagh against Armagh, in Lisnaskea. A big fellow toppled me over and as I lay on the ground, Dessie came over and hit him. As he helped me to my feet, Dessie said "I'm not so bad after all, Quinn." That's the way it always was and hopefully always will be, as everybody plays sport for the same reason, and we remained great friends until his death some years ago.

In February 1971, Fermanagh were playing Roscommon at the opening of a new pitch. When I arrived home, my mother told me that our close neighbour, Philip Gilleece, had been killed in a car accident. He was just 17 and, as an apprentice mechanic, had recently bought his first car. It was difficult to come to terms with such a tragedy. In February 1972, I was captain of Fermanagh a week after Bloody Sunday, when 13 people had been shot by British paratroopers in Derry, as we played Meath in Kells. It was a very emotional and memorable day: we all wore black armbands in remembrance of those who had been killed. By then the Troubles were at their height, and I was moving on from farming. Just as Northern Ireland became more and more divided and dangerous, I was embarking on a new business, in sand and gravel.

2

The 1960s were a momentous decade for our family. The cattle on my father's second farm in Ballyconnell had to be checked and foddered daily. As access across the border was curtailed after the bridge bombings, I had to cycle there every evening. At the time, some of the roads in the South weren't tarred, so bicycle punctures were commonplace.

Farmers were becoming more progressive, and Dad wasn't going to be left behind. In the early 1960s he bought a David Brown tractor and a Ford car. Dad drove the tractor, but he never drove the car. Peter was the only one with a driving licence, and as he was away at Queen's University Belfast from 1961, and Miriam was at St Mary's teaching training college in Belfast during the week, the car was only driven at weekends. I continued to farm with my father, and I saw the positives and negatives of farming life. I realised that it was a difficult life, without much financial reward. Farmers may have been asset rich, but they were certainly cash poor, and I'm not sure much has changed.

I had many dangerous encounters on our farms. One time, when I was about sixteen, while we were making hay on the mountain meadows, I was driving the tractor close to a deep glen. I remember losing control of the tractor, and it hurtling down a 60-foot bank. My father, my brother, and a neighbour called Phil Bannon, who was working with us that day, didn't notice that I was missing for a minute or so. When I started walking towards them, they all came running to see where the tractor was. When they saw that it was at the bottom of the glen, there was anger at the loss of the tractor, but it was offset by the joy that I had had the presence of mind to jump off on the high side. In those days, there were no safety barriers, and everyone knew what the result would have been if I had stayed on the tractor, or jumped on the low side.

When Peter graduated from Queen's in 1964, Dad did not seem to be thrilled, but he secretly was. At my mother's insistence, he took us all out to a celebratory dinner in the Royal Hotel in Enniskillen. It was the first time we had ever had such a family occasion. He also bought Peter a car, and when Miriam qualified as a teacher two years later, he and our mother bought her a car as well. At last, I had a car for myself, as when Miriam and Peter went to London to work for a neighbour, Gerry Gallen, who owned pubs in London, for the summer holidays the two cars stayed behind. After teaching my two sisters how to drive, and seeing them pass their test first time, they had a good laugh at me when it took me two attempts to pass mine, in 1964.

My horizons broadened in the mid-1960s. In 1965 there was a great family occasion: a visit from our cousins in America. Back in the late 1920s, when my father was in his twenties, his cousin who lived at Curran outside Ballyconnell died. Her husband was also dying, possibly from tuberculosis, and Dad went to visit him. Their relatives and neighbours began to talk about what would become of their seven young children. A relative on their father's side was already looking after their youngest, a newborn baby girl, and offered to keep her. Dad said that he would take the next youngest little girl, named Mina, but he was advised to go home and ask his mother, as she was the one who would look after the toddler. Dad's only sister, Cissie, was much older than he was and was married by this time, and their mother was delighted to take the child on.

Dad went back to the McManus home on his bicycle the following night and took home one-year-old Mina, officially Philomena, to rear as part of our family. Mina later became like a big sister to us until she emigrated in 1952 to Chicago, where three of her uncles lived. A few years later we were delighted to hear that she had met a wonderful man, a post-war immigrant from Czechoslovakia, called Tony Braunstein, and was getting married.

Dad had never been out of Ireland, and he refused to go to Mina's wedding in 1959, and Mina was very disappointed. Nevertheless, we always kept in close contact, and we looked forward to her coming home to Ireland with her husband and three sons. In the summer of 1965, they all came to stay with us for a month at Gortmullen. At the time, I had barely heard of Czechoslovakia, and never thought that someday I would own the biggest hotel in the Czech Republic, as well as a major plastic sheet business 50 kilometres from its capital, Prague.

The new house that my parents had built in the 1950s did not have a bathroom or indoor toilet, so a toilet was built specially for the Yankee visitors. It was a very exciting few weeks for all of us, but especially for Dad. He was thrilled to have Mina home, and it nearly broke his heart to say goodbye to her again. Before they left, they invited me to go to Chicago to visit them. Obviously, my parents wouldn't go with me so in July 1966, aged 19, I went on a visit to Chicago, on my own. It was my first time at an airport, on a plane or to leave Ireland. I wasn't even nervous as I was so exhilarated about what lay ahead. At the time there was a romantic idea of America as a land of dreams.

Spending two weeks in Chicago was an amazing experience. I was astounded by its skyscrapers, traffic, and pace of life. One of Mina's uncles died while I was there, and the family was thrilled that I, an Irish cousin, could help to carry his coffin. Their ties with Ireland were still very strong, even though many of them had never come home since leaving decades earlier. I learned what it was like to be an emigrant, how they yearned for home, and how Irish they still felt. I visited many sights in the city and was treated like a lord. In hindsight it was very unusual for an Irish teenager to visit Chicago, or even America, on a holiday. I was questioned by strangers about Ireland, work conditions, about the political situation and many other aspects of life that I had never even considered. I left with promises to return and a whole new set of relations I never knew existed.

Dad was very pleased to see me return home from Chicago. He had been convinced that I would stay in the USA for good, as all the people he knew who went to America only came back home for holidays, if ever.

I don't think he spoke to my younger sister during the couple of weeks I was away, as she had made my travel arrangements and he convinced himself I wouldn't come back. However, Dad was thrilled to hear all about Mina's life in Chicago, and to see my photographs. Maybe that trip to the USA was what motivated me, later in life, to stay in Teemore and create local jobs so that people were not forced to emigrate. Even at that stage, I felt it was very sad that so many people emigrated to America, many of whom never returned; and maybe unconsciously that planted the seed for me to see if I could create something at home that would allow people to stay in their own area. It never crossed my mind, however, that the Quinn businesses would transform the community in the way they did.

* * * *

By 1966 it was clear that Peter wasn't going to be a farmer, so my father sold his second farm for £3,600 – only £1,600 more than he had paid for it 16 years earlier. It was after this that land values started increasing steeply. When I bought the land back in 1983 to build the Slieve Russell Hotel, I paid £183,000 for it, although that included an adjoining farm of an additional 50 acres.

On 18 December 1967, barely a year after the second farm was sold, Dad died very suddenly, of a massive heart attack. My two sisters were at a dance in Belturbet, County Cavan, that night. When I was passing the house to drop a neighbour home, I saw our next-door neighbour, Charlie Reilly, whom my mother had telephoned, getting out of his car and running in through our front door. I ran into the house myself, but before I could run upstairs Charlie appeared at the top of the stairs and asked me to ring the priest. I rang Father O'Dowd, who it turned out had already visited our house earlier that evening. He asked me, "How bad is your father?" After seeing the expression on Charlie's face, I replied "I think he's dead Father."

Dad's death was an awful shock, and it took us a long time to get over it. Mina was in bed ill in Chicago when she received the news by telephone, and she later told Bernie, "The day I wanted him most, he wasn't here, and the day he wanted me most, I wasn't there." She would have liked him at her wedding, and she would have liked to attend his funeral.

Dad had only just started taking his pension, having turned 65. At the time of his death, I was only 21 and Bernadette only 18. Peter and Bernadette were in Belfast at the time. Miriam was teaching locally and home at night and I was at home full-time with our mother. I was forced to think seriously about where I would go from here. It was ironic that when I reached pension age, I also received it from Northern Ireland, as the southern government wouldn't pay it to me.

At least I inherited a farm that was in good shape financially. My first step was to further modernise, and mechanise, it. In 1968 I bought a second tractor, along with a trailer and baler, and started doing work for local farmers. But much of our labour was still physical. Jack Brough, who had worked on the farm for years, had phenomenal physical strength, and helped so much. I preferred the tractor work. On one occasion, after we had finished baling hay for some great local characters called Hugh and Jemmy Lee, they rewarded me with mountain dew, better known as poitín! After taking too much I headed off, but instead of going home I ended up, in high spirits, at the Wonderland Ballroom in Bawnboy, a village south of the border. I was unwashed, unshaven, and still in work attire after a 12- or 14-hour day, but I danced away, probably tramping on girls' toes. I doubt that I would be allowed into a nightclub or dancehall in such a condition today.

Despite these pleasures, by the end of the 1960s I was disillusioned with farming. I was not getting much satisfaction out of it, either personally or financially, and I often admitted that I was the worst farmer in Europe. I looked around me and realised that there were three businesses in the Teemore/Derrylin area making good money as sand and gravel merchants. One night, when sitting in the kitchen with my two sisters, I told them that I was thinking of starting a sand and gravel business myself. "What will Mum say?" was their immediate response. While Dad had willed me the farm, it was only to become mine after Mum's death. "Sure, I'll have to ask her", I replied. In fairness, Mum was a shrewd woman, who always supported progress, and she gave me her blessing, with more conditions than you receive from An Bord Pleanála!

My father had sold off one field of the original farm to T. Curry and Sons, a local sand and gravel company that drew good quality produce from that field, so I knew that there was valuable raw material in the remaining fields, and I was convinced that if a company could make good money having bought the material and drawing it away, it was a potentially successful business for someone who had the material free on his own land.

I bought a Bedford lorry from Jim Dolan of Loughside Garage in Enniskillen in 1973 for £1,800. John Curry and I went to Enniskillen to collect the lorry and I drove it home myself, having never driven a lorry before, which was probably not very sensible, and John drove my car home. I could only afford £100 of a deposit, and the rest was on hire purchase. I had a lot of support from the community, who wanted me to succeed and transferred their business to me. In the late 1970s, the British government gave Northern Irish farmers big grants to build concrete roads. Many roads that were built were unnecessary, and seldom used. Farmers also got grants for new cattle sheds, which we also supplied materials for. At the time, there was plenty of business for all of us.

I pressed ahead quickly with my ambitious project. Leasing was popular in those early days, and much of my equipment was leased. I bought a Finlay washing plant from John McCaffrey (later in life, I became very friendly with John and his wife, Carmel, and I was delighted when John became a sales manager for my company). Our greatest relationship was formed in 1973 with Pat O'Donnell, who represented Volvo industrial machinery on the island of Ireland. Fifty years later, in the company I started in 1973, you will still see dozens of Pat's machines onsite in Derrylin – loading shovels, dumptrucks, and track machines. The quality and service that Pat provided was first-class for those 50 years.

Doing work for and supplying materials to the local farmers was exciting, and they couldn't have been more supportive. The raw material was good quality and I set up a washer and started supplying farmers with material, mainly for land drainage. It was an exciting time, and I never really feared it would be a failure.

Once I was up and running, Seamus Burke, a long-time friend, came to drive the first lorry. (I had driven Seamus on his wedding day, but, unfortunately, his wife, Breda, died tragically some years later.) John Curry was my first shovel driver, and in later years he progressed to driving a lorry.

Not long after starting out, in 1973, I had what turned out to be my biggest break to date. Another local man, John Lee, came to work for me. John made a huge contribution to my business, and he was my eyes and ears on many occasions over the next 38 years. John Lee is roughly the same age as me and he had left school aged 15, as I had. Like me, John Lee was no administrator, but he was always a brilliant operations man. One of my biggest regrets is that John was not appointed to the main board of the company, and that he continued to report to people who had joined 20 or more years after he did, and who lacked his knowledge of and commitment to the business, which was totally wrong. He had little education, but he had common sense. John Lee carried on working loyally at the Quinn Group, as my company later became, until the very end. John finally quit following the appointment of Paul O'Brien as CEO. He started his own business, and it is no surprise that he and his son are very successful. He deserves all the success he gets.

A few months after hiring John Lee, I asked Hughie Lunney, a lorry driver who had driven for another company, if he would work for me, but his response put me in my place: "You have no water to wash the gravel with." He was partly right. My rivals had to spend a lot of time and money taking their gravel to a water source for it to be washed, but I had dammed a stream that ran through the farm to create a small reservoir, so the water came to me instead, through a filter pond. The problem was that in hot weather the stream would often run dry. Embarrassingly, it took me a while to realise that if I dug a well my problems would be solved. In fairness, boring wells wasn't common in our area at the time, but we ended up getting all the water we needed. Hughie soon became one of my longest-serving drivers.

In the first year I started, 1973, a young sixteen-year-old called Bernard McKiernan also came to work for us, doing manual work around the washing plant. I warned him not to drive the loading shovel, as he had neither a licence nor experience, but while I was delivering a load locally one evening, the regular shovel driver, John Curry, allowed Bernard to drive, and Bernard reversed the shovel into two yellow cars parked on the site. One of them belonged to John Lee, and the other to Alfie Little, another lorry driver. Bernard had practically squished the two cars into one, and when I returned, he hid behind the washing plant's wall. I saw him peeking out from behind it, went over to him, and told him to forget about it. Bernard certainly didn't forget about it, and he is now in his fiftieth year working for the company. There has never been a more loyal man than Bernard. Every day that he goes to work, it hurts him to see how the company has been run down in recent years. Speaking to him recently, I asked him if he remembered what his wages were in 1973, and he told me it was £16 per week! That is now roughly the going rate per hour.

Apart from keeping basic farming accounts, I had no experience in financial matters, and I realised early on that I needed administrative staff to deal with the secretarial work. Thankfully, my mother, brother, and sisters gave me great assistance during the early years. My mother took phone calls and orders at first, and Bernie did the accounts in the evenings and weekends. Miriam called in every evening on her way home from school and helped in any way she could.

My brother, Peter, was also an excellent help to me in the early days, but as an international business consultant with his own family, and a committed GAA official, he didn't have much time to spend on my business. In the early days customers came to the house to pay their bills, and I handed the staff their wages on a Friday evening, but for the first year or two, you could count the staff on your two hands.

I bought a caravan as an office, and my first administrative employee was a young neighbour called Dell Reilly, who was waiting on admission to teacher training. I remember going for a weekend to Ballybunion, a seaside resort in County Kerry, with my lifelong friend Jim Owens, and when we came home on the Sunday evening, we found that the caravan had blown over in heavy wind. My mother and sisters were frantically gathering up invoices, statements and so on from the surrounding ground. Patricia McKiernan was my first full-time office staff member. She was a sister of Bernard, and just as conscientious. Later on, a qualified accountant, Con Dolan, joined us, and in his efficient way kept us all on the right path until he left to establish his own accountancy business, which is very successful. This was no surprise to me, as Con was an excellent accountant, as well as being a perfect gentleman.

I faced many cross-border obstacles in my early years of trading, as the border road between Derrylin and Ballyconnell was an 'unapproved route'; to get across the border we were officially supposed to drive to Ballyconnell via Swanlinbar, a village on the southern side, which added about 15 miles to the journey. Frequently I chanced the unapproved road, and I was fined constantly by Customs and Excise when I was caught. Sometimes I delivered loads of sand and gravel myself in the evenings, and a local man called Pee McKiernan, with whom I used to play cards, asked me if I would bring him for a drive sometime when I would be delivering a load. So, one evening Pee and I headed for Redhills, a small village outside Cavan town, with a load of drainage stone. There had been a shower shortly before we arrived at the farmer's house, and after we tipped up the load of stones, the lorry skidded on the wet grass. We needed the farmer's assistance to get moving again. Once we had unloaded and were ready to head home, the farmer offered me a ten-shilling tip, which I refused. "That Quinn man must be paying you too well. What sort of a bloke is he? I hear different stories about him", he told me. "Ah, he's all right at times, I suppose", I replied, and headed off. Pee, who was listening, laughed about the fact that I hadn't admitted who I was. He insisted that we visit his sister's pub in Belturbet on the way home, and he enjoyed telling the other patrons about his evening's experiences. At the time there was only a fraction of the traffic on the road as there is today, and thankfully the breathalysers weren't as frequent, which suited us that evening. People locally were very supportive and my name was becoming known, and they applauded a young man starting a new business. Many just gave me a chance and obviously if they were pleased with the product and service, they continued to deal with me.

* * * *

The early 1970s were busy years in my personal life, as well as my business one. Searching for love, I travelled far and wide throughout Ireland, and I found the love of my life in the Olympic Ballroom in Dublin in 1973. She was Patricia Quinn, from Tyrone in County Galway, who was working as a secretary in Dublin. As it turned out on the night, she thought that I was too old for her liking, as I was twenty-seven at the time, and she was twenty-one. She told me later that the only reason she allowed me to bring her home was that her friend had already got a lift home, and she was happy to have company on her way home, so the old man's offer was accepted!

Although Patricia's surname was the same as mine, she was no relation; Quinn is a common name in Ireland. On my many trips to Galway as I was courting Patricia, I met her wonderful family in Kilcolgan, a small village on the shores of Galway Bay, about ten miles south of Galway itself. Patricia's mother (whose name was Mary Quinn, the same as my own mother) was a resourceful widow, just like my mother, and she had reared a family of ten children on a small farm. I loved going to visit them, and I soon realised that the two Quinn families had much in common.

Our wedding was in Galway on 12 October 1974. I was the last of my siblings to get married. Having done a Bachelor of Education degree at St Mary's, Belfast, my younger sister, Bernadette, taught for two years in the Convent Grammar School in Strabane before coming to the new St Aidan's secondary school in Derrylin. The following year, in August 1974, she married Brian Maguire, a local farmer. She took early retirement from her post as vice-principal in 2005 because of our mother's failing health, and Brian's multiple sclerosis. Bernie and Brian had three sons (Enda, Liam and Ruairí) and three daughters (Orla, Noreen and Áine). Sadly, Enda died in 2009 from pancreatic cancer aged 33.

Miriam had married Tom McMahon, who was also teacher, two years earlier, in 1972. Miriam taught in a primary school, in County Armagh to begin with, and then in two local primary schools, Derrybrick and Drumanymore, both of which closed because of falling pupil numbers, and she then transferred to the new St Mary's primary school in Teemore that replaced them. Tom also ran a furniture and fishing tackle shop in Belturbet with his parents. Miriam retired early to help look after Tom's elderly parents and help run the furniture business. Miriam and Tom had three girls (Tonya, Edel and Yvonne) and two boys (Ciarán and Seamus).

My brother, Peter, had also married in 1972, to Mary Clarke, sharing my mother's maiden name but not related. Mary was a highly respected and appreciated hospital and later district nurse. They had five children: Oisín, Miriam, Peter, Claire and Niamh. They were all very academic but sadly Miriam was the victim of a very serious car accident in the second year of her medical degree course and never succeeded in finishing it. Peter Jnr worked in the property division of the company with Kevin Lunney, and was in a senior position in the division at the time it was taken over. Both Peter Senior and Mary have now retired. Most of my nieces and nephews worked in some part of the business at various stages of their careers.

I'm lucky that Patricia didn't abandon our marriage plans on the morning of the wedding, as I wasn't ideal husband material that day. The previous evening, I had gone to Patricia's house and had a few drinks with her family, before leaving to go back to my hotel in Galway. It was traditional in those days for the groom not to see his bride on the wedding day until they met in the church. When Patricia's brother John Joe dropped me off at the hotel there were a few of my friends there, already in high spirits, and I joined them for a drinking session which lasted until the early hours before I finally went to bed.

The next thing I knew was seeing my brother, Peter, my best man, standing at the end of my bed in a fuming rage. He had knocked on my door fruitlessly without response, so he had gone to reception to borrow a key to enter my room. "Are you not fucking getting married today? The wedding's in less than an hour!" he shouted. I struggled into the bathroom, but when I went to take my crumpled clothes out of my suitcase, I couldn't find the key, so the lock had to be broken. I arrived at the church in a dishevelled state, ten minutes late and just as Patricia's car was approaching. Her brothers were not very pleased when I passed them at the church's entrance. At any rate, the wedding went ahead, and we then honeymooned for three days in the Downhill Hotel in County Mayo, just to the north of Galway – which seemed like a long way to travel for us at the time. In spite of all the ups and downs since then, Patricia and I have been very happy together, and are looking forward to our fiftieth anniversary shortly.

As we didn't have any surplus money, Patricia moved in with me to the family home in Derrylin. My mother had her own bedsit, and we had the rest of the house. Patricia joined me in County Fermanagh at a very turbulent time politically. The Troubles hit the area badly in the early 1970s. The house I had grown up in was only one mile from the border with the Irish Republic. Until the end of the 1950s, this had hardly mattered: the border was unmarked on most roads, and there were certainly no checkpoints. But after the bridge bombings this had all changed. From 1969 onwards many crossings had checkpoints run by the RUC, the Irish Gardaí, the British Army, or Customs and Excise. I was sometimes pulled over by British soldiers, who must have wondered "Where is this Quinn fella getting all his money from?" I remember my sister Bernie and her husband, Brian, telling me that when their insurance broker called to collect their premium he asked them if they knew Seán Quinn. They said that they did, but they didn't mention the relationship. He went on to tell them some very interesting information, including the fact that I was getting money from Charlie Haughey. A lot of false information has been propagated about me between then and now!

As well as much hassle crossing the border, there were several brutal murders locally in the early 1970s. In September 1972 Emily and Thomas Bullock, a Protestant couple living close to the border, had been brutally shot at Aghalane. In December 1972 a young butcher called Louis Leonard had been savagely dismembered in his Derrylin butcher's shop, an atrocity that terrified the whole community. The brutality of the killing, and the sympathy everyone felt for his widow, Betty, and their young son, were always talked about locally. In April 1974, George Saunderson, the principal of the Earl of Erne primary school in Teemore, was shot dead and there was much fear of retaliation. Both my sisters were teaching in local schools at the time, and there were constant warnings to be careful, and in Miriam's case to vary her time and route going to school as she was crossing the border. Only ten days after Mr Saunderson's murder, Jim Murphy, a very popular local garage owner, was murdered in his garage and his body dumped close by. As he was a neighbour and friend, his barbaric killing shocked us all.

Thankfully, none of these traumatic deaths touched my workforce directly, and Protestant and Catholic drivers worked side-by-side and delivered to both sides of the community, which was the practice in other local companies also. However, socially we kept mainly to our own friends and always had to be careful of where we went. Because of my links to the GAA, some Protestants distrusted me, and one of them confided in me that they didn't "want this Quinn boy to get out of his box." I had very good relations with my Protestant customers and employees, trying not to take sides. I was a nationalist who believed in a united Ireland, but I did not support the ongoing violence, which cost thousands of lives. Most of my friends were Catholic, but not all; one of my closest friends, Bertie Fisher, was a Protestant.

Bertie was a rally driver, and once he came with me to the funeral of Tom McGurk, whose family was very involved in rallying, in Ballyjamesduff, a small town south of Cavan. The church was full of racing fans, many of whom wanted to shake Bertie's hand because they were fans of his driving skills and success. In the local pub it was the same, and I said, "Bertie, if you think I'm going to drive a Protestant celebrity around Catholic churches, you can think again." There was no bigotry in Bertie, or in his wife, Gladys, who many years later succeeded my wife, Patricia, as lady captain of the Slieve Russell Golf Club. Gladys became one of the most popular captains there.

As well as having close Protestant friends, I was friendly with Harry West, leader of the Ulster Unionist Party and a long-serving Member of the Northern Ireland Parliament, representing Fermanagh and South Tyrone. He and I formed a strong relationship, and we did almost all of his work for a number of years. Harry once asked me why I chose green lorries for my business. The reason was simple: green was the colour of the Teemore Shamrocks, and of County Fermanagh. Ironically, the Fermanagh colours were chosen, as many county colours were, to suit the dominant team of the county, which was the Teemore Shamrocks from the 1900s to the 1930s. I replied by asking Harry, "Why are the school buses orange?" Harry shook his head with a smile, and he remained a good customer. In the 1980s Harry and I were once talking about politics, and I told him that he was 'well got' (very popular) in the area. "I am surely, Seán", he replied. "Ye proved that with Bobby Sands" (Sands was the IRA hunger striker, who had unexpectedly defeated Harry by only 1,000 votes in a by-election for the Westminster seat of Fermanagh and South Tyrone in April 1981, prompted by the death of the sitting Nationalist MP Frank Maguire). I had trouble replying to that one. Bobby Sands had practically total Catholic support in the election in an attempt to prove to Margaret Thatcher that her policy of allowing hunger strikers to die was wrong and unacceptable. His funeral was among the biggest ever held in Ireland.

Despite my friendships with many Protestants, my mother's fear for my safety was always on the back of her mind in the mid-1970s. "Sure, they'll shoot you too. They're out to get young Catholic businesspeople", she warned. The Troubles meant that all successful young men, both Protestant and Catholic, were potential targets if either side wanted to show that no one was safe from retribution. I certainly received threats to my life. I was once at Blakes, a bar at Derrylin, on a Good Friday night (I was drinking north of the border as no bars were open in the South on Good Friday). A neighbour arrived and told me a message had come from the Gardaí that there was a threat to my life. When I left the pub and went back across the border, I met the Gardaí, who escorted me home. Thankfully, the threat appears to have been benign. I once received a model coffin, just two inches high, in the post, with an unsigned note saying "Rest in Peace". I was certainly not happy to get it, but it did not give me sleepless nights. Somehow, I never felt that my life was in real danger because I was a businessman providing employment to all sides of the community and not involved in anything sectarian. Maybe it was a weakness I had, thinking that if I was doing everything right, I'd be treated right. Despite my nationalist persuasion, and my devotion to the GAA, I was able to navigate safely through the Troubles. Protestant church ministers, like Rev. Ken Robinson and Bishop Clarke, and RUC officers called on me periodically to thank me for providing so much employment to both sides in the area, increasing staff and building harmony, and for keeping our vehicles so roadworthy. I was pleased recently, when out for a meal with my siblings and their spouses, to be approached by the Rev. Robinson and his wife, both of whom were genuinely glad to see me. We talked over his visits and our chats in the office and they wished me well in the future. It was a warm friendly meeting and I appreciated it.

There were some murders and bombings locally in the 1980s: one local young man had his legs blown off by a bomb when he jumped on his digger one morning. The worst atrocity of the lot in County Fermanagh was the Remembrance Day bombing in November 1987, in which eleven people were killed and 63 injured in Enniskillen. I did not know any of the victims, but everyone in Fermanagh, both Protestant and Catholic, was horrified. Like others I became a great admirer of Gordon Wilson, who held the hand of his daughter Marie as she died in the bombing, and who later found it in him to forgive the bombers and become a peace campaigner. From 1993 until his death in 1995, Wilson served in Seanad Éireann, having been nominated by the Taoiseach, Albert Reynolds – an unheard-of honour for an Ulster Protestant.

Despite these atrocities, from the 1970s until the end of the Troubles there was much less violence or disharmony in County Fermanagh than in most of the other six counties. The growth of local companies like mine, with mixed workforces, was later seen as one of the main reasons why relationships were so good, and why the area was relatively peaceful.

The main problem that my business faced in the early years was not death threats, but opposition from established businesses in sand and gravel. I had three major competitors locally: Curry's, Mitten's and McCaffrey's, who had about forty lorries between them. While there was tremendous competition between us, we always respected each other, and we remained very friendly. Sadly, too many of the men I competed with passed away too young, including Brian McCaffrey. Brian and I may have been competitors, but when he once lamented the scarcity of raw materials and offered to buy some from me, I gave him 20 acres of sandstone in Toneymore free of charge. At that stage, sand and gravel was a small part of our business, and we had no plans to use this land. Brian and his family had contributed a lot to the area long before I had started.

I soon gained a bigger and bigger share of the local sand and gravel market. What was the secret of my success? My family's deep roots in the borderlands, and my links to the GAA, undoubtedly helped. A big factor was being the younger brother of Peter Quinn, who was seen as a 'local colossus' and 'local boy done good'. Peter was a folk hero across Catholic Northern Ireland, and his fame in GAA circles helped my businesses no end. The fact that Peter was the first Teemore captain to lift the New York Cup for more than thirty years, and that I had played with Fermanagh and was well-known in GAA circles myself, helped to attract customers. Having two sisters working as teachers in the local parish contributed to my success as well. Added to this, we always felt that we were providing the best quality and service in the products we were providing.

Peter was very busy in the early 1970s, however, he introduced me to an accountant friend, Raymond Flack. Raymond stayed over in our house every year when he was auditing the company accounts. We were both passionate about the GAA and we would sometimes sit up all night, with Raymond smoking and drinking coffee while I enjoyed Bacardi and coke. It was not great for a young mother with small children, but Patricia found Raymond very interesting, and great company.

Once my name started to get very well known, I was invited by Bryan Gallagher, the principal of St Aidan's secondary school in Derrylin, to give a careers talk in the 1970s. I was no public speaker, and I had no idea that the point was to encourage the boys to work hard at school so they could get good jobs. I'm afraid that I failed Mr Gallagher completely by stressing that neither John Lee nor I had any academic qualifications. One boy asked, "What is this John Lee like?", and I answered, "He's like myself, not much education, but lots of common sense, and he's hardworking and honest." I almost suggested that education was a waste of time for young-sters in the local area, and neither John Lee nor I were ever invited to give a careers talk again.

* * * *

By 1976 I wanted to diversify into higher-value products, so I started to make blocks and ready-mix concrete. Unfortunately, the local sand and gravel was too soft and porous to make high-quality concrete with, so we had to use much more cement to meet the required standard, which made our products very expensive. Rather than buy lots of cement from others, I decided that I needed to buy a limestone quarry that would allow us to produce far superior concrete products. In 1978 I bought 56 acres of lime-stone land for quarrying north of the border, half a mile from our head office.

Starting my own limestone quarry was just as important as finding gravel on my father's farm. But I had to overcome a major stumbling block: my existing bank would only lend me £5,000. Again, my brother, Peter, who was now a financial advisor to many banks, came to my rescue. He intro-duced me to Bill Price, from Northern Bank, who agreed to take on our business account and increase our overdraft to £50,000. It has since been said by a journalist that I gathered up this money from neighbours and friends, but there's not a word of truth in that, nor is there a word of truth in a lot of things he wrote.

I began spreading my wings beyond the borderlands, and buying quarries in other parts of Ireland. In 1977, while spending a weekend with Patricia's family, I took a drive on the Saturday up to County Mayo, where I knew there was a lot of good sand and gravel. I met a man called Frank Harrington in his sandpit. I forget what I said I was doing up there, but I remember Frank asking me if I knew a man by the name of Quinn, who was delivering blocks and ready-mix cheaply around Carrick-on-Shannon, an area that Frank's company covered. I said that I knew of him, but didn't know much about him. Frank later found out who I was, and he has been one of my best and most loyal friends to this day.

Later that day I drove to another pit not far away, and I met Cyril Gibbons for the first time (Cyril was another real gentleman, whose funeral I attended recently). I complimented Cyril on the quality of his gravel. He said, "It's OK, but the best gravel around this part of the world is in Williamstown, County Galway." I had never heard of the place, but Cyril gave me directions to Williamstown, a small village just outside Dunmore. I drove straight there and met an affable man by the name of Matt Geraghty, who owned the quarry. In the following weeks I bought it for £110,000. That quarry turned out to be very successful for over a quarter of a century, until the share receiver closed it down in 2011.

One of the best decisions I ever made was devising a system to pay my staff on performance. From 1978 onwards my drivers' pay was based on how many deliveries they did, the distance they travelled, and the volume they delivered, not how many hours they worked. There was once a rumour that all my drivers drove in the middle of narrow country lanes, because if they scratched the paintwork they had to pay for repairs. There was no truth in that, but it is true that if the lorries they drove were off the road for repairs, they earned no money.

In the interests of a workable arrangement, and for the scheme to work properly, staff were paid significantly more for older lorries (for example, someone driving a ten-year-old lorry was paid about 25 per cent more than someone driving a one-year-old one), but everyone gained. Not only did we get more output from our staff, our lorries and machines needed less maintenance. There were few arguments, because staff could earn a lot more by working for me than by working for anyone else for a straight salary. Although there were four or five other quarries within 20 miles, I never had any difficulty recruiting good staff.

The fact that my drivers were practically working for themselves meant that there was a great atmosphere in the company. My workers once organised an abseiling fundraiser one Sunday to raise money for a multiple sclerosis charity, through Seán McCaffrey, one of the salesmen. Participants abseiled from the top of the cement factory; if I recall correctly, Colette, my eldest daughter, was the first to abseil down.

However, there was also a lot of devilment, and my staff often carried out mischief and practical jokes. While we were building our first cement factory in Teemore in the late 1970s, a local farmer and customer called Benny Reilly called on me to pay his bill, shortly before the Christmas break. As he stayed for a few drinks he was given a lift home, and he returned the following day to pick up his tractor. He couldn't see it at first, but eventually he spied it on top of a concrete structure, which was part of the new building, 60 foot high. He couldn't understand how it had got up there, until he realised that it had been lifted by crane. Benny vented his anger and told me that I wasn't capable of running a business when I allowed staff to do what they liked. Little did Benny know whose idea it was! However, when he and his tractor were reunited there were no bad feelings, and he enjoyed telling the story in the pub many times afterwards.

We all worked hard – 60 to 70 hours a week – and we had no unions. My staff were very loyal to me, and I tried to be loyal to them in return. I was in Williamstown one day when word came through that my most hard-working and gifted mechanic had been involved in a horrific car crash on his way home from work. John Kellegher loved driving fast, and when a car had driven out from a side road in front of him he'd been seriously injured. Some days later I took his parents to the Royal Victoria Hospital in Belfast to see him. It was so heart-breaking to learn of the extent of his injuries that I had to leave the ward – I felt weak. When I returned to John's bedside he told me, with great sadness, that he would never be able to work again. I promised him that whatever the extent of his injuries he would have a job as long as I had a business. In spite of being wheelchair-bound, I am proud to say that John is still employed there, more than 40 years later. He rings me regularly, expressing his regret at the way things have turned out at the company I founded.

* * * *

In the 1970s Patricia and I started a family, and by 1977 we had two children: Colette (born in 1975), and Ciara (born in 1976). In 1977 we left my childhood home in Derrylin and moved south of the border to Ballyconnell, where our three youngest were all born (Seán in 1979, Aoife in 1981, and Brenda in 1987). I have lived in Ballyconnell ever since 1977, though our house was rebuilt in 2006.

Apart from Gaelic football, family visits and days out, I didn't have time for many pastimes once the children started arriving. But we used to go to Mullaghmore often on a Saturday for deep sea fishing, which was always enjoyable. As a family we played board games at night, and I always enjoyed a game of cards, often in McBarron's pub in Ballyconnell, with Pee McKiernan and others. When a friend, Mickey Lee, invited me to a game of cards in Paddy Drumm's house in Derrylin on a Tuesday night about 25 years ago, it became a regular appointment. Over the past 25 years, I'd have missed fewer than 25 Tuesday nights – I enjoy it greatly. We had great fun over the years, but a few of the original crew, Paddy Drumm (who played club football), and Paddy Maguire and Paul Corrigan (who both played for club and county), have since passed away. We had a lot of common interests! The game continues to this day, and Paddy's brother, Gerry, is the current host. Sometimes around Christmas, he could produce a bottle with clear liquid, which makes us all very merry!

3

The early 1980s were a time of falling living standards in Ireland, as an economic depression hit very hard, national debt rocketed, and unemployment and emigration increased dramatically. Employment in the construction industry fell by over 25 per cent and interest rates were in the region of 18 to 20 per cent. In May 1986, 'Self Aid', a benefit concert in Dublin, took place to highlight the problem of chronic unemployment. The event helped to restore some national pride, but what people really needed was jobs, not music: nearly 250,000 people were unemployed in Ireland at the time, and taxation was as high as 60 per cent.

In the 1960s and 1970s, most locals, including our football team, either had to emigrate, or travel to Dublin, Belfast or to factories in Enniskillen or Lisnaskea. Now in the 1980s this exodus was no longer necessary. I remember locals talking about how proud they were to see hundreds of cars driving to our area to work in Quinn's, Mitten's, McCaffrey's and Curry's businesses. At the time, it never dawned on me that the Quinn Group would be able to create 200 jobs per year on average for 37 years. Thankfully the border counties were largely sheltered from this crisis, and there was huge growth within the Quinn Group. In the early 1980s we built our rooftile and prestress concrete factories in Derrylin, followed by our first cement factory. I couldn't get finance from the Irish banks because of wealthy influential objectors – Irish Cement (part of CRH) and Blue Circle, the only two cement companies on the island – so Val Flynn, a young man born in the

UK of Irish parents, who worked in finance and who soon became a special friend, arranged the necessary funds from British and European banks. I will always be grateful to Val for achieving the almost impossible at the time.

Our first cement factory was seen by many as 'a step too far', but it soon expanded beyond the northwest counties of Ireland and grew into a national provider. I had a lot of major support from John Maguire, a Fermanagh man, then living in Dublin. John was the chief executive of the Independent Concrete Manufacturing Association (ICMA), which had been born out of frustration with CRH and Blue Circle, the two dominant cement companies, who sold cement much cheaper to the large users than small, family-run concerns. John encouraged his members, who were mainly small users, to buy from us and we made a commitment to sell cement to our smaller customers at the same price as CRH and Blue Circle were selling to the bigger customers. We soon gained a significant market share as our cost structure was much lower than that of our competitors; we had a very loyal workforce who worked as a team and were paid mainly on performance.

Before we started selling cement, RTE suggested that CRH flew helicopters over the factory site and approached our banks to discourage them from financing us; they also approached the IDB (Industrial Development Board) in Northern Ireland and successfully managed to have our grant dramatically reduced. The grant reduction and getting no support from the Irish banks hurt us very badly at the time, but, thankfully, we worked our way through it. Our company was a real cross-border business, with about 50 per cent of its workforce coming from the North, and 50 per cent from the South.

During those years, I decided not to move our quarry operations outside the areas we were already in – Fermanagh and Galway – which would only annoy our cement customers by becoming competitors of theirs. Instead, I concentrated on building market share, and battling with my larger competitors. Some years later, when John Bruton, leader of Fine Gael from 1990 to 2001, was Taoiseach, and Michael Lowry was Minister for Enterprise and Employment, my expansion plans were unexpectedly blocked. A licence for a new gypsum mine in Glangevlin, County Cavan, right beside our company headquarters, was granted to Gypsum Industries, a giant British company, despite the fact that David Mackey, on Quinn Group's behalf, had submitted a professional, fully financed proposal to develop and operate a gypsum factory at the same site. He received a letter stating that the licence had been granted to British Gypsum. A sod has never been turned on the site since and the British Gypsum monopoly continues. Bruton was a Fine Gael TD for County Meath, beside the location of Ireland's only gypsum factory, and normally, politicians like to create competition and jobs, and to help local Irish businesses. In this case, that didn't happen.

I made some mistakes of my own along the way: when a rival, Lagan Cement, wanted to open a cement factory in Kinnegad, near Mullingar in County Westmeath, I committed one of my most regrettable and embarrassing deeds. I gave money to a protest group because I was angry at misinformation that Kevin Lagan had given some of my cement customers in Fermanagh. Later, a judge accused me of "acting in a cynical, calculated and unscrupulous fashion" to get commercial advantage over Lagan Cement. I should have known better, and simply wished Kevin Lagan the best of luck. It was the only time that I ever objected to anything, and I deservedly got plenty of ridicule for it. Companies like Blue Circle, CRH, and Irish Glass seemed to get less ridicule for their objections to and attempts to stop the progress of the Quinn Group, but there's no excuse for me lowering myself to that level.

The Troubles were still at their peak in the early 1980s, and one day an unfortunate soldier on foot patrol along the Mountain Road, very near my birthplace, went into 'Stand-up's field', which belonged to a local man, called John James Curry. As there were so many Currys in the area, this particular family were called 'Stand-ups'. The soldier went into the field to investigate a milk tank and was blown up as the milk tank was booby-trapped. In February 1985 the IRA had killed Jimmy Graham, a bus driver and part-time UDR soldier, on the street in Derrylin, as he was waiting in his bus to drive children to a swimming pool. In June 1981 the IRA had killed Jimmy's brother Ronnie when he was delivering coal about nine miles from

Derrylin, and in November 1981 another brother, Cecil, was killed by the IRA.

In 1987 the writer Colm Tóibín published *Walking Along the Border*, an account of the journey he took in the border region the previous year. During his travels, he interviewed me. Journalists have claimed that Colm Tóibín found Ballyconnell and Derrylin "depressed and depressing" in 1986, but "the area was lucky in one respect, however: it had Seán Quinn." Tóibín himself described me as a "dark, good-looking, gruff man in his late thirties, wearing an old grey pullover … He didn't act like the boss. And he certainly didn't look like a millionaire." Tóibín was partly right: although my businesses were very successful from 1973 until 2007, increasing profits by more than tenfold in every ten-year period, I never woke up one morning and suddenly realised that I was either a millionaire or good-looking. Every morning I would wake up and just see lots of problems ahead and concentrate on solutions. I never felt it was helpful to be satisfied with what was already achieved, and I don't believe that's what life is about. Surely if someone has a talent to create something – academically, in sport, or in business – I believe that there is an obligation on them to maximise their full potential, rather than being the hurler on the ditch. I am a huge admirer of all of the people who devote their time for years to training and developing children and youth in sport and other activities – it's tremendously unselfish and contributes greatly to the common good. I believe that sport is a very important ingredient in life, and gives tremendous satisfaction to those who play it, as well as the many who watch. Having won a senior championship in 1969, all members of the team and supporters wanted us to win more, and we did, we won four more. While never being close to being Fermanagh's best player, I was lucky to captain the county team for three years.

I still have a great interest in sport, and take great pleasure in watching and following people like Leona Maguire, who not only put Ireland on the map for ladies golf, but was the leading player and inspired her continent to win the Solheim Cup. While Gaelic football was and is my favourite sport, I have been in awe of thousands of men and women who have excelled in their various fields, and I am unable, or maybe afraid, to mention them by name, as there are so many, but I believe that if a certain young man from Kerry keeps fit for another five years, he may well be the greatest Gaelic footballer of all time. I believe that one of the greatest games I have seen in any sport was the 2022 Munster hurling final between Clare and Limerick. It was high quality, hell-for-leather from start to finish.

Apart from sport, people like Adi Roche, Fr Peter McVerry, and many others also devote huge amounts of time to help the less fortunate, and again society, as a whole, benefits. I hope that they get more satisfaction from the joy they bring others than any businessperson gets from their success, because they certainly contribute more and have a bigger impact on the general population. I always loved being part of a team and sharing satisfaction, whether it be in sport, business, or community affairs, and I always felt that people who don't contribute in some way to the greater good are selfish, and I've been reminded of a quote by the actor James Stewart in the movie *Shenandoah*, "If we don't try, we don't do. And if we don't do, why are we here on this earth?"

When questioned I told Tóibín in 1986 that I "didn't think it was prudent" to do any business with the British Army or RUC. He asked me about the Saturday morning I had been held up at a border checkpoint while en route to a meeting followed by the funeral of a neighbour in Teemore, Paddy McGovern. Although my name was all over the green lorries moving concrete and gravel materials around the locality, this particular soldier told me to wait at the side of the road for what seemed like forever, and he even went as far as letting the air out of my spare wheel and taking the air breather off the engine. After half an hour I had missed my meeting, and I began to fear I would be late for the funeral. When John Gilleece came along in a company van, I told the soldier that I had a funeral to get to, and that I'd collect my car later. When I went to open the door of the van, the soldier caught me by the right arm and swung me around, and my left hand and his face collided.

The RUC were called to arrest me, but when the police sergeant arrived it was clear that he assumed the altercation had been with one of my staff, not with me. He was visibly surprised to see me. He went into the army building, and when he came out about ten minutes later he asked me to go with him to make a statement, while one of his colleagues would drive my car to my office, less than a mile away. I told him that I needed to go to a funeral. The police sergeant replied "That's fine, I'll meet you at your office in an hour. If you purposely hit that soldier, I'll be arresting you and taking you to Castlereagh [a detention centre in Northern Ireland], but if it was accidental and you were falling over, that'll be a different matter."

I had run the risk of being arrested for the altercation, but in the end there were no repercussions. Local people told Colm Tóibín that I had won a lot of respect for that, but, in fact, I heard very little talk about it.

Around two years later I attended a dinner for businesspeople at Hillsborough Castle in Belfast, hosted by the Secretary of State for Northern Ireland, Tom King. I was seated at Tom King's table, and when the Secretary of State went round the room to greet his guests I was introduced as Seán Quinn. Tom King shook hands with me and walked on, but then something registered with him, and he came back and asked, "Are you the guy who hit the soldier?" I said that I didn't think there had been any hitting done. He smiled and walked on. Later, he seemed interested in talking to me and we had a drink together. The soldier incident was never mentioned again.

* * * *

In the late 1980s, it became obvious that the Teemore pitch was too small for modern-day football. It also had sand and gravel underneath the pitch. So I did a deal with the club, offering them a full-sized pitch with a viewing stand, flood lighting, and a training ground on land I donated. In return, I got to draw sand and gravel from the old pitch. Some time later, two former Garda officers approached me and asked me if I could sell them some land for a new pitch in Ballyconnell. Again, I was pleased to donate it, because Ballyconnell was another community that had always given me massive support. It was always my view that having two-way respect with the staff and community was imperative for the success of any business, but particularly in a business like ours that generated a lot of noise and dust.

Later the Teemore Shamrocks was very proud when one of their players, Barry Owens, won two All-Star awards. He was a true Teemore and Fermanagh stalwart, and it was wonderful that he was joined by a fellow Fermanagh man, Ederney's Marty McGrath, on one of these occasions, as he is also from a family of outstanding players. There was many a tussle between Teemore and Ederney football clubs when Marty's father and uncles played. I was particularly pleased that both of these All Stars worked in my companies.

Marty's uncle Father Seán McGrath worked as a missionary priest, and it was a privilege for us to hold a golf classic at the Slieve Russell to raise funds for his mission in the early 2000s. During Fr Seán's playing career, he was one of the finest players around at that time. I attended his funeral in Ederney recently.

One of the proudest days of my life in GAA terms was 1 April 1990, when my brother, Peter, was elected as the president of the GAA, while still in his forties – it was a job normally filled by much older men. It was a great achievement for a man from Fermanagh, which was considered a Cinderella county in footballing terms, and for the Teemore community. Everyone in Fermanagh was ecstatic. When Peter came home to the little hall in Teemore as the GAA's president-elect he was greeted by bonfires, band parades, and representatives from every GAA club in the county and beyond. During his final year, the annual GAA Congress was held in the Slieve Russell. It was ironic that from 1950 to 1964, when he was a boy, he would have helped me, my parents, and my sisters to farm the land that the hotel was built on. It was very special for him and all of the family, to bring Congress back to the land that had initially been bought for him in 1950.

Peter had by now given up his globetrotting to return to Enniskillen and set up his own independent financial advice company, Peter Quinn Consultants. He turned out to be an excellent GAA president, thanks to his financial background and his business acumen, and he devoted himself completely to the rebuilding of Croke Park. I was a very happy man in 1991 on the day that Peter opened the new pitch in Teemore. A few years later I was also delighted when my son, Seán Jnr, was selected for the Ulster Colleges team, playing at full forward – the position I had played in throughout my own footballing career. While neither Seán Jnr nor I were great footballers, any success we had has been overshadowed by our attempts to defend what we thought we owned, and our related spells in prison.

I don't know how I found the time to be so involved in the GAA, as I was always so busy expanding my businesses. From 1973 to 1989 our management was local, and pretty amateurish. I always ran the show with John Lee, the Quinn Group's general manager. But in 1989 I had another great break by recruiting David Mackey to the new role of chief executive. David pretty much ran the company at my side for the next decade.

David Mackey was only two years younger than I was. He had been born in Letterkenny, County Donegal, in January 1949, and most of his career had been in local government. He had been a deputy county manager in Tipperary, before becoming county manager of Cavan County Council.

When I first met David in the late 1980s he was just forty, and softly spoken. Our first meeting was at his request, to discuss planning infringements at some of my quarries. There were strict rules over how much land I could quarry, how deep the excavations could be, and even over when and where I should spray water to combat dust. "Welcome to Cavan", I told Mackey. He returned the favour by telling me how welcome we were as a local employer, but he soon cut to the chase: he would not allow me to carry on cutting corners on planning regulations. Mackey had been firm but fair, without talking down to me as if I was a naughty schoolboy.

I was very impressed by his straightforwardness and integrity. I went home and thought about what he had to say, and soon an idea came to me: why don't I recruit David Mackey as my chief executive, to make sure all my operations complied with planning, licensing, and health and safety rules – he could take over the full administration of the business. At our next meeting I asked him if he would consider making a career move. He politely refused, but at our next meeting after that, I mentioned it again. David said that he didn't want to change career, but he did ask me what salary I was thinking of. I said that I didn't know what he deserved, but that I'd be happy to pay him double his current salary. He said that he'd think about it for a while. We finally agreed terms, and David started working for me in 1989.

I can say with no hesitation that David Mackey was the best individual who ever worked for the Quinn Group. He made sure that we always did everything by the book. I was always probably too relaxed about regulation – I felt that all we had to do was to find a way to live with them more easily than our competitors, and I could always rely on David to ensure we complied with every regulation to the letter. David and I never questioned each other's judgement. In reality, he was as much my boss as I was his, and in ten years, I never overruled him.

I considered David to be the only workaholic I ever knowingly met. I will never forget the day that David mislaid his Filofax in Cambridge; it was the day we signed the contracts for the Crowne Plaza Hotel, and we were probably full of adrenaline. David's Filofax was his indispensable personal organiser, and the forerunner of the modern smartphone. When I told him not to worry as we could replace it for him, he responded, "I'd rather lose my arm than that Filofax." All of his methodical details were recorded in it, and David was very relieved when it was found, and he and his Filofax could be reunited. I'd later tease him occasionally when I would see the Filofax in his hand, asking which arm he would have sacrificed for it! We stayed in close touch after David left the company, and I spoke to him the very week before he died.

Until the 1990s we did not have a proper company board, but David set one up. He and our then-accountant, Brian Delaney, recruited a young accountant called Liam McCaffrey, who arrived from Coopers and Lybrand in 1990, aged 27. Both for good and ill, Liam was to play a key role in the events of the next 30 years.

David was also very involved in the planning and construction of our first glass factory in Derrylin, and arranged the purchase of the site to build our glass factory in England, along with our second cement plant in 1999, just over the border in County Cavan. Having opened our first cement factory in 1989, with a capacity of 450,000 tonnes of cement per annum, the second plant had a capacity for 1.4 million tonnes a year. In the ten years between the two openings, cement production had become much leaner and more efficient: our first cement factory employed 100 people (plus drivers), but our second factory employed the same number, even though it had three times the capacity.

When I was building the first cement factory, we bought millions of pounds worth of equipment from Fisher Engineering and I soon became particularly friendly with Bertie Fisher, a former racing driver. Bertie and I spent many an enjoyable night out.

I can remember Gerry Reilly and Peter Weller, two senior managers, and I finalising a deal with Bertie for the purchase of a preheater for our first cement factory. The preheater cost £400,000-plus, and we had bargained down to the last £5,000. Bertie wanted to split the £5,000, but someone, probably me, suggested that it would be more exciting to toss a coin to settle the final price. We agreed, and Peter Weller threw the coin. "Sorry Bertie, you lose." We shook hands on the deal. A few years later there was another debate in Ballyconnell that was settled by the toss of a coin. Again, Peter Weller, an Englishman, tossed the coin and declared the winner, but someone who was watching disputed the call. It was an Irish coin, so the tail was in fact the harp, but Peter thought that the harp should be considered as the head. Peter shook his head, and said "Fucking hell, Quinn owes Bertie Fisher £5,000." When I shared this news with Bertie, he laughed it off and we continued to strike many deals worth millions of pounds in the years that followed, as he supplied steel for all of the factories we built over the following years.

As the Group expanded its workforce the need for more housing locally became very evident. Our workforce embarked on a big building programme, engaging other experts as they saw necessary. A big residential development called Doon Heights was built in Ballyconnell, and the Slieve View development was built in Teemore. The families who lived in these new houses were invaluable to our workforce and the area generally, as more and more people built houses in the area, with the result that within a five-mile area, the population has probably trebled in the last thirty years.

The Irish construction boom from the mid-1990s onwards certainly boosted Quinn Group's profits, but prior to that, we had started to diversify, having bought our first pub in Dublin, the Cat and Cage, in 1984. By the early 1980s I was a frequent visitor to Dublin, mostly on business and to attend sporting events. I was always amazed by how difficult it was to get a drink – every pub in Dublin seemed to be constantly packed, with long queues at every bar. It struck me that the pub business could be very lucrative, because people paid for their drinks upfront, before owners had to pay the brewery that had supplied the beer. I said to myself, "This has to be a simple business, because they are charging a ransom for the beer, and they get paid for the beer before they pay the supplier."

More to the point, pub buildings did not suffer the heavy levels of depreciation common in manufacturing. A piece of quarry equipment may cost £100,000, and it will be almost worthless within a few years, while real estate seldom loses its value, provided some sensible maintenance is carried out, and it normally only grows in value from day one. I realised that it would be better to own the freehold of pubs and lease them out, rather than manage them directly. That way, if staff stole money from the till, they would be stealing someone else's money, not mine.

My first pub, the Cat and Cage in Drumcondra, was very near to Croke Park, and to a teacher training college, so it was well-located for thirsty drinkers. It cost me £640,000. £540,000 of that was borrowed from the Northern Bank, and it was, at the time, the most expensive pub ever sold in Dublin. But in the years that followed I found that we could buy pubs relatively cheaply, and would get a double-digit return on the investment. By the end of the 1980s we owned six pubs in Dublin. It has been said that I never bought pubs with car parks, because I was worried that a crackdown on drink-driving would hit pubs which relied on driving customers the hardest. There is no truth in that, but I certainly liked city centre pubs with a lot of pedestrian footfall.

In the 1990s we bought six hotels and more pubs, as well as the 100-year-old Iveagh Baths in Dublin, which we converted into the Iveagh Fitness Club. The baths were housed in a beautiful redbrick, sandstone and granite building, and had been built to serve as public baths and a wash-house for the poor of Dublin. By the time we bought it, however, people in Ireland were becoming very fitness conscious, and were happy to pay for the use of elaborate equipment and advice from qualified instructors. Membership quickly reached capacity.

By the 2000s we had eighteen pubs and hotels across Ireland. From 1984 to the late 1990s we received double-digit returns from them, but as the property boom took off in the 2000s, our returns reduced to single digits, and we started selling some of them to buy our first hotel outside of Ireland – the Crowne Plaza in Cambridge – which we bought for £11.25 million sterling. It was a wise investment: the Crowne Plaza made more money in its first year than all of our Dublin pubs put together. In the end it was sold on by the administrators of Quinn Direct for £38 million in 2013, well over three times what we had paid for it.

Buying the Crowne Plaza was an educational experience; I learned much about the arrogance and distain with which Irish businesspeople can be viewed by some sections of English society. When David and I went to see the vendor's solicitor in Cambridge to finalise the deal, I gave him a bank draft deposit of £5 million, and he quizzed us on where we would get the other £6.25 million from. Annoyed, I asked him "Are you really implying that we might not complete the deal, considering that you have a non-refundable deposit of £5 million, plus your hotel, if we don't finalise it? Who'd be the loser there?" He looked a bit sheepish at that and treated us with respect from then on. It just made me wonder at the time if some of these guys with degrees had much common sense. It reminded me of a phrase that my brother, Peter, had said to me years earlier: there's little correlation between education and common sense.

Before long I had bought another English hotel, the Holiday Inn in Nottingham. However, my most important hotel was much closer to home.

The Fermanagh–Cavan area had long been seen as a poor part of Ireland. But by the late 1980s there was plenty of employment, and people had money to spend at last. The local population was expanding with new housing developments. Going out was now on the agenda for most young people. I decided to spend £183,000 in 1983 to buy back the 75-acre farm in Cranaghan that my father had sold in the early 1960s for £3,600. It now had an additional 45 acres, which included an old Protestant rectory. At the time, the Troubles in the North were at their height, and I had already purchased a number of Protestant farms in the area, so I felt that there might be opposition to me acquiring the local Protestant rectory. I approached a man I knew by the name of Patsy Forbes, who could have been perceived by some to be a Protestant, although he was actually Catholic. In fact, legend has it that when his brother, Mickey John, was playing for Tyrone against Dublin's Brian Mullins, he announced to Mullins that he was "Mickey John Forbes, the hardest wee man in Ulster", to which Mullins answered, "I am Brian Mullins."

I asked Patsy to attend the auction in the Farnham Arms Hotel in Cavan, which he did, and the land didn't reach the reserve price at the auction. In the hours following the auction, Patsy bought the land for £183,000 on my behalf. It took a little time before it was known who had actually bought the land.

The reason I bought the land was to build a hotel and golf course. At first no one encouraged me in this ambitious pipedream, as they thought that it would turn out to be a 'white elephant' in the middle of nowhere. I was determined to make it one of the best resorts in Ireland! I felt that a small hotel would not work; it had to be a destination hotel attracting clientele from all over and equipped with a beauty salon, swimming pool, and a championship golf course. While the land and hotel have been taken from our family, I believe that there would be no hotel in Ballyconnell only for Patsy Forbes, and I would sincerely like to thank Pasty for his achievement in acquiring that land.

One day in the late 1980s, I met my brother-in-law Brian Maguire on a road by the site and stopped for a chat. As Brian was a farmer, he was always interested in talking about land, so I told him of my intentions, and we went to the site. His seven-year-old daughter Noreen, who is my goddaughter, was with him, and I lifted her onto a gate, pointed to the field, and told her "You'll have your wedding reception there one day." She went home wildly excited at the possibility, and years later she did indeed have her wedding reception in the Slieve Russell Hotel. Unfortunately, it had been taken from us at that stage.

The hotel cost us £14 million to build. Its construction started in 1989, after the cement factory was built and we had sufficient resources to fund the project. When it opened in 1990 it caused much excitement locally, and many people wanted to visit and look around. A story was told about an elderly couple who were so impressed that they decided to treat themselves to a cup of tea and a biscuit. When the waitress came to take the order, the man asked how much it would cost. They were a bit taken aback by the price. "I think we'll go home for our cup of tea", he said, and walked out. But despite its grandeur, the Slieve Russell has only ever been a four-star hotel. In the early days, there was a disco on a Saturday night, and local clubs and charities were given the disco free of charge once a month on Friday nights, to hold teenage discos to raise funds. Some of my own children attended the disco in those days, and it was always well-attended, particularly around Christmas time, when all the young people from the surrounding area, who had perhaps moved away to work or study, would meet there on several nights over the Christmas period.

The Slieve Russell is a huge building, and I wanted it to feel very Irish. A historic tomb, estimated to be 4,000 years old, known as the Giant's Grave, was moved from one of my quarry sites, and I had it re-erected in the Slieve Russell's landscaped grounds in 1994. The hotel's Kells Bar had a reproduction of the Book of Kells, and in the hotel lobby was a bronze statue of Emer, wife of Cuchulainn, the warrior champion of Ulster. The media claimed that it became known locally as the 'beyjesus hotel', as that was the common reaction when people saw its huge scale, in the middle of nowhere just south of the border, for the first time. My mother certainly loved it, and she and her friends sat in the Slieve Russell's foyer on many a Sunday afternoon, enjoying a drink, chatting to the patrons, and probably feeling like ladies of the manor.

The hotel was another boost to the local economy, and particularly to students who wanted summer holiday work. Although John Lee was employed by my manufacturing businesses, he knew most families in the area, and he helped with recruitment for the hotel, ensuring that members of local families were given suitable positions. There were summer and weekend jobs available in housekeeping, the bars, restaurants, the leisure centre, the kids' club, which was open in holiday time, and later on at the golf course and in the golf club, as well, of course, as many permanent full-time positions. When fully complete the Slieve Russell had 222 bedrooms, a helicopter hangar, an 18-hole championship golf course and a function room that could seat 1,200 people. Rather than just a business, I saw the Slieve Russell as the social centre of the Quinn Group, and we often offered staff and top customers free stays there over weekends and midweek, which inspired a lot of loyalty from both groups. Years later I took the same approach at the Belfry, the English golf resort that I bought in 2005.

The Slieve Russell's swimming pool was very successful, and hundreds of young people learned to swim there. My niece Miriam coached hundreds of swimmers there until she was seriously injured in a car accident, and my daughter Aoife became a great swimmer who represented the county in many competitions. But most impressive of all was the golf course. Its architect, the late Paddy Merrigan, was a very bright man, and he assured me at our first meeting that we had enough land to build a championship golf course. But as the plans developed, he came requesting more land to make it a true championship course. The neighbouring farmers were very obliging, and I managed to buy the extra acres but later on he came asking for even more land. Again, I succeeded in procuring it but when he came a third time looking for two more acres my patience was wearing thin, and I told him there was no more land being bought. When he took me out to show me why he needed it on the third hole, I knew he was right, and went to my neighbour Benny Maguire.

I met Benny at his house. He was very popular locally, but he wasn't afraid to call a spade a spade. When I told him that I wanted a piece of his land, he asked me "What are you going to do with all that land you've ploughed up there?" I told him I was going to make a golf course on it. He said, "You should be fucking shot for destroying all that good land", so I steered the conversation towards farming and we parted on good terms. Around two weeks later, when one of the children answered the doorbell, she told me Benny Maguire wanted to speak to me. He refused to come in, but told me to take whatever land I wanted and turned to walk away. When I asked him how much he wanted or how much land he was selling he said, "I know you'll treat me right", and walked on. I'm afraid they don't make men like Benny nowadays. My wife, Patricia, and Benny's wife, May, became close friends, and they always attended the Slieve Russell's annual dinner dance at Christmas. For many years I visited Benny at Christmas, giving him a company calendar and a bottle of brandy. Sometimes the brandy bottle was lighter when I was leaving! Sadly, both he and May have since passed away, God rest them both.

I've never been very keen on playing golf personally, and I've only played about twenty rounds in my life – very badly, I may add. Patricia and my son were much keener (and better!) than I was, and Seán Jnr had a handicap of only two or three for a while. Twins Leona and Lisa Maguire lived locally, and they spent many long hours on the golf course, honing their skills. The Maguires are a very talented, hardworking family, ably led by Granny Kathleen, who is still inspirational in her nineties. Declan, the twins' father, is a local school principal, who spent many hours coaching football and camogie teams with great success. It was no great surprise locally that Leona gained world renown for her outstanding performance in the Solheim Cup. Many Irish people have represented their county and their country, but few have represented their continent, especially with such distinction. I am delighted that it was on the golf course I built that they practised their skills.

Over the years I met many celebrities at the Slieve Russell. In 1991 the film *The Playboys* was filmed at nearby Redhills (the home of its scriptwriter, Shane Connaughton, who had earned an Oscar nomination for *My Left Foot*, and whom I knew well). Both the film's big stars stayed at the Slieve Russell: Albert Finney and Robin Wright, with her then boyfriend Sean Penn (the couple later married). Sean Penn had recently been divorced from Madonna, after a turbulent marriage. He told me much about Madonna, and on many an evening our daughter Ciara babysat Wright and Penn's baby daughter, Dylan.

One of my big heroes has been the country singer Johnny Cash; I always love watching the film of his performance to the inmates at San Quentin State Prison in California in 1969, which became an iconic album. I could watch forever his entrance into San Quentin with his accoutrements on his back, accompanied by his wife, June Carter. What excitement he generated! It was such a heartwarming performance and the inmates responded so enthusiastically. Since Judge Elizabeth Dunne put me in prison, I appreciate it even more. About the year 2000, I was delighted to meet Johnny when he played and stayed at the Slieve Russell, and I was flattered when he asked me "Are you the guy who owns this place?" I took the opportunity to speak to him for a short while, and could tell during our short exchange that he had lived a hard life. Many Irish bands and groups played at the Slieve Russell over the years and there were many sell-out concerts and performances. Ireland has, in my view, produced some of the best country and western singers in the world, and both myself and Patricia could listen to them all night. While I don't want to single any of them out, as there are so many, I remember one night at the Quarryman's Ball at Ashford Castle in Cong, Joe Dolan was playing and joined a group of us for a drink when the dancing had stopped. We all might have felt the next day that the drink lasted too long! When the craic was at its height, I said jokingly to Joe, "You'll play free of charge some night for me in the Slieve Russell", and Joe replied "Jesus, I will Seán, but Ben [his brother] is very expensive." He had my measure!

* * * *

As well as helping to expand the Group, David helped the local community to develop several other local projects, including the Teemore Business Park and the Ballyconnell Medical Centre. He had tremendous contacts, and of course those contacts would have known all about David's skills and knew that if he was involved in something it would be a success. A major development, in terms of the company, was a move into glass production.

Part of my interest in producing glass was my growing knowledge of plastic. In the late 1980s I read an article about plastics potentially being a bigger killer than cigarettes, because they are 100 per cent oil-based. The article explained that plastics can create cancer cells in the body and cause fertility problems, for both men and women, and I believe that this has been proven over the past thirty years. At the time the late George Bush Senior was American president, but as he was a shareholder in the oil company Halliburton he did little to hinder the production of oil-based products. I am surprised that there hasn't been more discussion of the plastics problems in the 30 years since then. Scientists have been advising of the impending problem of global warming, but there has been less attention paid to the dangers of plastics.

Once I read that article in the late 1980s, I started discouraging my children from drinking from plastic bottles. Soon another new idea was sown in my mind: to build Ireland's largest and soon to be only glass plant, as I saw glass as an inert product, with no health risks and 100 per cent recyclable.

In those days there was a glass monopoly in Ireland – the only production facility was the Irish Glass Bottle Company in Ringsend, near Dublin, owned by a company called Ardagh. My plan to open a rival plant in County Fermanagh was opposed by the British Glass Confederation, who said that it would lead to over-capacity and job losses. It was strange for a British glass confederation to oppose the opening of a new glass factory in Ireland. But despite their opposition we opened our first plant in Derrylin, with the capacity to produce 800 million bottles a year, in 1996. It soon employed 340 people, and after Ardagh's factory in Dublin closed in March 2002, our plant became the only glass factory on the island of Ireland, taking in all the used bottles from every hotel, pub and home in Ireland. All glass for recycling on the island now comes to the factory in Derrylin, which current Quinn management agreed to sell to a Spanish company. It and the Slieve Russell were the two local businesses I had the most pride in.

We then embarked on the construction of a new glass factory in Elton, near Chester, which opened in 2000. With the capacity to make 1.4 billion bottles a year, it was the first in Britain to have its own bottling lines, and continues to be Europe's highest quality glass factory. The only new glass factories to be built in Britain or Ireland over the past 80 years were built by the Quinn Group. The Elton plant encountered strong opposition. A well-known director of Irish Glass, Paul Coulson (who was also a director on the Fine Gael Board of Trustees), tried to have the Elton plant demolished once it was found to be 20 per cent larger than the approved plans. After some comings and goings between us and the local council, in the end it was given the official go-ahead. By 2011, Quinn Glass had a 28.5 per cent share of the UK's glass bottle market.

We also opened Ireland's second on-shore windfarm (the first having been built in County Mayo) in the 1990s, on the slopes of Slieve Rushen, the hill behind our head office in Derrylin. Ten small turbines, each of 0.5 megawatts, were built in 1994. In 2008 I replaced these turbines with eighteen much larger ones, each of 3 megawatts, generating 54 megawatts in total and selling electricity to the national grid. Following the administration of Quinn Insurance, the administrators, on behalf of the Irish government, sold the windfarm four years after I had built it, for approximately twice what it had cost to build. It also meant the end of a 35-year construction programme within the Quinn Group, as from 1973 to 2008 there was never a year that there wasn't at least one ongoing building project, but there has been none in the past fifteen years.

In 1994 we decided to apply for an insurance licence. While we had an excellent relationship with our broker, I had never been happy with the claims settlement process regarding our premises, equipment or vehicles, and we felt strongly that we could have settled a lot of claims ourselves for less than what the insurance company settled them for. For smaller claims, we often paid for the repair ourselves, as the hassle of making a claim, as well as increasing future premiums, was too much. We were effectively insuring ourselves. We realised that if we can do this for ourselves, we can do it for other people. By the mid-1990s, David and I had moved on from self-insurance to the idea of running our own insurance company to offer cover to others.

David moved quickly to meet the appropriate government officials throughout 1995 and by the end of the year we met all specified requirements and were granted a licence to commence trading in January 1996. Quinn Insurance Limited (QIL for short) started trading under the brand name Quinn Direct. "Mighty Quinn takes on giant killing role again with life insurance venture" reported the *Irish Times*, noting my "long history of taking on established interests".

From day one we tried to involve the policy holder in all claims; this worked really well with new staff but those who came from other companies were reluctant to change from the traditional practices.

Once again, an upstart from County Fermanagh was disrupting an established industry. Unusually, QIL was not a standalone company, like most insurance companies, but part of a wider group. And many of the people who worked at QIL came, like me, from a farming background.

Quinn Direct was consciously modelled on dealing directly with the customer, and minimising broker and legal costs, while keeping overheads down. This model allowed us to charge lower premiums. About 90 per cent of our motor insurance policies, and 70 per cent of our commercial policies, were sold directly. Overall about three-quarters of our business was private motor insurance, and we had a deliberate policy of taking on young drivers, whom some other insurers refused to insure at all. We soon had more young drivers on our books than any other Irish insurer, which turned out to be lucrative for us: although young men at the time commanded premiums eight times higher than older drivers, they only represented six times the risk.

Any new insurance company on the block always attracts its fair shares of fraudsters, who assume that it can be taken advantage of. To combat fraud, in the early 2000s we hired 600 regional claims managers (RCMs): 300 of them in Ireland, and 300 in the UK. Other insurance companies did not normally have any claims managers out on the road. Most of our RCMs were retired police officers.

Whenever anyone made a claim they would be visited by a claims manager, who would ask to see the vehicle that was being claimed for. This helped to eliminate fraud, and it also sped up the settlement of *bona fide* claims – a process that traditionally always went 'from Billy to Jack' with no one ever making a decision. Most of our RCMs formed pleasant working relationships with clients. The longer claims go on, the more expensive they are so fast-track settlements were very welcome; 85 to 90 per cent of claims were settled within a week, and very few claims ended up in the courts, where legal, medical and other professionals were costing more than the injured party would receive.

The RCMs soon saw off the fraudsters, and they were a key reason for QIL's success. They thoroughly investigated any claims in which there was a suspicion of fraud, and in some cases they found that claimants who appeared on crutches in court had in fact been playing football or dancing within hours of their court appearance. Most of the fraudsters soon transferred their business to other companies, which meant that our book improved dramatically following the introduction of the fast-track model.

It has sometimes been claimed that Quinn Direct refused to pay out on claims. This is certainly not true: we had very well-defined protocols in place; typically, our claimants were paid out much faster than any of our competitors, and often within 24 hours of an accident occurring. This reputation for not paying out on claims likely came from the fact that when we felt a claim was fraudulent, we investigated that claim thoroughly. I felt that honest claimants should not be penalised by paying premiums that were inflated by the dishonesty of others. Of course, our RCMs and all of us did make some mistakes, which made headlines and were sometimes disparaged in court, but the vast majority of our customers renewed their policies annually, and most were very pleased with the quick and efficient service they received. They tended to be particularly impressed at being kept informed of and involved in any payouts on their policy. Of course, anyone who was dissatisfied still had recourse to solicitors, but it soon became obvious that we faced fewer legal cases than any other insurer, and as a result our premiums could be made even cheaper. The company was very successful and became Ireland's second largest insurer in a very short space of time.

One of the early recruits to QIL was a young technical engineer called Kevin Lunney, who had been born and bred in Derrylin. Having started his career at Andersen Consulting (later known as Accenture), Kevin joined Quinn Direct in 1996, aged 28. He soon rose through the ranks of Quinn Direct, becoming its head of operations and then replacing Noel Curley as its chief executive. Along with Liam McCaffrey and Dara O'Reilly, Kevin would play a crucial role in the disasters that befell our companies in the 2000s. But I couldn't have known that at the time.

By the end of the 1990s David and I had built up a very strong team, and the Quinn Group was the largest single employer in both Counties Fermanagh and Cavan.

As well as being Quinn Group's chairman, I ran its operations. I regularly visited our factories, and if there were problems, I would visit them three or four times a day until the problems were sorted out. I was happiest and at my most productive when walking around the factories and talking to the management and staff. I left the administration of the company and the office work to others. When David decided to leave after ten years at my side, to start a construction company with two other men he was very friendly with, it was a huge blow to our company. In hindsight, I should have offered David and a few other people who had helped develop the business in the 1970s, 1980s and 1990s a shareholding in some of the companies.

David's departure later turned out to be a disaster. He had always had an exceptionally good handle on all of our businesses, and I now realise that the blunders that followed would simply not have happened on his watch. Having put all the necessary safeguards in place at our insurance company I know that he would not have allowed any money to be invested without board approval. David and I continued to have a great relationship and I appointed him to the main board of the Quinn Group and Quinn Insurance until they were taken from us. Within two years of him leaving, around €50 million was invested in shares without the approval of either the board or the Financial Regulator, and, as he was still a non-executive director, he was quite annoyed that the board had been kept in the dark.

I fully accept that he should have been kept informed.

4

I n 1995, Patricia and I had decided to transfer the entire business into the hands of our five children, with each of them taking a 20 per cent share. If I lived for seven years after the transfer, it would be tax-free, and so it was.

By the early 2000s all my children were working for my businesses (except for my youngest daughter, Brenda, simply because she was still at school). Colette was managing the hotel and pub businesses, having trained in hotel management in Shannon, Galway and Switzerland. Aoife, who had graduated in sport and leisure, worked at the Iveagh Fitness Club. Some years later she returned to her studies and qualified as a solicitor, though because of later events she never practised as one. Ciara qualified as a nurse and went to Romania, while Seán Jnr spent a year in America after graduating in business management. Ciara, Seán and Aoife all ended up working in various positions in Quinn Direct, and Brenda later joined them after graduating.

Ultimately, they all became claims managers in Quinn Direct, including Colette, as there was nowhere else in the businesses where they could contribute as much. They proved to be very successful at fast-tracking settlements quickly and efficiently, as many of our corporate customers liked dealing with a Quinn, as did many of our panel of solicitors and regional claims managers (RCMs). The family developed a great team around them in the claims department, and were well-supported by extended family members. Many of the children's friends from school also worked there, and there was a tremendous atmosphere in the company.

The turn of the millennium saw an end to the Irish Troubles, thankfully. A series of temporary IRA ceasefires in the 1990s led to a permanent cease-fire in 1997. There were still bombings and killings after that: in August 1998, the 'Real IRA' detonated a bomb in Omagh which killed 29 civilians, but it discredited the dissident republicans and it was the last major bombing in Northern Ireland. In April 1998 the Good Friday Agreement was signed. Once it was ratified by a referendum both north and south of the border, in May 1998, it led to the restoration of self-government, on the basis of 'power-sharing', and the renaming of the RUC as the Police Service of Northern Ireland (PSNI), with a requirement to recruit at least a 50 per cent quota of Catholics for ten years. In the border counties, redundant British Army barracks and observation towers were closed, and gradually most British troops were withdrawn. Having one half of my businesses a kilometre north of the border and the other half a kilometre to the south, with an army post in between, meant we often faced delays, varying from a minute to an hour. With so many of our vehicles crossing the border daily, the removal of the army posts was a Godsend.

I was, like most people, all in favour of the Good Friday Agreement. Nowadays my grandchildren don't know the difference between Protestants and Catholics, which can only be good, and in fact my own children have very little interest in religious differences. What a difference in a generation! While occasional sectarian attacks continue, there have been hardly any in Fermanagh in recent times, and the county's murder rate is now among the lowest in Europe.

The turn of the new millennium also saw an important change in our companies' senior management. After David Mackey's departure in late 1999, I made what I believe to be one of the biggest misjudgements of my life. Firstly, I promoted Liam McCaffery, who had been hired in 1990 as a junior accountant to help David, to the position of the Group's chief executive. Liam was still only 34 when he got the top job. I blame myself for this, as I knew that until 1999 Liam had spent his time preparing figures for David – and he was very good at that – but he had had no experience in or input into the running of the business. I then made another misjudgement by appointing a relatively inexperienced young man, Dara O'Reilly, as finance director. Dara had only joined the company in 2000. However, I trusted them both, as they were both chartered accountants, to continue to manage the administration of the company as David had set up all of the systems necessary for managing the business over the previous ten years. I felt they would be able to continue with the strong structures in place. While David had assisted me in developing many projects, after he left I employed new management to assist me in the operational side of the business, which meant that Liam and Dara were not distracted from their administrative roles.

Kevin Lunney had been managing Quinn Direct since Noel Curley had retired, and I noticed that he was getting bogged down in fixing IT problems, and was not up to speed with underwriting or claims. I appointed Colin Morgan as Quinn Direct's CEO in Kevin's place. Liam told me that Kevin was very disappointed, and asked me if I would appoint him to the main board. I immediately agreed, as Kevin was a hardworking, friendly man with whom I got on very well, and I wanted it to look as if it had been a promotion, rather than a demotion. At the time, as Kevin told Cyril Hardiman of the *Irish Independent*, he was still involved with Quinn Direct at Dáil Committee level and in the various government insurance initiatives. In 2004 Kevin took charge of our property operations, searching for suitable assets for us to buy, and fitted the job very well.

I always managed the operational side of the businesses, and I enjoyed it immensely. I never found it particularly difficult. I had great friendships with all the loyal, hardworking managers and staff, and I always called on them for updates and general chat, normally learning more from them than they learned from me, which generally resulted in us coming to an amicable agreement on the decisions of the day. I seldom ever overruled my managers as I felt it could ruin their confidence, and sense of initiative, but when I felt that they were making wrong decisions, I would try to plant a different seed in their mind, which normally worked. This backfired on me once when a good customer and friend, Frank Harrington, told me that one of my best sales reps, Tony McLoughlin from Sligo, was being threatened with dismissal by his manager. I asked another director to ensure it didn't happen, but it did. I should have followed through, and while I apologised to both Frank and Tony later, the damage was done. Thankfully it did not affect Tony's popularity, as he was later elected as a Fine Gael TD for Sligo–Leitrim. Tony's sacking didn't do him any harm, but it appears that it may have affected my standing with the Fine Gael party.

At first I got on very well with Liam, Dara and Kevin, who I soon started calling 'the executives'. In the early 2000s I went to all their weddings. In return, all three of them came to the weddings of some of my children.

The year after Dara started, I suggested buying shares, and Liam and Dara facilitated the purchase and managed the transactions, investing Quinn Direct money in shares. When the 'dotcom crash' (which became known in the company as the 'dotcom disaster') happened in 2001, the company lost between €40 and €50 million in short order, and in 2002, I was sanctioned by the Office of the Financial Regulator for allowing the solvency of Quinn Insurance to drop below the required level, for which I took full responsibility, even though I was not on the relevant committees. I was never on the compliance or audit committees of Quinn Group or Quinn Direct, and never even attended their meetings, as everybody in the company was aware, and as the Central Bank acknowledged in 2019, when they sanctioned Liam and Kevin and discontinued their investigation into me.

In 2002 Pat Brady, an official in the Office of the Financial Regulator, asked me to resign from the investment committee, because of our dotcom losses. I did so; as captain of the ship, it seemed to be the best thing for me to do, rather than apportioning blame elsewhere. I only met Pat Brady three times, and in any discussion I had with him the administration or compliance of the company was not the central part of the discussions, which were mostly about market share and profits, as he seemed to know that I wasn't involved in committee affairs. So, I have great difficulty understanding why he focused on me only, rather than the two qualified accountants who were managing the finances, as responsible for the losses at Quinn Insurance.

In the years that followed we pressed on and bought shareholdings in a number of other companies. They were not dotcoms, but many of them were in the high-tech field. In the early 2000s we bought shares in a number of other companies, including Airtricity, an online payments business called Alphyra, and Powerscreen, a business that manufactured plant for the quarry industry, which was very close to my heart. We also bought a shareholding in NCB stockbrokers and in Ryanair. I met the chief executive of Ryanair, Michael O'Leary, at the Slieve Russell, where he was visiting with his wife, and we had a long and interesting discussion. Any shares that we bought at this time were bought outright by Quinn Group, Quinn Direct, or the family, with no borrowing, and they were generally very profitable.

Again, I relied heavily on Liam and Dara to do the administration on all of these deals. We had two significant deals with Eddie O'Connor, chief executive of Airtricity, whom I always found to be a very interesting man, and I enjoyed his company. We bought a 13 per cent share in Airtricity for €36 million, as well as a 13.5-megawatt windfarm, which we bought outright. I appointed Liam to make all the financial arrangements at our end, while Eddie appointed his finance director, Senan Murphy, to look after his end. Liam and Senan formed a close relationship, and Senan later moved to CRH.

From 2000 onwards, most of our expansion was in buying property overseas, rather than buying companies in Ireland. The Irish hotel and pub market was too hot for my liking, with very high prices, and I realised that we could make much higher returns from offices, warehouses, shopping centres and hotels in the UK, India, Russia, Ukraine, Czechia, Bulgaria, Poland and Turkey than from Irish pubs and hotels. At that time, many Irish investors were buying villas or holiday apartments on the Spanish Costas, but I was looking to central Europe. Holiday villas weren't my style, as I wanted bigger and more regular returns.

Between 2002 and 2006 some €800 million from QIL was paid out to my five children as dividends to buy property overseas. None of my children ever received a penny of these dividends – about €450 million of the money was spent on property in central and Eastern Europe, Russia, Ukraine, and India, which was kept in the family's own name, but the rest was ploughed back into Group projects. I was involved in all of these acquisitions and deals, but, thankfully, the money to finance them was never a problem. It came from three different sources: Group profits, bank borrowing, and the

€800 million of the family dividends. To this day I do not know how all the money was spent, but I do know that none of the family received any of it, not even the profits from the family assets, which were also reinvested into Group projects.

By the early 2000s I had learned that buying existing hotels was better than building them from scratch. As the old saying goes, 'Fools build hotels, but wise men buy them.' The Crowne Plaza in Cambridge and the Holiday Inn in Nottingham whet my appetite for buying managed hotels. We bought hotels in Czechia, Bulgaria, and Poland, which were managed by the top hotel companies across the world, including Hilton, Sheraton, Crowne Plaza, Holiday Inn, and Ibis.

The Hilton hotel in Prague was by far our largest hotel investment, with 791 bedrooms. We bought it, and a smaller nearby two-star property, in January 2004 for €145 million – at the time the biggest property trans-action in Czech history. We only had to pay Hilton 5–6 per cent of our turnover each year, and Hilton was responsible for the management of the hotel and routine maintenance on the building.

The Prague deal seemed a no-brainer, given the huge growth in tourism there since the fall of the Iron Curtain in the early 1990s, particularly as the hotel carried the well-respected Hilton name. In Dublin profit margins from hotels had fallen to about 6 per cent, but in Europe we made double-digit returns, and the management contract with Hilton worked very well. In 2006 we gave the Hilton a €50 million makeover. By then, I had decided that our main future growth lay in buying large hotels anywhere in the world and having them managed by international hotel companies. I saw three major upsides to that: firstly, we got a good and safe return on our invest-ment; secondly, it took up very little management time; and thirdly, property assets generally increase in value over time.

In the space of only a few years we bought lots of property, deliberately spreading the risk by buying assets in many different countries. I only wish I had taken the same approach to my other investments, and not invested so heavily in Anglo!

In Sofia, the capital of Bulgaria, we bought another Hilton hotel, and also a Sheraton in the Polish city of Krakow (without ever visiting the place, as the hotel there never had an official opening ceremony). In Moscow we bought the Caspiy business and shopping centre for €40 million. In Bahçeşehir (a suburb of Istanbul, Turkey), we bought the Prestige shopping centre, which was always fully let, and very successful. In Kazan (the capital of Tatarstan, 800 km east of Moscow) we bought a big warehousing complex, and a number of Stroiarsenal DIY stores across Russia. In Ufa, the capital of Bashkortostan, 1,200 km east of Moscow, we bought a retail, logistics and leisure development. We started building a €400 million chemical factory in Leuna, near Leipzig in Germany, with the capacity to make 100,000 tonnes a year of MMA (methyl methacrylate), a liquid used in the making of plastic. It was supposed to be up and running within two years, but it was postponed in January 2009 because of the credit crunch, after capital investment of €210 million, and its construction was never completed.

One of our largest projects was the Q Centre, a huge office complex in Hyderabad, a growing centre for high-tech industry in India. With more than 1 billion people, I saw India as a safe investment. Construction costs are only 30 per cent of Western ones, which meant that we were making higher returns than on most of the investments we were making. Hyderabad is a city of six million people, and we soon chose a site there and started building. I found the Indian people I met were very strait-laced, but very hard-working. I remember seeing women carrying building materials on their heads on building sites, and felt sorry for them. The Q Centre in Hyderabad could have been a great success, and it could have been leased twice over. But in the end it was only completed in 2009, just as our troubles began, so we never gained any big returns from it.

Looking back, I have no regrets about having invested in overseas property. The only thing I would do differently if I had my time again is buy more property that had already been built, rather than build from scratch. We would have made money out of the biggest new-build projects (the Kutuzoff Tower in Moscow and the Q Centre in Hyderabad) in the end, but managing them from thousands of miles away was a lot of hassle. We were making profit from day one in all of the hotels and shopping centres that we bought, with very little input required because of the management contracts in place.

Although I had visited the USA on many occasions, I had no ambition to buy property there, as the returns were much lower than in Eastern Europe. I also steered clear of China. Having read stories of organ theft, and the death penalty being given to bicycle thieves, I had an instinctive aversion to doing any business there, and never even looked at it. I believe now that my instinct at that time was correct. I cannot say the same about Russia – with all that has happened since February 2022, my instincts were horribly wrong.

In the former Soviet Union people often lived very simply, but they were always very well turned-out. On my many trips to Moscow, the Russian vendors and potential vendors always looked after us very well, but, despite the hospitality, our investment decisions were not influenced!

I liked the Ukrainians most of all, as they were more friendly, genuine and relaxed than the Russians. I went to Ukraine five or six times. The property we built in Ukraine was always a struggle, but the operating shopping centre that we bought was a huge success from day one.

One big mistake I made in the overseas property market was trying to make a success of an Irish pub in Berlin. I bought an old building in the early 1990s in a working-class area and spent €5 million on it. There were no bars in the area, and there was a local population of more than 100,000. But the bar failed to make much money; I soon realised that the Germans do not have an 'after work' drinking habit, preferring to go out later in the evening in the city centre, with their spouses or partners. Berliners simply don't drink the way that Irish people do. I never went for a drink in the pub myself, but I heard that drinkers would sometimes go in, order one bottle of mineral water between them, and sip it over several hours. We didn't have many of those sorts of guys around Ballyconnell or Derrylin!

By the early 2000s, there were a number of senior executives travelling to fourteen countries to manage and oversee our various operations. Our policy was that a minimum of two people, but usually more, would travel together. At some point, it was agreed that given the amount of travel that executives were undertaking, it made sense to purchase a corporate jet. A situation could have arisen where I and others would be full-time travelling, which we did not want to happen.

Gene and Ray were our reliable and trustworthy pilots on all these trips, and they were always courteous and respectful, with meticulous preparation. Kevin Lunney normally accompanied me on these trips, and he made sure they went like clockwork; he couldn't have managed them any better. I looked forward to them, but I never wanted to go away for more than four days at a time, and I always liked coming home at the end of them. I enjoyed visiting all of the cities, but geographically and culturally Cambridge and Prague stood out – I always liked walking around their streets.

We always worked hard when travelling abroad: we'd normally be in meetings or visiting sites between 8 a.m. and 6 p.m., and then grab a shower before dinner, either with colleagues or people with whom we were doing business. Late nights in bars or nightclubs were rare, and only on the final night, when we could sleep on the way home the next day. I was never there long enough to make friends in any of these countries, as my visits were short. I never learnt to speak any foreign languages, as the people with whom I was doing deals generally spoke perfect English – in most cases better than mine! I never liked computers, and I barely ever learnt how to switch them on; my staff always furnished me with detailed hardcopies of documents. I specialised in what I am good at: running the operations, making business deals, maximising profits, and planning for the future. I never believed in the theory that you could be jack-of-all-trades, and a lot of people who think they are, are often good at nothing.

I never felt like the richest man in Ireland, even though I was presented as such. I never thumped my chest and said, "This is brilliant", as I was always too busy thinking of problems that needed solving. I felt that local people did not envy me, although maybe I was wrong about a few. I was always a regular in the Angler's Rest, my local pub in Ballyconnell, where I have socialised for over fifty years. Even at the height of my wealth I would still spend Tuesday evenings at Drumm's in Derrylin, playing cards for 50 pence (or 50 cent) stakes, and I still do. When the children were young

I was probably too keen on pubs, and I often went out for a drink three or four nights a week, when I should have been at home helping Patricia. I believe that this is one of the greatest improvements in family life over the past couple of generations, where fathers are now far more involved in raising their family than my generation were.

I did not flaunt my wealth. Whether I was talking to Barack Obama (whom I met at the Prague Hilton in 2009) or to a brickyard labourer, I would always try to treat people the same. I avoided looking up to, or down upon, anyone. As one writer once observed, Seán Quinn "seemed to wear his massive wealth with ease, as if it didn't matter to him. His lifestyle was somehow the opposite of ostentatious, a trait that endeared him to many, even if he did own a corporate jet and helicopter." I would like to think that this is true, because I despise people who look down on others, and as I have found out in recent years, it is these people, who believe that they are superior than the average, are also the people who are dishonest and are not blessed with a strong moral compass. I believe these characteristics have served me well over the past twelve years, since my business empire was taken from me.

The acquisition that I felt would have a highly positive effect on our English business was a golf course in the very heart of England, the Belfry. As a young man, I always thought that I would rather be a national sportsman than a rich man, and I always watched sport on TV: mainly Gaelic football, but also a lot of golf. After the turn of the millennium, I decided that I wanted to buy a major English golf course, to emulate what we had in Ireland.

In 2004 we tried to buy Wentworth in Surrey, probably the most exclusive golf course of the lot, for £135 million, but I was beaten to it by Richard Caring, a millionaire in the clothing industry who has gone on to become a successful restaurateur. In April 2005 we succeeded in buying another prestigious English course, the Belfry, for £186 million. The deal was reported approvingly in *The Economist* as part of a 'Celtic reconquest' of the English property market.

The Belfry has three golf courses. The Brabazon, which has hosted the Ryder Cup four times, is the main tournament course, alongside the PGA

National and the Derby. The Professional Golfers' Association headquarters was also on the site, along with a four-star, 324-room hotel, tennis courts and a spa. They are all set in 550 acres between Sutton Coldfield and Tamworth, close to Birmingham Airport and only about ten miles from the centre of Birmingham itself, so the Belfry is very well-located.

We didn't get brilliant returns from the Belfry in the few years that we owned it, but it gave us a profit of £9 or £10 million a year. We never made the same kind of returns that we did from other foreign property assets in India, Ukraine, Russia, Turkey, Bulgaria, or Poland, but it was a safe investment, and the value of the Belfry was not just financial. The course hosted the British Masters golf tournament in May 2006, sponsored by QIL, and we met several world-class golfers. The Belfry gave us a certain status, and, like the Slieve Russell, it also gave us a place where we could hold meetings with our RCMs and solicitors, and where we could reward loyal customers of our businesses with complimentary weekend or mid-week breaks.

I stayed at the Belfry half-a-dozen times over the five years we owned it. By 2008 we had plans to rebuild some of its hotel accommodation, which I thought was a bit old-fashioned, but we never got around to it before all of our businesses were taken from us. The Belfry was acquired from the receiver by KSL Capital Partners in August 2012, and in 2013 its hotel underwent a £26 million renovation. I've never been back since.

* * * *

Closer to home, in 2002, 900 of my employees – the bulk of Quinn Direct's workforce – moved to a new office complex called the Q Centre on the Cavan Road in Blanchardstown, a western suburb of Dublin. At the Q Centre's opening ceremony, the ribbon was cut by none other than the Taoiseach, Bertie Ahern, who was fulsome in his praise of our contribution to Irish society.

Alongside Ahern was Brian Lenihan Jnr, who was then Minister for Children and a TD for the Dublin West constituency, which covers Blanchardstown. Lenihan was part of an important political dynasty: his father, Brian

Lenihan Snr, had been a long-serving Fianna Fáil TD, and a candidate for the Irish presidency in 1990. Soon after Lenihan Snr's death in 1996, his son inherited his Dublin West seat. Although I did not know it, within a few years, Lenihan would be holding the fate of my business empire in his hands.

I had met Bertie Ahern three or four times by 2002. Our first meeting was in about 1987, ten years before Bertie became Taoiseach, when he was already an ambitious young politician. Although we'd never met before, I recognised him in our Dublin pub, Quinn's of Drumcondra, before a GAA match, and he recognised me. "How are you, young Quinn?" he asked, as if I was a twenty-year-old; in fact, I was older than him. It was typical of Bertie's 'Hail fellow, well met' personality. After that I met him in the Slieve Russell a couple of times. Although I've since lost confidence in many politicians, I have to hand it to Bertie, who has the rare distinction of being elected three times as Taoiseach. He was also ridiculed for building too many houses in the new millennium, but where would we be now without them? I believe that he also deserves huge credit for his part in the Good Friday Agreement.

Many of my operations were north of the border, and in the early 2000s I also met the Queen when she opened a new factory at Fisher Engineering in County Fermanagh (a year after the death of its chairman, Bertie Fisher).

By the mid-2000s I had bought a bit of extra land from a neighbour, and in the summer of 2004 planning permission was obtained for building a new house. The new house was much bigger than the old one, and in hindsight, it was far too big. I now wish that I had the money it cost at the time!

My mother, Mary Quinn, died in May 2005, aged 92. Every day until shortly before her death, she used to visit the offices we had built on either side of her house, and she was quick to comment on anything she thought was astray, as she always did to me and my siblings throughout our lives. The staff were always very courteous to her, and in her failing years they watched out for her and visited her regularly. After consulting with my siblings, it was decided that it was preferable to demolish the house, and integrate its site into our office complex, rather than see it neglected and derelict. The house was right on the verge of the road, and traffic had increased so much that it was no longer a good family home, or a safe place for children to visit; however, my mother loved tending to the garden she had cultivated over many years.

I always looked closely at our monthly and quarterly profit figures, and I was usually pleasantly surprised by them. From 1973 to 2003 our profits grew by more than 30 per cent per year on average and the last three years before the financial crash – 2004, 2005 and 2006 – saw average growth of 38 per cent per annum, from €164 million to €433 million of pre-tax profits (excluding our property businesses). By 2007 the turnover had reached more than €2 billion, and the Quinn Group had a workforce of more than 8,500. Quinn Insurance had offices in Cavan, Enniskillen, Dublin, Meath, Cork and Manchester. By 2007 we were the second largest insurer in Ireland, with more than 1 million customers. This 38 per cent increase was among the highest three-year profit increases the company ever enjoyed, and was influenced by the energy and commitment the family brought to the table, and particularly their input into the fast-track claims model. It was a very exciting time, and, whether by accident or design, all of the family members became involved in the business in the five years prior to the crash, during a tremendous growth period.

Things did not always go perfectly. In August 2005 we had a clash with the Labour Court, to do with overtime and the lack of sick pay for a small number of staff, but the dispute was resolved quickly. Our growth continued. By 2008 the Group had a total of 6,000 direct employees, plus another 2,500 indirect employees, whose livelihood depended on me. Most of the indirect ones were in our foreign hotels and Irish pubs; they were technically employed by the hotel or pub operators, even though we owned the properties.

My expansion into hospitality and insurance made my companies a lot less male-dominated. In the early 1970s men had outnumbered women by twenty to one in my quarry operations, which only employed a few women in the office. Most, though not all, of the people who worked making construction materials, and driving lorries, were men. However, by 2008, 3,000 of the 6,000 direct employees were women, most of them in insurance and hospitality operations. I have always believed in gender equality, and the fact that I had four daughters reinforced that view.

Because of my hands-on style of management, I stupidly kept myself and all my family in the operations parts of the business, and none of us were ever involved in the administration of the company. All of the administration was left to the staff in head office – to such an extent that we wouldn't even have known about the companies that existed in Sweden, the Channel Islands, Cyprus, or Madeira. What we did know was that all of our businesses were run to the highest standards, producing higher profit margins than our competitors in any of the fields in which we operated. As we were making €10 million a week of profit, I didn't realise that our administration department was going to become the problem that it did.

From the 1970s onwards I had always trusted accountants. With hindsight, I now realise that I was very naïve, and that I'd become over-reliant on Dara and Liam. Having worked with Liam since 1990, I trusted him, just as I did all the others before him.

From 1973 onwards our main bankers had been Ulster Bank, and later Northern Bank. We used AIB (Allied Irish Banks) and Bank of Ireland for our day-to-day banking in the 2000s. But gradually we had more and more to do with Anglo Irish Bank, always known as Anglo for short. We had inherited Anglo with the acquisition of Lite-Pac in 1994, a company in Longford that produces insulation products for the building industry. That was an unusual and interesting deal, as I always liked haggling over price and I usually offered much less than what I was willing to pay, and much less than the vendor asked. I knew and liked Lite-Pac's owners, Niall Enright and John Reilly. They had told me that they might consider selling and I told them I'd be interested in buying. Months later, David Mackey and I met Niall, John and John's wife, Chrissie, for lunch in the Kilmore Hotel in Cavan. I asked them a number of times how much they wanted for the company. Niall, who was spokesman on the day, kept on saying "It'll be dear, Quinn." Eventually he looked at me and said, "It'll be five million Quinn." I immediately stretched out my hand to shake on the deal. There was absolute silence and shock in the room. Niall, John and Chrissie couldn't believe that they had sold their business, and David thought that I had gone completely mad, paying the full asking price. But I was happy, and Niall, John and Chrissie were willing to help run the company for the first year. We completely rebuilt the factory with new efficient technology, and the acquisition of Lite-Pac was a great deal for the Quinn Group; it was just a pity that Anglo came with it. Lite-Pac had a pre-existing banking relationship with Anglo Irish, so the relationship between Anglo and the larger Quinn Group developed from there.

Anglo soon became more and more active in financing our property developments. I was quickly impressed by them. From the late 1990s until the subprime crash in 2007, Anglo loaned us €450 million to purchase or refinance property assets in Ireland, England, Prague, Turkey and Ukraine.

Established in Dublin in 1964, Anglo was never a consumer bank. It had no branches, only a number of regional offices. I don't think I met anyone senior at Anglo until after we bought the Prague hotels in 2004, when I met the bank's chief executive, David Drumm, for the first time. He and I agreed that deal, but our other deals in the 2000s were generally transacted between Liam McCaffrey and Michael O'Sullivan, the Anglo manager in charge of our account, whom I met a few times. John Bowe, a senior manager at Anglo, met with Dara and Kevin on dozens of occasions, but he never met with me or any of my family; as usual, we simply signed everything that we were asked to. In fact, none of my family ever met anyone from Anglo in an official capacity until after they took our business, despite the fact that the family had been 100 per cent owners for the previous nine years.

David Drumm had been unexpectedly promoted to become Anglo's chief executive in 2005, after Seán FitzPatrick had moved from the chief executive's office to the bank's chairmanship. I felt at the time that he was a good operator. Tiarnan O'Mahoney, who had been tipped to get the chief executive's job ahead of Drumm, left the bank. His new venture, the International Securities Trading Corporation (ISTC), was an investment vehicle, not a bank. We decided to invest in it. ISTC was not immune from the growing storm clouds over the Irish economy; it went bust in 2007 and, unfortunately, we lost all of the money we had invested.

I didn't get to know Seán FitzPatrick particularly well. In the 1990s and early 2000s I met him at a couple of dinners, shook hands with him, and found him friendly and courteous. He always struck me as a man who could get things done, a characteristic I always admired in others. But I did not meet FitzPatrick professionally until September 2007, when I informed him of our huge CFD shareholdings. Even then, he showed a mature attitude, and it was obvious that he was a man of the world.

Our relationship with Anglo seemed to be a good one, and as with many other things, I was happy for the management team to manage it day-to-day.

In 2004 I rang Dermot Desmond, offering to buy his shareholding in Barlo, a publicly quoted company that made radiators, plastic sheeting, and packaging for the food industry. He told me that he was going to the Cheltenham racing festival the following week. As I and five other local lads had decided to go to Cheltenham that year, I agreed to meet Dermot there in his hospitality box, while Albert Reynolds, former Taoiseach, and Charlie McCreevy, a former Minister of Finance, were visiting him. Reynolds and McCreevy encouraged us to meet halfway between the asking price and what I was prepared to offer, and we sealed the deal in a few minutes. While I only met Dermot Desmond a few times, I found him to be a very honourable man, and I have reflected on many an occasion on a comment he made when I met him one time by chance. He addressed me as "the man they couldn't hang." I asked, "have they been trying", and he replied "yes, they have." I thought he was joking, but maybe he knew more than I thought at the time.

It was later reported that I socialised with Dermot for a number of days, when, in fact, I met him for less than half an hour. It makes one wonder if the people who are writing such rubbish make it up themselves, or are they told it by others? The same writer said that in 2008, Quinn management were concerned about my mental health, and stated that I hadn't appeared at work for a week, and that they were concerned that I was going to 'top' myself, while in fact, I never missed a day at work, apart from holidays, and, thankfully, stress never kept me from work. Do people like this not have any responsibility, to be getting on with such rubbish? I later closed the existing radiator factories in County Tipperary and Belgium to build a state-of-the-art factory near Cardiff, with the capacity to make four million radiators a year. Barlo's packaging plant was relocated to Ballyconnell, and I attracted some criticism from the media, politicians, workers and local people in the areas from which we moved the businesses, particularly from Clonmel in Co. Tipperary.

In 2007 we bought Bupa Healthcare's Irish operations, and we soon rebranded them as Quinn Healthcare. With the Bupa acquisition I took over 475,000 clients in Ireland. The deal was "not without controversy", according to sections of the media. Bupa had decided to back out of the Irish market, saying that the payments it had to make to the state-owned Voluntary Health Insurance Board (VHI) made it unviable. As VHI has an older customer base with more health problems, all other Irish insurers were obliged to compensate it via a system called 'risk equalisation'.

Critics, and I was one of them, have long claimed that this gives VHI an unfair advantage, allowing it to hang on to 75 per cent of the health insurance market in Ireland. As the new owner of BUPA's Irish operations, I expected to be exempt from making any payments to VHI for the first three years, as the insurance rules that were then in force stated. In the end I wasn't allowed to, thanks to an emergency change in the law in the Dáil, which stayed in session until after midnight to finalise the change, though I did get Bupa to cut its sale price by about half.

Despite all this controversy, during our takeover of Bupa Healthcare the regulators looked at all our books in Quinn Insurance; we were given a clean bill of health, and the purchase went ahead. While I could understand some of the reasons why the government wanted to protect VHI, I and many others in the industry were unhappy that we were propping up a subsidiary of the Irish state, which ran a very inefficient operation with practically no solvency. We had one of the highest levels of solvency in the business, and when we were later taken over by that same government, shortly after our demise, VHI had to be bailed out by Warren Buffett, the veteran American investor, to the tune of €270 million, to meet solvency margins that they had never met in the preceding ten years. As late as 2013, in order to meet a deadline agreed with the European Commission of being regulated by the Central Bank, the government had to make a commitment to invest around €100 million in VHI. The Central Bank demanded that the VHI increased its reserves before it would regulate it, and the European Commission demanded that it meet the same rules that applied to other insurers. The difference in how the VHI, with a history of having lengthy periods of insolvency, was dealt with, and the way we were dealt with was stark. They were given time, we were taken out, despite the fact that we had the highest reserves in the country, and, by the Central Bank's own statistics, we had an 80 per cent higher reserve per claim than our competitors. This may well be at the heart of the matter. Here was VHI, a government-owned health insurer, which never met its solvency requirements. They, FBD, and RSA, who were in business for decades before us, had to borrow money to stay afloat, while we, in fact, received €800 million of dividends and still had €1.56 billion of assets and cash to meet our liabilities. In Ireland, this equated to €15.92 per claim. Based on the same metric, FBD had €8.55 and RSA had €4.39 per claim, yet we were the company that was taken out.

In the media I was often referred to as 'the sandman', implying that I was still just a sand and gravel merchant in County Cavan. Shane Ross once wrote that although I had "made billions from nothing" and had taken "the staid Irish insurance world by storm ... few wealthy Irishmen have ever been able to hide so successfully from the national media." The Quinn Group eventually engaged a public relations man, Brian Bell (the company he worked for, Wilson Hartnell, had a name that sounded like a provincial solicitors, but it was in fact part of the giant WPP public relations and advertising empire, owned by Martin Sorrell). PR was not a high priority for me, and I never cultivated the media, or had lunch with newspaper editors, as many people did – an approach that may have cost me.

On 7 March 2007 I was cajoled by Vincent Reynolds, the chairman of the Cavan County Enterprise Board, into giving a speech at the Slieve Russell Hotel. It was a very rare public appearance by me, and in the Slieve

Russell's ballroom, and a large crowd attended. I had not spoken in public for many years, and hoped it would be as long before I would do so again.

I don't remember much of what I said in that speech, but I do remember trying to give an honest appraisal of my life and the growth of the businesses, and to show that we depended on our staff and their work ethic. I think it was in that speech I first mooted the idea of allowing staff to share the wealth they had helped us create. These attempts sadly came to an end shortly afterwards, when all that we had was taken from us. I have been reminded by listeners that my final words were: "We came from a very simple background, and we tried to make business always simple." Maybe I had kept it too simple and trusted too many? I also stated during that speech that I was always greedy for success, and I make no apology for that; money was never my motivation, success always was, and that was demonstrated by the fact that I was the lowest paid director in the company, and never took money out of it. Success to me was always about achieving goals, never money. Building projects like the Slieve Russell Hotel, a glass factory, a cement factory, and an insurance company in our local communities were always what gave me the buzz, particularly when it was felt by others that these projects would not succeed. Apart from financial matters, winning county senior championships with my local club gave me as much satisfaction as any of my financial achievements.

Having shunned the media spotlight for so long, in 2008/2009 QIL started sponsoring Ireland's most famous TV chatshow, *The Late Late Show*, which had been presented by the legendary Gay Byrne from 1962 to 1999. It symbolised how far I had come, in the space of 35 years, from a farmer's son to an international businessman. My companies had seen their profits grow by more than 30 per cent each year on average for over 35 years, and the media began to speculate on my success. Some wondered how I had achieved so much, having come from such frugal beginnings, how I had challenged monopolies, and how I had succeeded in such a poverty-stricken area, close to the border.

While some of the media coverage was negative, many journalists acknowledged how I had helped to stem emigration from the border counties, how I had given the area one of the best-designed hotels and golf courses in Ireland, and how Quinn businesses had helped other businesses to spring up locally. I had disproved the theory that one had to come from a rich, privileged background to succeed, and above all I had shown how monopolies could be broken.

But as I was about to find out, the biggest success stories can quickly turn into nightmares.

5

From 2004 onwards the Quinn Group's relationship with Anglo Irish was a two-way street. As well as Anglo giving the Quinn Group finance for its expansion, the Quinn Group also became one of the bank's biggest investors, and that was mainly due to my ill-advised belief in the bank.

We did so not by buying conventional shares in Anglo, but by buying contracts for difference (CFDs). CFDs are, according to their dictionary definition, a type of financial derivative in which two parties exchange the difference between the opening and closing value of an underlying asset. In plain English, a CFD is a bet on a share price, not an actual share.

A buyer buys a CFD at a set fraction of the share price (in our case, 20 per cent). If the share price increases by 20 per cent, a CFD holder can sell their CFDs at the high price and pocket the difference, making a profit of 100 per cent. However, if a share price falls, it is the seller of CFDs (the company you are investing in), rather than the buyer, who pockets the difference. If shares start consistently falling in value, CFDs soon become a disaster as buyers are liable, by a legally binding agreement, for all the losses. This was the fate that befell us from 2007 onwards.

Although some 30 to 40 per cent of big financial transactions these days are CFDs, they were barely heard of, let alone understood, outside banking. Until 2005, I had never heard of them myself, and I certainly did not know what the letters CFD stood for. Good, bad, or indifferent, I was simply never told about the idea of buying CFDs until it was ready to start.

The CFD concept needed some explanation, but once I understood the idea I liked it, and my senior financial men seemed equally excited and positive about it. In 2005 Liam and Dara set up a new company in Madeira, called Bazzely, through which CFDs were bought. The Madeira company did not have any non-executive directors, as it should have. Although I was one of its directors, alongside Liam, Dara and Kevin, my children only learned about the company's existence when they read stories in news-papers. I was told at the time that we were following a legal tax efficiency scheme, recommended by our accountants PwC, as Madeira's corporation tax rate is only 3 per cent.

I agreed that we should go ahead with buying CFDs in Anglo Irish Bank. After all, we knew and respected Anglo. In the heady Celtic Tiger boom years of the early 2000s everyone expected its share price to keep rising. I was besotted by Anglo, and I admired its initiative, its management and its cost structure. Other banks had twice the loan book that Anglo had, but ten times the number of customers. At every opportunity, I encouraged manage-ment to buy Anglo shares.

Anglo was not Ireland's biggest bank (it was never more than the third largest), but it was considered to be its best, having been named as the World's Best Small Bank at Davos in 2007. By 2005 I had started studying Anglo's financial reports assiduously and I was always impressed by what I read. Their cost structure was less than half of their competitors, which was something that impressed me greatly, as I followed a similar principle in my businesses.

The first CFD deal was done in October 2005. As the CFDs did not need to be publicly reported, neither the Quinn Group board, nor the Financial Regulator, were informed about them. This, of course, was the start of our problems.

Another important decision was made within the Quinn Group in 2005, relating to its finance arrangements. We reached an agreement with Barclays Bank and American bondholders to replace our existing banks, which allowed us to borrow up to three times our annual profits. I attended the first meeting at our head office alongside Liam, Dara and Kevin, when the arrangement was explained to us. To me it seemed to be a much simpler and cheaper way of borrowing money than anything we had done so far. I also remember that the Barclays representative raised the fact that the loans could not be secured against 'regulated entities' (assets belonging to Quinn Insurance), something which we had already known.

While there were no guarantees given in the associated documentation, which was approved on our behalf by our solicitors, A&L Goodbody – a point which Liam McCaffrey made at the Central Bank Inquiry in 2019 – unknown to us there were contingent guarantees (third-party guarantees) given by subsidiaries (hotels and office blocks) of Quinn Insurance, which was a regulated entity. Both PwC and Moore Stephens, a global financial consultancy company, would later find that these contingent guarantees had no effect on the solvency of Quinn Insurance, and the Regulator never showed us any evidence that they had.

From its peak of €17.31 on 24 May 2007, Anglo's share price fell to €11.90 in late 2007. Around that time, it became known that the Quinn Group was holding a large number of Anglo CFDs, and by September, Anglo was becoming increasingly concerned about our CFD position, and I was becoming increasingly concerned myself about the bank's falling share price. David Drumm asked to meet me to address his concerns. Liam McCaffrey and I met Drumm and Seán FitzPatrick at the Ardboyne Hotel in Navan on 11 September, and we told them that we controlled 25 per cent of the bank shares through CFDs, and we had no further funds available to support the margin calls. They appeared shocked at the revelation, and they asked me what my intentions were. I said that I had bought them because I had felt that they were cheap, based on the performance of the bank, and I enquired if the bank was continuing to be as successful as it had been. They assured me that it was, and that it would be reporting record profits at the end of that month, which they subsequently did. They told me that my CFD holding was much too high, and said that if it became known in the market, it could collapse the bank's share price. They asked me if I would reduce our holding to single digits when the share price recovered, and I agreed to do so. They headed off in their cars, and stopped at the County Club, where they decided that they would tell their board and all relevant government agencies about our shareholding. They concluded that they weren't worried about the Quinn Group because of the profits they were producing. It didn't cross my mind at the time, but I have since realised that when they asked for the meeting they would have known we had used up a lot of cash and that we would have had to start to sell off some CFDs to meet our margin calls. They obviously would not have wanted this to happen, and they knew that with our low level of borrowing, they could afford to lend us money to protect the share price. Whether or not they had discussed this with the Regulator or the Central Bank in advance of that meeting, I have no idea. That very evening, they held a board meeting to inform all of their directors. Those who couldn't attend were informed by telephone.

Within two or three days the bank had contacted all relevant government institutions, namely the Regulator, the Central Bank, the Department of Finance, and the Domestic Standing Group,* so now the scene was set for our destruction, as there is no argument as to what happened subsequently. Apparently either by verbal agreement, or implicit in silence, it was decided that Anglo could provide funds to the Quinn Group for the specific purpose of supporting the shares by paying the margin calls, thereby misleading the market. I feel that this was an astonishing decision to make – by trying to portray that they weren't supporting the share price, and by funnelling the funds through the Quinn Group to support the share price, it seems to me as if it was criminal from day one. (This would later be referenced by Judge Martin Nolan, who heard the case relating to the purchase of our shares and those of the Maple Ten.) If they had not injected these funds illegally into their own shares, we would have had no option but to sell the CFDs. There was no third choice – they either had to give the money to support them, or we had to sell them. They certainly didn't want to sell them, as a flood of shares

---

*   At the outset of the financial crisis in 2008, representatives from the Central Bank, Financial Regulator, Department of Finance, and National Treasury Management Agency (NTMA) began investigating how they would cope with a run on or collapse of a bank. This group became known as the Domestic Standing Group, and it became the Government's financial war cabinet during the crisis.

on the market would have affected the share price, and potentially the bank. Their determination to not allow the shares to be sold was later evidenced by the fact that they didn't allow their finance director, Willie McAteer, or our CEO, Liam McCaffrey, to sell their shares – they financed them also, rather than allow them to come onto the market. In *The FitzPatrick Tapes*, Seán Fitz-Patrick acknowledged that when he first heard about our shareholding that day in Navan, we believed that the shares would have to be sold. "'We were shocked', FitzPatrick says. 'Both of us were. I certainly was because I was never led to believe it was that figure. And I believe David [Drumm] was also shocked. The point that they made then at that stage was that they were going to have to get rid of [the shares].'"

Simon Carswell claims in his book *Anglo Republic* that, "The bank was in contact with the Central Bank and Financial Regulator by phone every day, sometimes several times a day, following the share price collapse." Later in the book, he says that interactions between David Drumm and John Hurley, Governor of the Central Bank, show "how cosy the relationship was between bank and state." It is concerning that the Central Bank and the Regulator would remain silent about their involvement in the share support scheme, and it is even more concerning that there were no repercussions for the actions of these state agencies. It is unrealistic to believe that the Central Bank and the Regulator were not fully apprised of the situation.

There is a very telling description in Tom Lyons and Brian Carey's *The FitzPatrick Tapes*, which describes Seán FitzPatrick's reaction to the conclusion of the Maple Ten deal:

> 'In hindsight I kill myself. I should have brought it up. We should have had some session on the whole thing – let's look at that whole thing again and say what happened with that, what are we doing, how is it being done, are we happy with that.'

He went on to say that he had no idea that there was anything "dodgy" about the Maple Ten deal – they had taken advice from Matheson Ormsby Prentice and from Morgan Stanley.

'We had [also] got clearance from the Irish Stock Exchange,' he says. ... 'If you take all of that and all of the legals, the Irish Stock Exchange, the Financial Regulator and the Central Bank were all aware of it. ... There was no sense of, Oh Jesus Christ this is a bit dodgy. ... No one on the board felt that there was something irregular here or something that needs to be sort of hushed up.'

Lyons and Carey also reveal that a source close to the Irish Stock Exchange confirmed that it knew about the deal and allowed it to go through because the Financial Regulator told them to allow it.

As Shane Ross, who would become a senior government minister, would later say in his book *The Bankers*, "Anglo was now treading a dangerous path. It was lending money to clients to buy shares in itself. The whole operation looked like a share-support scheme. Anglo was misleading the market."

On 22 February 2008, Pat Whelan, a senior director of Anglo Irish's Ireland operations, wrote to Liam McCaffery to ask the Quinn Group to dispose of assets worth €500 million, so we could repay some of the money we owed. I was very annoyed with this request, as they had surplus security on the €450 million loans that were legally provided for assets in Ireland, the UK, Prague, Turkey, and Ukraine, and they were now looking for repayment of money they had provided to support their own share price. So, instead of selling the shares, they wanted us to sell assets. It is interesting that from the time David Mackey restructured the administration of the business onwards, to my knowledge, I never received any letter from any bank, auditor, or solicitor, nor did any of my family.

Anglo Irish and the Quinn Group were then overtaken by events beyond our control. In March 2008 Bear Sterns, an investment bank in the USA, collapsed, and bank share prices began to fall across the world. The so-called 'St Patrick's Day Massacre' on 17 March caused €3.5 billion to be wiped off the value of the Irish stock exchange. Anglo's share price fell dramatically – by 23 per cent in a single day – and in the next few weeks it almost halved, from €9.20 to €4.85. Anglo then invested a further €375 million, taking Quinn Group share support funding to €1.15 billion. There was so much urgency that one of the loans had to be channelled through a company that we owned in the UK, as all Irish banks were closed because St Patrick's Day is a holiday.

On 18 March, the day after the St Patrick's Day Massacre, Liam McCaffrey, Quinn Group CEO, wrote to Michael O'Sullivan, granting the bank share pledges over the family's share in the Quinn Group. Liam had signed over control of the Group to the bank in return for the money advanced for share support. This made no sense, as Liam would have known that the money was not for the Quinns, this was done to support Anglo's share price; they were also doing the same thing to support Liam's own personally held shares. Neither I, nor any member of my family, nor the Quinn board, knew of this arrangement. None of us approved his actions, or even discussed them, nor at the time were we aware that Liam was in deep financial trouble with Anglo with his own shares. Nor were we aware that he even owned CFDs in Anglo in his own personal capacity, which ultimately led to him transferring €500,000 from a Quinn Group company to cover his own margin calls, and fifteen years later, none of my family have ever seen a copy of that letter.

Later, Simon Carswell would write, "the fundamental problem with the shares underlying the Quinn CFDs was that nobody wanted to buy them." After the 17 March crash Anglo had hoped for a bailout by Dubai financiers. Anglo and the Regulator decided that some of the Quinn CFDs should be sold, and Drumm travelled to the Middle East to see if he could find interested parties to buy some of them. While he was in Dubai, he was contacted by Patrick Neary, the Financial Regulator during the crisis, asking for an update on progress. Drumm said that progress was poor: there was no demand for the shares. Even at this stage, when the shares had been supported to the tune of over one billion euro, the government and Anglo insisted that the shares should not be allowed to go onto the market. While Drumm was in Dubai, I expressed my concerns about trying to sell the shares at a point where Anglo had supported them by over a billion euro, rather than allowing them to be sold in 2007, and when that message was relayed to Drumm, he advised, "Tell that fucker to have some manners. I'm up to my bollocks in sand trying to get some credit to fill the black hole." Whatever else may be said about Drumm, at least he had a sense of humour, and was trying to resolve a problem that was caused by me buying such an amount of CFDs, and agents of the Irish government agreeing to their support, knowing that that support was illegal.

To overcome my resistance to the sale of the shares, the bank then decided to take a Power of Attorney over the shares. This meant that the bank had full control over the shares, and the family had none whatsoever.

Matt Moran, Anglo's CFO, told Con Horan, head of banking supervision at the Office of the Financial Regulator, that the bank had agreed a new deal with us to unwind our CFD position, and he sent Horan a copy of the signed agreement, which had been executed that afternoon. The agreement was that each of my five children would buy 3 per cent of the shares outright. Moran needed the Regulator's assurance that he would allow my family to own the shares, and an acknowledgement that the individual family members were not acting in concert, which was against stock market rules. Anglo had the benefit of professional advice from their investment banking and legal advisors, but my wife and children had no say whatsoever as Anglo had Power of Attorney over the shares. The Regulator encouraged the bank to get the shares dealt with as soon as possible, raising no objection when the bank made him aware that Anglo itself would have to fund the children's share purchases. According to *Citizen Quinn*, "Drumm told Quinn he had little option; the Financial Regulator had cleared the planned transaction and warned the bank not to lend any more money to Quinn under any circumstances. The bank board had approved the CFD unwinding and had the power of attorney to do it, even against Quinn's wishes." I still find it hard to believe that the Irish state could find my family responsible in any way for the €488.5 million paid to complete this transaction when they knew that the family had zero input into it. We read more about the details of the transaction in a national newspaper, the *Sunday Business Post*, in an article written by Richard Curran and David Clerkin, than we were given by Anglo Irish Bank. Curran and Clerkin stated that they had seen the document where a charge was granted on 27 June and filed in the Companies Registration Office on 9 July, just six days before the deal with Anglo was made public.

Later, when a government inquiry was set up, I wrote to the Taoiseach, Enda Kenny, asking him to broaden the investigation. He replied saying that they had already broadened their investigation, and they weren't going to broaden it any further. This meant that the investigation was only looking into events from ten days after Patrick Neary announced his retirement, at which point the horse had well and truly bolted! To me, that told its own story. The government knew that investigating happenings before that meant that they were investigating the actions of their own agents – the Central Bank and the Department of Finance.

We weren't alone in being misled by the state. Department of Finance documents from that period show that the Central Bank and the Regulator were actively engaging with the CEOs of Irish banks, to explore options that might be available in a crisis situation, and to ensure that a collaborative approach would be taken in response to any issue that arose within the banking system. The chief executive of Irish Life and Permanent, Denis Casey, met John Hurley, Governor of the Central Bank, and Patrick Neary as part of that engagement process, and in a later affidavit sent to the Gardaí and the ODCE (Office of the Director of Corporate Enforcement) Casey would say that, "In March 2008, the chief executive of the Financial Regulator and the governor of the Central Bank requested the Irish Life and Permanent Group to participate in a 'Green Jersey Agenda', under which Irish financial institutions were asked to provide each other with mutual in-market support at a time of unprecedented turmoil in global financial markets in order to maintain financial stability."[†] Later, in the affidavit, Casey stated that he advised his board members the Regulator had said the "green jersey agenda" should be considered highly confidential as it would likely be viewed negatively in the international markets, so the extent to which government agents went to, to first encourage the banks to act inappropriately, is very clear. Of course,

---

[†]   There was much camaraderie among Irish banks, the Department of Finance and regulators in those days, which was dubbed the 'Green Jersey'. If an Irish bank had financial difficulties, Irish regulators, civil servants and politicians would often do all they could to prop it up, to stop embarrassing stories appearing in the media, or at least to prevent a bank's collapse.

they then denied all responsibility. Denis Casey paid a high price for doing what his superiors asked of him in this regard, by going to prison. This was probably one of the most blatant injustices perpetrated by the Central Bank and the Regulator during the crisis.

David Drumm had received the same message from Hurley and Neary: Irish banks should help each other out. He emailed his management team after his meeting, asking John Bowe, his head of treasury, to consider some mechanisms. Drumm advised his executives that he wanted to begin "dialogue" with the Central Bank and the chief executives of other banks "sooner rather than later". At a meeting between the Regulator, Drumm and Willie McAteer, Anglo's finance director, on 24 September, McAteer told the Regulator that he would be managing the balance sheet at year end, and that he was doing a treasury arrangement with Irish Life and Permanent. Patrick Neary's response was "Fair play to you, Willie." This clearly shows that the bank was trying to solve a problem that the Irish government knew about, and indeed encouraged, from 2007. David Drumm, Willie McAteer, and John Bowe also served prison sentences for carrying out a scheme which they believed to have had the approval of the Central Bank and the Financial Regulator.

The deal to unwind the CFDs was transacted on 13 July 2008, and in addition to my family buying 3 per cent each of the shares outright, the other 10 per cent of CFDs that we had were to be unwound by being purchased by a new consortium of ten investors, most of them big Irish property developers. These 'trusted pals' of the bank were later known as the 'Golden Circle' and later still as the 'Maple Ten' (after the codename Maple, which was used by merchant bankers from Morgan Stanley, who were masterminding Anglo's rescue). At this point, the matter was out of our hands, and my family and I had no control.

Anglo got each member of the Maple Ten to buy a 1 per cent stake in the bank – a tenth of the 10 per cent stake they were selling. They did so with a loan of €451 million from Anglo itself. The Regulator directed the Irish Stock Exchange to allow the Maple Ten deal to go through, which seems incredible, even though it would, under normal circumstances, be considered unlawful for a bank to loan money to external parties to buy its own shares. No action was ever taken in relation to this. None of the legal advisors have ever faced any sanctions for their role as far as I know.

The 3 per cent that were being put into my family's names were transacted via six Cypriot companies that Liam and Dara had set up. This transaction was implemented without any meeting or discussion with the family. The family signed whatever documents were emailed to them, as they had been doing for the previous six years. Some €488.5 million of debt was put in the names of my wife and five children, without it ever being mentioned to them. We had been left in an impossible position. It is important to emphasise that neither Patricia nor any of our five children ever met anyone from Anglo, agents of the state, or legal advisors regarding these transactions at any stage from when the first CFDs were acquired in August 2005 until after Quinn Insurance was put into administration in 2010.

I was asked to issue a public statement approving the 'Maple Ten' plan, which had to be agreed beforehand with the Regulator. The following week I sought legal advice about the possibility of issuing proceedings against Anglo, but it soon became clear that no renowned Irish legal practice would take our case on, as they all appeared to be very reliant on work from the state. Knowing that it would be difficult to find a high-quality legal team in Ireland to represent us against the Irish government, we turned to an English firm, White and Case, who were highly recommended for complex financial cases.

I met them in London, and they assured me immediately that we had a very strong case on multiple grounds, and wrote to Anglo with a view to issuing proceedings. White and Case couldn't believe that agents of the Irish government were involved, and that these deals had been done without any meetings or discussions with the shareholders of the company in whose names these investments had been made. Within days Seán FitzPatrick had sought a meeting with me, at Buswells Hotel, where he suggested that we reach an agreement without the need for any legal proceedings. Later, David Drumm and Patrick Neary had similar meetings with me, and I agreed that we would repay all of the debt, even the €2.34 billion that the bank had invested in their own shares, which I felt at the time wouldn't have been due if we had followed the White and Case advice. However, pride wasn't going to allow me to owe money, whether perceived or otherwise, as our reputation was more important to us than money, as we felt that even with paying the illegal loans, we would still have plenty of money.

FitzPatrick was very complimentary towards my approach, and said that, within reason, he would give us all the time we needed, that the Quinn Group had been very successful over the previous 36 years, and that we should have no problem repaying the loans. Within about four weeks, I had met all three of them – Neary, Drumm and FitzPatrick – at least twice. At all of these meetings, it was very clear to me that both the bank and the Regulator knew they had a major problem if this case was to go down a legal route, and we made it clear that we were prepared to repay all of the loans. Later, Dara O'Reilly, our finance director, admitted in court hearings in both Sweden and Ireland that in the ten months to July 2008, Anglo loaned us €2.34 billion to support their shares, with the full support of the Irish government, the Governor of the Central Bank, the Department of Finance, and the Regulator. He said that he rang Anglo every morning to assess how things were going, and to tell them much money was needed to cover our margin calls. In the Swedish court, the judge warned him not to incriminate himself.

It was only through reading books, written years later by investigative journalists, that I became aware of a 77-page document that Liam McCaffrey sent to the Quinn Group bondholders in May 2008. The document implied that it had been written with my support and input, but to this day I have never seen a copy of it, nor did I ever hear it being discussed. It seems strange that journalists have seen this document, while neither I nor any of my family have ever seen sight of it.

According to journalists, Liam's lengthy presentation made confident predictions of future growth. It forecast that Quinn Group's revenues would reach €2.4 billion in 2008, and €2.65 billion in 2009. It admitted that without any board or regulatory approval, it had invested €398 million in Anglo shares – using money from QIL – sometime between May 2007 and July 2008.

Liam felt that when the Regulator became aware of who was responsible for withdrawing so much Quinn Insurance money, which at this stage had all been lost, both himself and Dara would be struck off as accountants by their regulatory board. I believe that this was potentially one of the biggest cover-ups in the whole debacle. Later, the Gardaí, on behalf of the ODCE, interviewed myself, Patricia, and our children regarding our knowledge of and input into the whole affair, and found that we had no input, as all transactions were agreed and implemented by Quinn and Anglo Irish Bank executives. In fact, myself and the rest of the family were ultimately witnesses on behalf of the state in prosecuting Anglo executives, so how or why did the state and the media come up with the idea that I had a part to play in the administration of the Group? As is well known, I was never on any of the compliance, audit, or investment committees, but, more importantly, when the Central Bank spent years investigating who was responsible for the multiple breaches, they found that I wasn't involved, and in fact had me as a witness for a second time on behalf of the state during the Central Bank's investigation into Liam and Kevin, so how was it ever felt that I was responsible for the administration side of the business, and if I was, what were Liam, Dara and Kevin, who were main board directors, paid to do? Does this mean that the Taoiseach of the country is responsible for any breaches that occur in any government department, or in RTE for that matter?

In 2013, the Central Bank found against Quinn Insurance regarding a number of offences. The Central Bank and Quinn Insurance entered into a settlement agreement on 18 February 2013 in relation to breaches of financial regulations, including taking the €398 million without either board or regulatory approval, and Quinn Insurance was fined the maximum penalty of €5 million. The individuals responsible were not identified publicly, and I believe that this was a critical miscalculation, as over the five-year investigation, they would have known exactly who was responsible, but decided against prosecuting them, which left the impression that it was me who was responsible for everything. Ten years later, they are still not being investigated for any wrongdoing prior to 2013, or since 2013. More about that later. This has created a belief in the community that justice is not being served evenly, something that I strongly believe. As Derville Rowland, Head of Enforcement Division at the Central Bank, commented in 2013, at the time of the Quinn Insurance settlement, "... firms and individuals must expect full public disclosure of all relevant facts in successful enforcement action. There is powerful deterrent impact from such disclosure. We also owe it to consumers and investors so that their confidence, so damaged in recent years, is restored in Ireland's financial services sector." It does lead one to wonder why those responsible were not named at the time.

Liam's document to the financiers also outlined the fact that QIL's board hadn't met for six months, and the flimsy excuse given was the absence of one member. The document admitted the multiple wrongs that had been committed by the executives, but for which I was later blamed, with zero supporting evidence.

While I had very little contact with the banks or bondholders, Liam and Dara flew on our private jet to meet them in New York and Delaware (whose low taxes have always attracted lots of financiers) a couple of times a year and had regular discussions. While they were reckless in pledging these QIL guarantees, I don't believe there was any malice in signing them over, but I think that it was unforgiveable for them to say that I was involved, as Liam and Kevin did in the Central Bank Inquiry in May 2019. By Liam giving the Group's share pledges and guarantees on the family's properties, he also protected his own position, since he himself was heavily indebted to the bank and the Quinn Group. Trevor Birney's *Quinn* has stated that the €500,000 Liam took from a Quinn Group company in 2008 has been written off. As this €500,000 wasn't written off during my time at the Quinn Group, when was it written off, and was the person who wrote it off aware that the circumstances required examination? Did they not feel that this should be investigated by the ODCE or the Gardaí?

The Quinn Group's solicitor for many years, A&L Goodbody, had approved the legal agreement that included the guarantees to the bond holders. I am still annoyed that they did not advise the company that it should contest the appointment of the administrator knowing that the inclusion of the guarantees shouldn't be considered a legal basis for the administration of the company as they didn't appear to have any legal standing, as verified in detail by PwC and the Moore Stephens report. Liam McCaffrey gave evidence on this point at the Central Bank Inquiry in 2019, where he said that he depended on A&L Goodbody to keep him and the board right.

The Irish government was in a panic of its own after the fall of Lehman Brothers in September 2008, and it gave a blanket guarantee on the assets and liabilities of six Irish banks. The Irish economy, which had grown fast during the 'Bertie Boom', was suddenly in serious trouble, because it was so exposed to the worldwide banking crisis. The foreign borrowings of Irish banks had risen from €15 billion to €110 billion between 2006 and 2008. Much of the money had gone on a construction boom, which we had largely steered clear of. In 2008 the residential property market slumped dramatically, but we were not affected directly, as we had bought no new property assets in Ireland in the previous few years, and had in fact sold a number of assets in Ireland.

The Quinn and 'Maple Ten' deals were described in the media as a "hall of mirrors", an "extravagant scam", and a "good old-fashioned carousel", Fintan O'Toole has argued. Many of the Maple Ten had strong Fianna Fáil connections, which has fuelled many conspiracy theories. But I personally only knew three of the ten: Seán Reilly, a Cavan man; Joe Reilly (no relation), who came from County Longford and had held his wedding reception at the Slieve Russell; and Seamus Ross, who was a customer of mine, buying both building materials and insurance policies from Quinn Group. I didn't know any of them particularly well, and I certainly had no communication with any of them about shares; however, I believe that they rightly felt that they were doing no wrong.

Anglo was not out of the woods by any means. In September 2008 a meeting was held between Finance Minister Brian Lenihan, Anglo's chairman Seán FitzPatrick, and David Doyle, secretary of the Department of Finance. FitzPatrick suggested a merger between Anglo and the Irish Nationwide bank, but Doyle asked him "And what about the sandman, Seánie?", referring, as Shane Ross puts it, "to the billionaire Quinn's recent acrobatics in Anglo shares". According to Ross, the "beleaguered chairman of Anglo shrugged his shoulders", and Anglo were shown the door by the Department of Finance. I believe it was harsh to show them the door, as the Department of Finance was fully aware of these loans from September 2007, and had in fact supported them. The huge amount of money Anglo invested in the CFDs had apparently kiboshed a rescue deal for the bank.

Drumm and FitzPatrick did not survive long after that. Funnily enough, it was not the huge amount of money invested by Anglo in the Quinn Group that finished them, but a separate scandal, in which I had no involvement.

In September 2008 it became apparent that for several years Anglo had been receiving a short-term loan twice annually from Irish Life and Permanent, a big bank and insurance company, to make its balance sheet look better. Each time, the loan would be repaid a few days later. By 2008 the size of loan had reached €7.2 billion.

In early October 2008, according to Simon Carswell, a member of Anglo's treasury department called Ciaran McArdle spoke with Claire Taylor, who worked in the Office of the Financial Regulator. According to Carswell, Taylor was looking for information regarding a figure of €8 billion on Anglo's balance sheet. McArdle went into some detail advising her that the number was there in an attempt to "manipulate our balance sheet for our financial year-end last night." McArdle explained that when the snapshot of the bank's performance was produced in December, they were trying to make it look "as good as possible", and that "it is not a real number". The figure was excluded from the bank's ratios, and would be taken off the balance sheet within a couple of days. Taylor's response was "that's grand, right, I think that's everything." Obviously, the Office of the Financial Regulator was aware of the manipulation that was going on, and seemed comfortable with it.

Simultaneously, the unusual balance sheet entry was also brought to the attention of Kevin Cardiff, one of the most senior people in the Department of Finance. He did not believe that the balance sheet manipulation was a 'red flag' issue, and he did not inform the then Minister for Finance, Brian Lenihan. The chairman of the Dáil's Public Accounts Committee would later say that it was "incredible" that the balance sheet manipulation had happened, and that it was known to "the controlling hand of the department", who did not inform the minister. Kevin Cardiff was later promoted to secretary general of the Department of Finance after the incumbent, David Doyle, retired in February 2010. He continued to wield huge power in the department, and it was he who subsequently appointed Matthew Elderfield, and we now know what he was hired to do.

Of course, Anglo's accounts were audited annually, and their auditors at the time were Ernst and Young (EY). EY received €4.6 million in fees from Anglo between 2005 and 2008, but these fees provided no guarantee that EY's audit would be as thorough as one might expect. The unusual transactions, made in an attempt to manipulate the bank's balance sheet, were not noticed by its auditors, or if they were, they were not referred to, nor was the €2.34 billion Anglo invested to support its own share price. EY gave Anglo a clean bill of health for its original 2008 accounts, which I and thousands of other investors relied upon. EY were later forced to reissue Anglo's 2008 accounts, which came with a health warning. EY resigned as Anglo's auditors shortly afterwards. Following their resignation, EY were appointed to advise the Regulator the following month, as well as being appointed as receivers to Moran Hotels; then, in April, they were appointed by the government to conduct a forensic review of Irish Nationwide. They later refused to appear in front of the Public Accounts Committee and tried to halt the inquiry into the banking scandal after the Comptroller & Auditor General stated that they had a case to answer. Then in 2011, they were appointed to the Quinn Group, where there was an immediate direction given that the new Quinn Group board could not sue Anglo Irish Bank, so it doesn't appear to matter what they do, they will still be on the government's favoured list, and have helped them out of hot spots with all of the information they had about the Quinn–Anglo relationship.

In late 2008, the scandal was soon all over the front pages of Irish newspapers, and Anglo's reputation was badly tarnished. Until then, Anglo had been the best-respected bank in the world, according to the World Economic Forum. If I had known about the bank's longstanding arrangement with Irish

Life and Permanent, I would not have agreed to Quinn Group investing a penny in Anglo shares or CFDs, but I did not hear about the scandal until it was too late.

The Irish Life and Permanent scandal was too big for the Green Jersey to cover up. Ultimately, heads had to roll. In July 2016, after years of legal wrangling, Anglo executives John Bowe and Willie McAteer, and Irish Life and Permanent's former chief executive, Denis Casey, were jailed for between two and three years, after being found guilty of a conspiracy to defraud. Casey's appeal against the conviction later failed in the Supreme Court.

I believe that what was done to Denis Casey was outrageous. I have never met Mr Casey, but I believe that he is an extremely honourable and decent man, and I find it difficult to understand why he was imprisoned for participating in the 'green jersey agenda' when this was done at the request of the Irish financial authorities.

In the short term, David Drumm and Seán FitzPatrick had to go. FitzPatrick resigned as Anglo chairman on 18 December 2008, and Drumm followed suit on 19 December. FitzPatrick also admitted that he had concealed his personal borrowings from the bank. Patrick Neary, the Financial Regulator, went the following month. It's interesting that just three months prior to that, in September 2008, Seán FitzPatrick invested over €1 million in Anglo shares, so obviously he still believed in the bank, even though it was later stated that he must have been aware that the bank was in trouble – but surely if he was, he wouldn't have invested so much only a few months earlier.

The trouble is that my final meetings with all three individuals – FitzPatrick, Drumm and Neary – were informal and unrecorded, and within a few months all three of them had resigned their positions. With hindsight, I should have asked for an agreement in writing from them at the time, but it never occurred to me that they would all resign within weeks, so when I met Donal O'Connor, Drumm's successor, and an honourable man, in January 2009, I assured him that I would honour the agreement I had made with FitzPatrick, Drumm, and Neary. He seemed very comfortable with that, as he had been the managing partner in PwC, who were the Quinn Group auditors for many years, and he would have been fully aware of our profit growth over many years. With all that was going on, I should have gone back to White and Case and made sure that we had a proper legal agreement signed on a way forward, but at that stage, I didn't see any problems with the bank, which was now owned by the government, which was appointed by the public, as we had made a full commitment to repaying all of the loans in full, even those for the share support. In hindsight, while I was very demanding for forty years on those who worked in the operational side of the business, unfortunately, that wasn't the case for the executive side of the business.

* * * *

In October 2008, Pat Brady from the Office of the Financial Regulator fined Quinn Insurance €3.25 million and me €200,000 for various breaches. While everyone knew I wasn't responsible for the transactions, as owner and chairman of the company, I never objected. As I had always taken the glory when things had gone well, I felt I should carry the can when things went wrong. It was never my style to blame somebody else, something that I paid a heavy price for later, as covering up for others was never appreciated. "We will pay the fines and move on", I told RTE.

The only thing I resisted was a sanction that Brady wanted to levy on my son, Seán Jnr. At a meeting with the full board present, I asked Brady why Seán Jnr was being sanctioned too, seeing as he only ever worked in the operational side of the business, not the regulatory side. Brady accepted my argument, and he agreed that Seán should not be sanctioned. I think that this proved what sort of men Liam and Dara were; it was me who had to interject to say that Seán wasn't involved in the administration of the company. Surely these men, who were present, should have accepted some responsibility for what had happened at that stage. It was only two months later that Liam offered me his resignation on the basis that when the Central Bank investigation would be complete both he and Dara would be struck off as accountants.

I found Brady to be a bit abrasive in private meetings, but he was always complimentary about Quinn Insurance, telling me that we were the Ryanair of the insurance world, and a breath of fresh air. I had good relationships with Patrick Neary and Con Horan, Brady's superiors at the Office of the Financial Regulator, and I had several meetings with them in 2008. Gavin Daly and Ian Kehoe claimed that in 2008 Patrick Neary had a light-touch reputation, and that his office "was reluctant to censure Quinn" because they did not want to further destabilise Anglo, or the Quinn Group itself, which was both one of Ireland's biggest insurers and one of its biggest employers.

But I had now received a 'red card' from the Regulator, and I was sacked as chairman of Quinn Insurance. I was succeeded by Jim Quigley, an existing non-executive director of QIL, and a veteran at the insurance giant Axa. I had not recruited Jim, who was an amiable, cool character, and a victim, not a villain, of this story. Jim and Colin Morgan warned me on a number of occasions that the new Regulator might be keen to put a spoke in my wheel, and with Pat Brady and the new Regulator receiving regular calls from the Financial Services Authority (FSA) in the UK, in hindsight, this was a useful warning. Unfortunately, as the insurance company was doing so well, I underestimated their advice.

While none of the non-executive directors on either the Quinn Group board or the Quinn Insurance board wanted to get involved in the blame game, I knew they were concerned about their hard-earned reputations being damaged, and we decided to appoint new additional directors to the main Quinn Group board, to make sure that what had happened would never happen again, and that all important decisions would be agreed at board level in future, which hadn't been happening since David Mackey's departure. The new non-execs were Brendan Tuohy, an ex-senior civil servant, and Pat O'Neill, the ex-CEO of Glanbia, who were both well-known and respected by my brother, Peter. They joined another long-standing non-executive director, Paddy Murphy, who was an ex-Bank of Ireland senior executive. All of them were around my own age, and I felt that they were excellent choices, and that they would enhance the board and be allies of the family, just as David Mackey and Peter were.

Shortly after, Liam offered his resignation, during Christmas week 2008. There was general disappointment all around, amongst the non-executive directors and my own family, that I didn't accept Liam's resignation. They all knew that I wasn't involved in the administration of the business. Wrongly, I felt at the time that there were two reasons for not accepting it. One was that it would add to the negative stream of reporting on the Quinn issue in the media, and secondly, I felt that as it was Liam, as chief executive, who was responsible for what happened, that it would be wrong of him to walk away without trying to resolve some of the issues. Now, I feel it was a mistake not to accept his resignation.

Brendan Tuohy and Pat O'Neill began in early 2009, after I had left the QIL board. The first board meeting they attended was in March 2009 at Buswells Hotel in Dublin. I didn't attend that meeting, which was called to sign off our 2008 accounts. From the start, Pat and Brendan would have known that I wasn't involved in the day-to-day administration of any Quinn companies. We had further operational meetings in June and September, which I chaired, and in December I wanted to introduce the Quinn board to my family, who came to the final part of the board meeting. My children chatted informally with the directors about golf, insurance and the hotels – the parts of the businesses in which they worked. Everything seemed hunky-dory, and none of the directors asked any questions about our Anglo CFDs, or our debts.

To our disappointment, these three men, Pat O'Neill, Paddy Murphy and Brendan Tuohy, who had been friendly, cooperative and helpful, later took a position where they were moving to have the family removed from the organisation, without speaking with any of us again. Not even to Peter, who was the one who invited them to join the board. Pat O'Neill would later become Quinn Group's chairman. It was later reported in various publications that they were unhappy about not being made fully aware of the CFD position. But in fact, most of the nation was aware of our CFDs, as a result of constant reports in the media over the previous two years, and, in any case, it would have been Liam, Dara, Kevin, and our auditors who would have been familiarising them with any details they needed to know.

Regarding the €500,000 that Liam had taken from a Quinn Group company, to cover his losses in CFDs, it was always, in my view, wrong and highly irregular, but that was not my main concern at that time. Why had he given Anglo share pledges on the Quinn Group and guarantees on my children's foreign properties? Had his personal debts to Anglo created a conflict of interest with his role at the Quinn Group, and skewed its whole relationship with Anglo? When I confronted Liam about the €500,000, his reaction was to say, "I know that it was wrong, but it's small beer in the grand scheme of things."

With hindsight I should have told Liam on the spot that it was not acceptable and sought his resignation.

Separately, the Central Bank did indeed subsequently investigate who was responsible for signing the guarantees to the American bondholders, and they reached a settlement with Liam McCaffrey and Kevin Lunney in 2019. At that stage, they would also have known for definite who was responsible for the breaches regarding the €398 million that was taken from Quinn Insurance.

6

Despite all the disappointments and setbacks of the previous two years, I started 2009 in a positive mood. On 30 January I told RTE, in a short interview, that our Anglo CFD investments had been a "bad mistake" and that the financial losses had been "hurtful". But in a new year message to staff and customers, I boasted that I would invest €2 billion in new technology over the next decade. I also promised that our profits would continue to increase by more than 30 per cent per annum, which they had for the previous 36 years, and that our debt would reduce significantly, year on year.

I believe that the Irish government bust the country between 2007 and 2012, when, in practical terms, they closed down the Irish banks and, by doing so, essentially closed the country. This resulted, for example, in AIB losing 95 per cent of their value in two years. How can a country survive in a situation where there was no bank lending? AIB said that it was "nationalisation by stealth". At the time, because of government policy, the banks were taking businesses and homes from tens of thousands of citizens, many of whose loans were never in default, and handing them to hedge funds at a fraction of their value, ruining the lives of many who had bought houses and built businesses, and the country is still paying a high price for those injustices, as the hedge funds that bought those loans have failed to develop them over the years, and has left the country in a housing crisis.

Because we had agreed to repay the full €2.8 billion, from our point of view 2009 was going to be a fairly dull year, but we continued to invest in our manufacturing and property operations, as well as doing the final commissioning on our new 54-megawatt windfarm, which had cost us €67.5 million in 2008. We were also increasing our cash in Quinn Insurance on a monthly basis, going from €600 million in 2008 to €1.1 billion in March 2010, when the administrators were appointed.

Of course, Drumm and FitzPatrick had both resigned from Anglo Irish Bank in December 2008, and the bank was nationalised on 16 January 2009, which meant that we were essentially dealing with the Irish government rather than with a private bank. It never occurred to us that now that we were dealing with the Irish state, they would renege on a deal they had been party to devising and overseeing the implementation of, and that they would appoint the outgoing Attorney General to represent them. Whether or not they were ever advised on White and Case's legal letter and the agreement between myself, Seán FitzPatrick, David Drumm, and Patrick Neary from the Regulator's Office, we still don't know, thirteen years later. Everything changed after the departure of FitzPatrick, Drumm and Neary.

In December 2008, the Irish government had announced plans to inject €1.5 billion of capital into Anglo, in return for a 75 per cent stake in the bank, which never happened, and the offer was withdrawn. The nationalisation was made official on 16 January 2009. The Taoiseach Brian Cowen announced that it was "business as usual" at Anglo, and that the bank was still solvent. But by then the Dublin and London stock exchanges had suspended trading in Anglo Irish's shares, whose closing price – just €0.22 – was 98 per cent below its peak.

Anglo had become another casualty of the worldwide banking crisis. It was later estimated that of the €78 billion cost of bailing out the country, €50 billion was estimated to be for the banks. If anything, I can't understand why it wasn't more than €50 billion, as so many of the bank's loans were later sold to vulture funds for between 10 and 20 per cent of their cost. With Mike Aynsley stating that he had sold €95 billion of assets, predominantly to vulture funds, and AIB having their book reduced from €180 billion of loans to €90 billion, what other result could we have had? I believe that this was one of the biggest mistakes that was made during the banking crisis, as many of the assets that were given away then are still retained by vulture and hedge funds, and have not been made available to Irish citizens in the midst of a housing crisis.

The nationalisation was a catastrophe for Anglo, and, as it turns out, for me. What had been a private debt between me and a commercial bank now became a political issue. I now effectively owed €2.8 billion to the Irish taxpayer, and I now had the Irish government to deal with. Until 2009 I had never borrowed a cent from the Irish state, and indeed I had paid it €1.3 billion in taxes over the years.

In May 2008 Anglo had announced record profits, but just a year later, in May 2009, Anglo's interim results showed that it had made a colossal loss of €2.8 billion in the space of only six months. €368 million of these losses arose from a write-off, because "ten long-standing clients" of Anglo (the Maple Ten) had bought Anglo shares which were now effectively worthless, "with money lent to them by Anglo after Seán Quinn unwound his CFD position in the bank", Shane Ross wrote in 2009. Ross seemed to imply that by now I had severed my ties with Anglo, and that I no longer owed any money for my CFD debts. Whether we owed it or not, we were always prepared to pay it, and never asked for it to be reduced by even one cent.

There were several changes of personnel at the same time, both in the bank and the Regulator's office. On 9 January 2009, just as Anglo was being nationalised, Patrick Neary, the Central Bank of Ireland's head regulator, announced that he would be retiring at the end of that month.

At Anglo itself a new chairman, Donal O'Connor, was quickly installed to take Seán FitzPatrick's place. O'Connor was a former managing partner at our auditors PwC until 2007, so would have seen our profits increasing by more than ten-fold every ten years.

O'Connor showed no fear of us not being willing or capable of repaying our loans. But he did ask me to consider selling off assets so I could repay the bank faster, but the timing was all wrong: amidst the banking crisis the value of all our assets had suddenly plunged, and I felt that I should wait until a better price could be obtained. It has been reported that the meeting was cordial, but that towards the end I told O'Conner I could be difficult if

I was forced to repay the money, and that I added words about how rats behave when backed into a corner, which was effectively a threat to the bank. I don't recall any threats being made, and I would be surprised if that was O'Connor's recollection of the meeting as repayment was never an issue. However, it is true that I didn't want to sell assets in such a depressed market.

As well as a new chairman, Anglo urgently needed a new chief executive to take David Drumm's place. The government quickly vetoed Anglo's own choice, Declan Quilligan, the head of Anglo's UK operations. Instead, the government, and the Regulator, wanted an outsider to run Anglo. Mike Soden, a former chief executive of Bank of Ireland, was consulted for advice on who would be suitable to run Anglo. Soden recommended Mike Aynsley for the job.

Born in Australia in 1960, Aynsley had started his career at the Commonwealth Bank of Australia. He had then worked at the French BNP's Sydney office, the Rotterdam Bank in Holland, Security Pacific (which was one of the financiers of my first cement plant) and at its stockbroker Hoare Govett, where he had befriended Soden. In the 1990s Aynsley had worked alongside Soden at National Australia Bank, which then owned the National Irish Bank. He later worked at Deloitte, and at the Australian and New Zealand Banking Group (ANZ), before gaining an MBA.

Aynsley came to Ireland from Australia with a huge salary plus bonuses, relocation expenses, a generous pension and free flights back and forth to Australia, at a cost of almost €1 million annually. Aynsley began on 7 September 2009. Aynsley soon brought in Tom Hunersen, an American known as 'the gunner', who had worked with him at National Australia Bank, as well as Richard Woodhouse.

The only meeting that I had with the new management of Anglo prior to them taking my businesses was in February 2010, when I met Mike Aynsley and Richard Woodhouse, and, after the meeting, I couldn't believe that this man had been appointed as CEO to a major Irish bank. The week before he left IBRC (as Anglo later became), on 4 August 2013, he was interviewed by Tom Lyons of the *Sunday Independent*. When asked "What did you and your management team achieve at IBRC?", Aynsley's response was incredible. Aynsley replied, confidently, saying he was proud that IBRC had sold off €95 billion of assets at a fraction of their real value. The frightening thing is that he seemed to believe that this was an achievement, and the consequences have since come home to roost, with sites throughout the country that were bought for nearly nothing being hoarded for years by American hedge funds. It all begs the question about the whole approach that was taken to deal with financial turmoil, which was a problem for every country in the world, but the Irish government turned it into a financial crisis.

It has been said that at Mike Aynsley's first meeting with Finance Minister Brian Lenihan in 2009 he was told that the government had not yet decided whether it wanted to ask him to save Anglo or shut it down. I'm sure that Lenihan soon realised what Aynsley's abilities were, and that helped him make the decision. This was news to Aynsley, and to Donal O'Connor. However, Aynsley was determined to save Anglo, and he appointed Richard Woodhouse to oversee the rescue. Officially, Woodhouse was Anglo's new head of specialist lending, but in practice he was Aynsley's number two. When Woodhouse first heard that I owed Anglo €2.8 billion, it has been claimed that he asked Aynsley "Did you say billion?" incredulously.

Citizen Quinn says that Woodhouse found me "as he portrayed himself – a man of the people, open, direct, apparently simple to understand" – but that I did not understand the serious situation I was in. But surely he must have known that it was Anglo Irish Bank and the state that put me in that position, but despite putting me in that position, I was still willing and able to rescue the position for myself, the bank, and the nation. Although Woodhouse felt I "had built a tremendous business", he "could not fathom how or why he had gambled it all on a secret investment in Anglo Irish Bank." He is right there, as I can't understand it myself, but maybe he should have asked himself why his predecessors put €2.34 billion, 78 per cent of the total investment, into supporting these shares, while the Quinns invested 22 per cent, less than what we had received in dividends between 2002 and 2006. Surely he would have known that his predecessors were being investigated for criminality regarding this investment. Apparently, Woodhouse considered our insurance business to be the jewel in the crown, and he was also right in that view.

He felt that it was ripe for disposal, but I could not countenance it being sold, as it was the most profitable business I had ever owned, generating profits of between €200 million and €300 million a year, around half of our annual profits. Selling it would have extended the repayment of our loans by several years. Thirteen years later, I still can't believe that not only was it given away for nothing, but that it has cost the Irish taxpayer more than €1 billion through the Insurance Compensation Fund, while in fact, it should have made profits of between €3 and €4 billion over the past thirteen years.

At my first meeting with Aynsley and Woodhouse on 19 February 2010, I restated my plan to repay all the money we owed to Anglo, plus interest. I forecast that in the next three years the Quinn Group would increase our pre-tax profits back up to €500 million a year, reduce our debts by €400 million, pay at least €300 million in Irish tax, spend around €500 million to complete all our outstanding projects in both manufacturing and property, and create 1,000 new jobs. My proposal was realistic – as in the previous 30-odd years, we always projected figures much less than what we eventually achieved – and I confirmed my offer in writing to Aynsley, who replied to me on 26 February to say that he was "delighted that the core Group has continued to trade robustly in a difficult economic environment, and that performance relevant to peers continues to be pleasing." He had had access to a review that had been completed by KPMG, and was obviously impressed by its contents. Aynsley added that he looked forward to meeting with me again after his meeting with "our shareholder", who was of course the Irish government. Surely, if the bank wanted a workable solution, we were offering them the perfect scenario in writing: paying our interest; reducing our debts substantially; increasing employment; making a huge contribution to the taxman; and, if we didn't meet our projections in full, they would have known that the €400 million debt reduction was safe in any event, as all we had to do was reduce our €500 million of capital investment. We had for the previous 30-odd years budgeted conservatively, and we were highly confident of beating our projections again going forward, so it was win–win for all sides.

Another new face at Anglo was Alan Dukes, a former leader of Fine Gael who had been Irish Finance Minister in the early 1980s, during Garret FitzGerald's time as Taoiseach. Dukes was one of Anglo's 'public interest' board directors. Much has been made of the fact that Dukes was also a director of Wilson Hartnell, the big Dublin public relations company which worked for the Quinn Group from 2006 onwards. Quinn Group was still Anglo's largest shareholder, and some have claimed that this created a conflict of interest. According to Shane Ross's book *The Untouchables*, Dukes did himself no favours by replying tersely to questions from a journalist, the *Sunday Business Post*'s Kathleen Barrington, by asserting that he wasn't a "lobbyist". When she asked to see a list of all Wilson Hartnell's clients, he replied that "this is none of your business." Dukes later gave local politicians from the border area incredible information about why the company was taken into receivership, and supplied figures about how Ireland would benefit from the appointment of a receiver. It was scarcely believable at the time, and it has become less believable every day since. From January 2009 until February 2010, and from February 2010 until April 2011, I had no meetings whatsoever with Anglo, despite what Alan Dukes has stated. It is very concerning that Alan Dukes, Richard Woodhouse, Mike Aynsley and Murdoch McKillop are all stating very clearly that they had multiple meetings with me during this time period, meetings which never happened. This is obviously an attempt to convince the public that they tried to negotiate deals with me, when, in fact, they never even met me during this period of time. I only met them after the takeover of the Quinn Group. The meetings I did have during this period were: one in February 2010 with Mike Aynsley and Richard Woodhouse, and a board meeting in April 2010 with the Quinn Group board. No other meetings took place with Anglo or the Quinn Group board until after the company was taken over. The day it was taken over was the first day I met Alan Dukes.

On 7 April 2009, the government announced the creation of the National Asset Management Agency (NAMA). After this, regardless of how strong a bank was (and I am no great supporter of the banks!), when a government body would reduce the value of a large part of their lending by around 50 per cent, no bank in the world could sustain that, no matter how strong they were, and so it proved, as all of the Irish banks were pushed under water, as they were practically closed for business, and many of their assets were given away to vulture funds. This was done at a time when the majority of mortgages were performing, but as more and more people lost their jobs, and the banks all but closed, non-performing loans naturally increased and there was such pressure on the banks that they even foreclosed on some performing mortgages.

Through NAMA, the Irish government took a similar approach to other Irish entrepreneurs, such as the disgraceful approach taken towards Paddy McKillen, an Irish hotelier and property developer, whose companies owned four of London's grandest hotels: the Savoy, Claridge's, the Connaught and the Berkeley. In February 2011 McKillen won a landmark Supreme Court case, which blocked NAMA from seizing his €3 billion empire. This showed an Irish government under such serious financial strain that they were willing to cause the collapse of the McKillen Group. The full force of the Irish state was brought to bear, with the government bringing in its Attorney General, Paul Gallagher (who had drafted the NAMA legislation), to argue against McKillen. Ann Nolan from the Department of Finance was also brought in to testify against McKillen. Paddy McKillen eventually won, but not before a High Court case, which ultimately went to the Supreme Court, and cost millions of euros in legal fees. While other countries were trying to help and support their entrepreneurs, Ireland was trying to destroy theirs. To this day, I still can't understand who was pushing this agenda, or why it was being pushed. Interestingly, at the time, an Irish Supreme Court case, which, unusually, was heard by all seven Supreme Court judges, gave a landmark decision outlining how a government cannot override citizens' rights during national emergencies, and surely this must also apply to the hundreds of thousands of people who lost their homes or businesses during that period. Is it coincidental that Paddy McKillen and myself, who were both regarded as billionaires, were both born and reared in Northern Ireland?

McKillen's case wasn't a one-off. They did the same thing with Cork developer Michael O'Flynn, who they also tried to bring into NAMA.

Michael was fortunate to have both the human and financial resources to defend himself and was able to keep his company away from the claws of NAMA, and has continued to be very successful since, as has the McKillen family.

Ann Nolan, who testified for the Department of Finance during the McKillen case, was one of Michael Noonan's top officials, and she had played a key role in the formation of NAMA in 2009. She also played a key role in the handling of the banking crisis. In July 2013 Daniel McConnall from the *Irish Independent* published transcripts of phone calls between Ann Nolan and John Bowe of Anglo. These conversations took place around the time of the bank guarantee, three weeks before Anglo was nationalised. The transcripts show how cosy the relationship was between the Department of Finance and Anglo. Ann Nolan enjoyed friendly conversations with Bowe, showing sympathy and camaraderie with him. McConnall concluded that Nolan's conduct was disgraceful, and he questioned Nolan's competency and her suitability for such a senior role.

I also had my own problems with Ann Nolan. As a senior representative of the Department of Finance, she attended meetings of the Domestic Standing Group. Within a month of my meeting with FitzPatrick and Drumm in the Ardboyne Hotel in Navan, Nolan was aware of my CFD position.

On 29 January 2009 Brian Lenihan requested a report from Donal O'Connor, the new chairman of Anglo, on the extent of lending by Anglo for the purpose of CFD acquisitions. O'Connor provided a draft reply to Ann Nolan on 3 February 2009, which O'Connor intended to send the following morning to Lenihan, with a covering note saying, "As requested, I enclose a report on the extent of lending for the purpose of share acquisition and contracts for difference generally, and Anglo shares in particular." The reply was an admission by O'Connor that the bank was lending funds to support its own share price. Nolan agreed to read the draft report and revert to O'Connor with her comments. What happened in the following 24 hours is anyone's guess, but the final version of the report, sent the following day, denied that the bank had advanced any lending for the purposes of supporting its own share price. The new version of the report said, "We do not lend for the purpose of taking positions in contracts for differences." Why was the letter changed? It appears to prove that the Department of Finance had known that Anglo had acted illegally, but it suited them to turn a blind eye.

Not much happened over the following months, as the recession deepened. We were stabilising the company, but still making very hefty profits. At the same time, an official inquiry into the collapse of Anglo began. In November 2008 Anglo's solicitor, William Fry, sent a huge number of documents, through Dara O'Reilly, to the Quinn Group's head office. The documents were for me and several members of my family to sign, to confirm that we had received legal advice about the share support transactions. They had not been signed at the time the share support transactions went through. In February 2009, Fry's tried again to have the documents signed, and made contact with a Quinn Group employee to see if she could assist. Again, they weren't signed. On the third occasion the subject was broached, they were forwarded by Liam McCaffrey and Dara O'Reilly to our local solicitor in Cavan, Michael Ryan (a family friend of many years standing, who was a former captain of the Slieve Russell Golf Club).

Thankfully, Michael was very professional. He rang me to tell me about the documents he had in front of him on his desk, and we met later that day. Michael and I agreed how wrong and inappropriate this would be, given that the family had received no such advice.

Michael replied to Fry's as follows:

Dear XXX,

We confirm that we received a formal request to attend with members of the Quinn family for the purposes of completing independent advice letters, by way of security.

We confirm that we attended firstly with Mr Sean Quinn Senior, at his offices in Cavan on 4th September 2009.

When the writer enquired as to the background, as a part of an enquiry incidental to the furnishing of legal advice, it became apparent that the documents which were sought to be completed, were in effect "post facto", and furthermore, it appeared that the Quinn family and their associated interests, were not getting any benefit in late 2009, incidental to the furnishing of independent legal advice and any subsequent legal advice letters.

It was therefore my respectful opinion, that it would be inappropriate for me in the particular circumstances, to provide independent legal advices relating to transactions which had long since taken place, and the related documentation apparently already in place, including those documents relating to the matter upon which the certification as to the giving and obtaining of independent legal advice was now being sought.

Yours sincerely ...

Looking back on this correspondence, I have to ask the question: whose idea was it and why was it necessary? It appears to me as though there may have been a number of solicitors and accountants involved. For once I had overruled Dara and Liam, and I told them that we could not obtain retrospective legal advice as Anglo had requested. The incident was a reminder to all of us that over several decades I had signed thousands of documents given to us by the executives without reading them or understanding them. I had formed this habit as far back as the 1970s, from my early years in business, and, unfortunately, the children felt that it wouldn't go down well if they didn't follow suit. Considering all that happened before and after this, it makes you wonder what inadequacies, deficiencies or discrepancies are either overlooked, covered up or ignored by the very institutions that are supposed to protect us.

* * * *

Amidst all of this upheaval, my travels around Asia and Europe reduced, as we were purchasing no new properties, only developing existing ones.

However, in April 2009 Barack Obama, who had been elected as US president five months earlier, came to stay at the Prague Hilton during a state visit to the Czech Republic, along with the First Lady, his wife, Michelle. I was invited to welcome them to our hotel, and I was delighted to do so. The Obamas were accompanied by Hillary Clinton, who was then the US Secretary of State. What you see is what you get with Obama. Both he and Michelle were charming. He certainly likes to keep in good shape: he was in the hotel's gym at 6 in the morning. Both he and Michelle exuded class, and it is no surprise that he was considered to be an excellent president.

Back in Ireland, there was little respite from my problems. From January 2010 there was a new Financial Regulator in Dublin, to replace Patrick Neary. On 4 January 2010, the very day that Richard Woodhouse began at Anglo, an Englishman called Matthew Elderfield arrived as the new Deputy Governor of the Central Bank of Ireland, in charge of regulation.

Aged 43, Elderfield had studied and worked on both sides of the Atlantic, though I believe he has never passed a finance exam in his life. It was the only thing that he and I had in common! After a long stint at the Financial Services Authority (FSA) in London, he was the chief executive of the Bermuda Monetary Authority from 2007 to 2009. But he is said to have suffered from 'island fever' in Bermuda, and to have become reluctant to sign another three-year contract. In early 2010 Elderfield swapped Bermuda for Dublin. He soon hired Jonathon McMahon, another Englishman who had worked at the FSA in London, as his 'enforcer'.

I never met Matthew Elderfield, and I never sought a meeting with him, but QIL's chairman, Jim Quigley, always kept me informed about what he was up to. It was no secret that QIL's growth in the British insurance market had caught the attention of Elderfield's former employer, the FSA (which regulates insurance companies in the UK). Elderfield seems to have brought these complaints with him to Dublin. In early 2010 Jim Quigley told me that he and Colin Morgan, QIL's chief executive, were regularly getting calls from Pat Brady, passing on the concerns of the British FSA.

Citizen Quinn and other journalists claim that "The FSA ... had raised concerns over Quinn's operations in Britain. It was undercutting all its competitors there on price, building up market share but losing significant sums. The FSA wanted to know if the paper billionaire could cover the losses. Elderfield knew enough about Seán Quinn to have his doubts." We were indeed undercutting British insurers on price, but we had the highest reserves of any insurance company in Ireland, or the UK; we had the lowest cost base; and we had higher profit margins than any of our competitors. This was mainly achieved by using our fast-track claims model.

The first quarter of 2010 was one of the best quarters in QIL's history. The company increased its cash balances by over €20 million, and significantly reduced its open claims, which had peaked in Week 3 of 2010 at 30,262. On 27 March 2010, three days prior to the appointment of the administrators, the open claims count fell to 27,428, a decrease of 2,834 claims from the peak. A month before the administrators were appointed, we had written our largest premium ever, of over £10 million, in the UK. This may have irked the industry enormously, as would our sponsorship of *The Late Late Show*. On the day the administrators were appointed, there was €1.1 billion of cash in Quinn Insurance's bank account, as well as ownership of €464 million of property assets. I believe that this was higher than any other insurance company in Ireland, and certainly higher per outstanding claim than any other company.

As Elderfield was being employed to serve the interests of the Irish taxpayer, what was he doing getting his orders from his old bosses in London? On the day that he sent administrators into Quinn Direct in March 2010, he barred Quinn Insurance from doing any further underwriting of insurance in the UK, which to my mind was assisting UK insurance companies.

Shortly after we were taken over, RSA had to raise €500 million for their Irish operations; FBD had to raise €300 million; and VHI, who never had meaningful solvency over the previous decade, had to raise €270 million from Warren Buffet. Although QIL's cashflow and profits in the first quarter of 2010 were at record levels, I had made powerful enemies in the insurance world. The stage was being set for QIL to be put into administration.

7

2010 seemed to get off to a great start, as my manufacturing businesses were past the worst point of the recession, and QIL was making record profits.

Just as I was reassuring Anglo at our February meeting that I would pay them back in full, the Irish people were taking to the streets to protest against the bank's mismanagement and the Irish Life and Permanent scandal. On 20 February 2010 some 120,000 people marched in Dublin. On 24 February the Gardaí raided Anglo's head office, and in March Seán FitzPatrick and David Drumm were arrested and questioned. FitzPatrick was later prosecuted but he was never convicted of any crime, and it was only in 2018 that David Drumm was prosecuted for his part in the Irish Life and Permanent scandal and jailed for six years. This was ten years after he and Denis Casey were instructed to work together to create an impression of high deposits in their respective banks.

Events then moved very quickly. On a Thursday, our executives were notified that there had been contingent guarantees given by subsidiaries of Quinn Insurance, and when it was checked out, both PwC and the American bondholders agreed that these guarantees had no standing – they were from subsidiaries of a regulated company – and that they would be released, but there were many bondholders, and it would take a couple of weeks to get the paperwork in order.

How had these illegal guarantees ever been made in the first place? At the Central Bank Inquiry in 2019 Liam McCaffrey blamed A&L Goodbody, and he may be right, as A&L Goodbody were principally responsible for approving the guarantee documents on our behalf. However, Liam and Kevin Lunney were also paid to read these documents, and to protect the interests of me and the rest of my family while we were busy running the businesses. How do these executives feel about failing to meet their fiduciary duties? At least Kevin Lunney had the honesty to tell the Central Bank Inquiry, in 2019, that his failures were something that he would have to live with for the rest of his life, but it still didn't stop him from being part of the gang that planned the betrayal of our family and our community in 2014–2015.

The Regulator had to move quickly before the guarantees were lifted, so Elderfield wasted no time. Before these twenty American banks and bondholders could release the guarantees, on 30 March 2010 Matthew Elderfield obtained an *ex parte* application in the High Court. I believe that his lack of relevant financial experience and knowledge was demonstrated on the first day, when there was no evidence to prove to Judge Kearns that there was a deficit, and also when he directed the administrators, who were appointed by the court, to stop underwriting in the UK.

Elderfield had made an *ex parte* application to the Courts, which meant we were not allowed to respond to it because Quinn Insurance was not represented at the hearing. If he was acting as a representative of the Irish government, why would he have to go with an *ex parte* application regarding the second biggest insurance company in the country, and one of its biggest employers? He obviously had a reason. Surely an experienced, qualified regulator would not have behaved in this manner, and would certainly not have played to the gallery by stating publicly "show me the money."

Despite the fact that the Regulator stated to the Court that "On the basis of currently available information the Financial Regulator is not in a position to verify the true extent of the impairment of the Insurer's assets by reason of the guarantee", Judge Nicholas Kearns granted Elderfield's wish, and he agreed to put QIL in administration. It is clear that by his own admission he could not verify whether the assets were impaired or not, and thirteen years later, we still have not received that verification. This was despite the fact that this statement is in stark contrast to the professional opinion of PwC and Moore Stephens. The company was put into administration on the basis that the €448 million of property assets should be excluded from QIL's reserves, rendering the company insolvent. PwC and Moore Stephens were stead-fast in their assertion that this was incorrect. Michael McAteer and Paul McCann, from Grant Thornton, were appointed as QIL's joint administrators.

In fact, QIL was anything but insolvent. Far from being broke, QIL had increased its cash reserves by half a billion euros between 2008 and March 2010. It was never short of cash: in 2008 it had €600 million of it, and in 2010 €1.1 billion. It also owned property assets worth €464 million, and in March 2010 it had cash and assets of €1.564 billion. None of these figures have ever been disputed.

So, what really happened with Quinn Insurance? Correspondence between our auditors, PwC, and the Financial Regulator after the admin-istration showed that PwC believed that the guarantees did not impact the solvency of QIL. In two reports to the Regulator, PwC maintained their view that their accountancy treatment of the guarantees, and their audit opinions, were appropriate.

A PwC report sent to the Financial Regulator, dated 21 June 2010, states on page 2 that "PWC is of the view that its audit opinions in respect of the years 2005, 2006, 2007 and 2008 were appropriate." On page 10, it states that:

> PWC was aware that PWC UK undertook audit work each year on covenant compliance as part of its assessment of the going concern status of Quinn Group. As this work had been successfully completed in each year, _PWC had no reason to believe that the existence of cross company guarantees of any type would have any financial impact_ [my emphasis].

In a later report, on 26 July 2010, PwC answered questions posed by the Financial Regulator. Question 1.4(b) asked PwC to "confirm whether PwC agrees that, in accordance with the valuation Rules contained in Annex III of the Regulations, the assets of the relevant subsidiaries should have been excluded for valuation purposes".

PwC's response was:

In respect of the years ended 31 December 2005–2008 (inclusive) PWC is not aware why an adjustment is requested to the valuation of the net assets of the relevant subsidiaries recorded in Forms 6 at those dates to which the respective forms were drawn up.

On the basis of the information currently available to it, PWC does not agree that the application of the valuation rules contained in Annex III of the European Communities (Non-Life Insurance) Framework Regulations 1994 would require the assets of the relevant subsidiaries to have been excluded from QIL's calculation of assets admissible as representing technical reserves as at 31 December 2005–2008 (inclusive).

In a further report, dated 29 October 2010, which was again submitted to the Regulator, PwC went further. They stated that the Regulator *instructed* the administrators of QIL to write the assets down to zero, thus ensuring that there was a solvency deficit [my emphasis.]

This matter had arisen when PwC submitted a regulatory return on 18 June 2010, and the Regulator sought further information on what gave rise to the report. PwC responded stating:

On 24 May 2010, PWC received a copy of QIL's monthly return to the Financial Regulator for the period ended 30 April 2010. The Valuation of the net assets of the subsidiary companies which had provided guarantees in respect of the liabilities of Quinn Group Limited down to zero in the return. On enquiry, PWC was informed that the net assets had been written down to zero in the return for the period ended 31 March 2010 on the instruction of the Financial Regulator, and that the joint administrators of QIL had required that the 30 April 2010 return also be completed in accordance with the instruction. As at 24 May 2010, the joint administrators had not, however, prepared a formal assessment of whether a _liability was required to be recorded in respect of the guarantees, taking account of all the relevant facts and circumstances,_ which PWC required for purposes of complying with its responsibilities under Section 35(1) [my emphasis].

On 14 June 2010, PWC received correspondence from QIL which stated "it is currently our view that the existence of the guarantees has a material impact on QIL's ability to ensure full value for its investment in subsidiaries. In this context we anticipate that from both an accounting and regulatory perspective that it would _be prudent to account for a complete impairment of the investment leading to a nil net book value_ of the investments as recorded in the books of QIL" [my emphasis].

On the basis of an instruction by the Financial Regulator on 18 June 2010, two-and-a-half months after the administration, PwC filed a return writing down the subsidiary assets to nil. The basis of the nil valuation was an instruction from the Regulator to QIL's administrators. On 24 May 2010, PwC noted that the administrators failed to prepare an assessment on whether a liability was required in respect of the guarantees. Two weeks later, PwC received an instruction from the administrators, in line with the Regulator's instruction to write down the assets to nil.

Pertinent questions that arose and were put forward to Matthew Elderfield by the local support group and David Mackey have never been answered, queries that bring into question the legality of the administration process, and the impartiality of the Financial Regulator. What we wanted to know, then and now, was:

1. On what legal or professional advice did the Regulator seek to have the value of QIL subsidiary companies written down to nil?
2. The administrators were court-appointed, and answerable to the court. Why were they taking instructions from the Financial Regulator, and not allowed to independently assess the situation?
3. On what grounds did the Financial Regulator give a direction to the administrators to stop underwriting business in the UK?

That day was very hard for me; one of the most difficult days of my life. I happened to be in the Quinn Insurance building in Dublin that morning when I heard the news. I rang Patricia immediately and there was complete silence for a while. Patricia was very shocked and in no mood for talking, and I then rang Colette, who was at our hotel in Krakow. Again, she was shocked. I contacted Ciara, Seán, Aoife, and Brenda, and asked them to meet me in the boardroom, and while initially they were bombarding me with questions, they soon realised that I didn't know much about what was happening either. They wanted to understand how or why the company had given the guarantees that were the cause of the administration, and I just wasn't able to provide answers for them. We all decided that it wasn't going to be in anybody's interest to get involved in the blame game, and they all went back to their desks.

Within days, the de-Quinning of Quinn Insurance started. Files were removed from the family, access to computers were blocked, and they were left sitting at their desks with nothing to do. Fabricated redundancies and demotions were implemented, and within a short period, they were all gone, with minimum redundancy payments, despite the fact that it appeared that the administration was a mistake.

After the appointment of the administrators, we commissioned Moore Stephens LLP, one of the world's major accounting and consulting networks, with network firms in over one hundred countries, to review the regulatory and statuary returns of QIL and assess the impact of the subsidiary guarantees on QIL's solvency.

The Moore Stephens' report categorically stated that the existence of the guarantees did not impact QIL's solvency, which was absolutely contrary to Matthew Elderfield's contention and his reasoning behind placing QIL into administration.

Unfortunately, the report was obtained too late. The administrators were already in place, and shortly afterwards the Quinn family effectively lost control of the Quinn Group board to a nominee of the lenders, Murdoch McKillop. Had the Quinn family had the benefit of this professional report upon the appointment of the administrators, it certainly would have vigorously contested the ex *parte* application.

Moore Stephens were asked to "State [your] view of the impact of the existence of the guarantees in calculating the Solvency ratios of QIL as a matter of proper account".

At Para 8.2.23 of its report, Moore Stephens concluded that:

Under FRS 12 a liability in respect of a guarantee should only be recognised if it is considered more likely than not that it will crystallise. Therefore QIL's solvency is only impacted if it is considered more likely than not that the Guarantees will crystallise and result in a payment by the QIL Guarantors. The mere existence of the 9 Guarantees does not impact QIL's solvency [my emphasis].

And at Para 8.2.34 the report stated:

The impact on QIL's solvency requirements is driven by the treatment of the Guarantees within the audited financial statements of QIL and the QIL Guarantors. On the assumption that the probability of the Guarantees giving rise to economic outflow was less than 50% then the audited financial statements of QIL and the QIL Guarantors for each of the years ended 31 December 2005, 2006, 2007, 2008 did not need to recognise a liability in respect of the Guarantees [my emphasis].

As for QIL's 2009 returns, the report stated that the calculation would be more difficult to assess as an "event of default" had occurred. Moore Stephens LLP stated that the event of default that had occurred was the Regulator's decision to place QIL into administration, not the existence of guarantees. At Para 8.2.28 the report stated:

An Event of Default has occurred because QIL was placed into administration on 30 March 2010 upon petition by the Financial Regulator.

Notwithstanding the fact that the Regulator had triggered an event of default with the Group's lenders, the report goes further, and states that an event of default does not automatically result in a contingent liability. At Para 8.2.28 it stated:

> *To determine whether this (Event of Default) impacts QIL's solvency requirement it is necessary to assess the liability that would be required in the QIL guarantors' financial statements. <u>This requires a detailed assessment of the financial position of each of the 35 Guarantor companies within the Quinn Group</u>, the likely amount of any shortfall and the proportion of any debts that would be recovered by QIL from the QIL Guarantors on their liquidation which requires consideration of ...*" [my emphasis].

Moore Stephens' report couldn't be clearer. Even after the event of default was triggered by the Regulator, in order to assess the potential impact on the solvency position of QIL, if any, a *detailed assessment of 35 Group subsidiaries would be required*. It's important to note that Matthew Elderfield acted within three days of being notified of the existence of the guarantees.

* * * *

It had taken only three working days, from when the guarantees were noticed until the administrators were appointed, even though they had been there for five years. Almost thirteen years later, we are still waiting to see or hear the legal advice that the administration was based upon.

I lost the profits of almost fifteen years' work overnight, but as I had effectively been sacked as a QIL director over a year earlier there was nothing I could do. I now found myself barred from the offices of the insurance company I had set up in 1996.

Over the weekend prior to the administration, I had contacted Brendan Smith, a TD for Cavan–Monaghan and the then Minister for Agriculture, with whom I was friendly at the time. On the Saturday Smith came to visit me at the Quinn Group's head office in Derrylin, and he agreed to talk to the

Taoiseach, Brian Cowen, and Brian Lenihan on my behalf. Smith and I then went to the Slieve Russell and had a few beers. Unfortunately, although he was a senior government minister at the time, he didn't make any progress. In hindsight, if he had been able to arrange a meeting with either Brian Cowen or Brian Lenihan, we could have given them the necessary assurances that everything relating to the contingent guarantees would be released within a couple of weeks. If they needed to, they could have sent someone into Quinn Insurance for those few weeks to make sure that everything was OK, if they felt it necessary. While I accept that nobody could have stepped in to overrule the Regulator, a delay might have been beneficial. We were only given a few days, over a weekend, to resolve the contingent guarantee issue before the administrators came in. Elderfield had bypassed all the usual due process in order to achieve his objective.

Two days later, just after the administrators had been appointed, a friend of mine, then Senator Donie Cassidy, told me that he had been talking to Brian Cowen, the then Taoiseach. Cassidy asked me if I would speak to him, as he was uneasy about the administration. I said yes, and Cowen himself rang me on my home number ten minutes later. Until then I only had a very minimal relationship with Brian Cowen; we had just acknowledged each other in passing. But Cowen was sympathetic on the telephone that day. When I told him that QIL had €1.1 billion in cash and €456 million in property assets, he went quiet for a few seconds, then replied, "Are you sure about that Seán?" I said that I was, and he then said that there was little he could do to get QIL out of administration: "If I overruled Elderfield I'd be done [as Taoiseach] within days", he said. Irish regulators had been seen as a 'soft touch' for too long, and calling them off would have been politically disastrous. Some books about the Quinn affair have claimed, probably rightly, that in March 2010 Elderfield simply told Cowen's Finance Minister, Brian Lenihan, that he was sending in administrators, rather than seeking Lenihan's permission. At the height of the Irish financial crisis, politicians were taking a back seat for once, and I understood that.

The only help that Cowen could offer was organising a meeting with Hugh Cooney of Enterprise Ireland, a state-run investment agency. Within a couple of days, four of us met with Cooney and showed him our figures. At first glance, he seemed reluctant to believe the figures, and asked, "Why would anyone put this company into administration?" Cooney agreed to get back to us in a few days, and he did, but no progress was made. It was apparent that there was going to be no backing down on QIL's administration. The die had been cast and we had to go.

I made contact with a good friend and a good customer of mine, Ray O'Rourke, who had agreed our biggest policy ever of over STG£10 million just a few weeks earlier. Ray was born in Co. Leitrim beside me, and had purchased Laing Construction some years earlier. He was turning billions of pounds on contracts all over the world. At the time he was doing work in Australia, and as Mike Aynsley was an Australian, he told me he would try to make contact with Aynsley. Within a week of the administration of Quinn Insurance, he had arranged to meet Aynsley in his offices in Dublin. Before the meeting, he and I met in Buswells Hotel to discuss the overall position. When he returned from the meeting, he was very concerned, and said that they were going to take all of the businesses. I questioned him on that, saying that couldn't be right, but he was adamant, and said that they were going to take everything within weeks, and make me an offer of around €30 million to move on. Shortly after Ray's meeting, the Taoiseach's office arranged a meeting in Government Buildings, attended by myself, Liam McCaffrey, the Taoiseach himself, Brendan Smith and Rory O'Hanlon (Cavan–Monaghan TDs), and Frank Ryan, the chief executive of Enterprise Ireland. A number of other people were there, I forget who they were. The meeting was chaired by the Taoiseach. The main item on the agenda was the security of the Quinn manufacturing and property businesses. Between then and 14 April, John Bowe, an Anglo executive, made contact with Kevin and Dara, with a change of tone, saying that anything that would be done would be done consensually, and that they were going to put plans in place for Quinn Insurance to be returned to the Quinn family. At the same time, Murdoch McKillop arranged a meeting on 14 April in the Slieve Russell, with all of the directors of the Quinn Group, saying that he had a deal done to get all of the financial facilities renewed for the Quinn manufacturing businesses.

At the meeting, which I chaired, the attendees were my brother, Peter, David Mackey, Paddy Murphy, Pat O'Neill, Brendan Tuohy, Liam McCaffrey, Dara O'Reilly, Kevin Lunney, and McKillop himself, who was representing the bondholders. After I welcomed the group, McKillop said that he had good news for us, that he had agreed a deal with the banks and bondholders that they would refinance for a further five years at similar terms as we had had over the previous five years on the condition that there would be changes to the board. I was delighted to hear this, and offered my resignation immediately, because I felt that this was going to be a solution to the guarantee issue in the insurance business as well. A refinance deal would exclude the guarantees. Pat O'Neill took over as chairman. I felt that my presence on the board wasn't necessary, because I had the full support of the remaining directors.

We felt at the time that everybody believed this was very good news, but over the following few weeks McKillop also got rid of Kevin and Dara and changed David's role from a director to an observer of the board. To our dismay, the three Dublin directors – Paddy Murphy, Pat O'Neill, and Brendan Tuohy – supported McKillop in his plan to oust us. Then McKillop started adding his own directors to the board, and within a couple of weeks, he had taken complete control, with only my brother, Peter, as a non-executive and Liam as an executive director. Peter and David were ignored from that point on, and I don't know what Liam's position was from that point on, but at the time, it was considered to be supportive of me. I later found out that McKillop, Murphy, O'Neill, and Tuohy had a meeting on 20 April, six days after McKillop had committed to the refinancing, so obviously they had their minds made up at that stage. It came as complete shock to all of us that these three non-executive directors would not support the family who had appointed them only a little over a year earlier, in order to strengthen our board to ensure that what happened in 2007 and 2008 wouldn't happen again. The result of the appointment of the new board was that the company couldn't take any action regarding the share support or the illegality of the administration. In the meantime, John Bowe was assuring Kevin and Dara that he was making plans to get Quinn Insurance returned to us. So, within two weeks of the administration, when they weren't allowed to take the Group, they had us completely tied up anyway.

At the same time, Kevin and Dara lobbied as many politicians and people of power as they could, but all to no avail. At least some politicians spoke up for me in Dublin. In the Seanad, Fianna Fáil's chief whip, Diarmuid Wilson, said "I want fairness for [Seán Quinn] and I want justice", adding that I was a "patriot". I also had huge support from throughout the country, including from household names. However, bit by bit and week by week, as the media and the political establishment ground us down, and ridiculed people who supported us, our supporters became less vocal. I could understand that as the majority of people don't want to be arguing against their own government.

At the same time, Quinn employees, and many other people in the border counties who relied directly and indirectly on the Quinn Group for their livelihoods, set up a number of pro-Quinn protest groups, including Concerned Irish Citizens. This group was set up initially by Patricia Gilheany and Kevin Lunney, and was supported by thousands of people. In fact, on the day the Quinn Group was taken over, there were 93,000 signatures on a petition presented to Michael Noonan, the then Finance Minister, to return Quinn Insurance to the family. On that day, there were hundreds of people in Dublin protesting against the 'Financial Wreckulator', as he was described. It is notable that Patricia Gilheany and Kevin Lunney worked very closely together during this period, and spoke every day. Years later, when Patricia was still campaigning on my family's behalf, but Kevin had jumped ship, he used the Quinn Group to issue proceedings against Patricia, when she made unfavourable comments about the company.

Despite all this opposition to the administrators and the Regulator, it became apparent that the Regulator was in no mood to change tack and that McKillop, Murphy, O'Neill and Tuohy were reneging on the deal they had agreed with the board on 14 April 2010. The Irish economy was in deep trouble, and Cowen and Lenihan were powerless to stop the regulators, even if they knew that the administration was wrong. Even a decade after he'd left his job as my chief executive, I relied on David Mackey, who was still a non-executive director of some of my companies, for advice. David met with Matthew Elderfield and Kevin Cardiff on my behalf in 2010. He gave Elderfield a copy of the Moore Stephens report and asked Elderfield for the legal advice he had received relating to the administration, but to no avail. Elderfield was not for turning and David never received the legal advice.

The Regulator and administrators placed a value of zero on the property assets of Quinn Insurance, and built up a narrative that there was a €600 million shortfall in solvency, due to an impairment on Quinn assets. In fact, there was no impairment, and Quinn Insurance had the highest reserves of any insurance company in the country. They kept throwing up this €600 million figure and media outlets ran with it, and so it soon became 'fact', although there was no evidence to support it. Astonishingly, at all times up until then, the Central Bank's own statistical reviews showed Quinn Insurance as having the highest reserve per claim of any insurer in the country, and yet the same Central Bank put in an administrator on the basis that we didn't have enough reserves.

Citizen Quinn states that "in a parallel universe, Murdoch McKillop and Seán Quinn could have been friends." McKillop was only a year younger than me, and very persuasive, but much more presentable-looking than I am. "Like Quinn, he was broadly built and physically strong, a man with presence, used to taking charge of situations", Gavin Daly and Ian Kehoe wrote.

They didn't seem to appreciate the fact that McKillop had promised us he would be able to get refinancing in place. I have since learned about the type of man he was. It has been said that he found me to be one of the most difficult men he ever met. I don't know how he found me so difficult, considering that I never met him again after the day I resigned in order to allow the refinancing that he promised would take place. On that day, I had offered my resignation immediately, without any argument or even discussion. It has also been reported that I asked him to go to London to make a new proposal to the banks and bonds, which in fact is totally untrue, as I never met him after I resigned in April 2010. When we belatedly realised that this new board had totally reneged on their commitment made on 14 April, we made arrangements with Shay Bannon from BDO Financial Services for him to make contact with the banks and bondholders in London, where we could ask them to consider a new proposal where we would repay them 100 per cent of all loans and an interest margin of 3.5 per cent, up from the 0.8 per cent they had been previously promised. It was so disappointing for our family to see these men, who had such reputations, and who were invited into the company as supporters of the family, to dismiss us in such a manner, as they would have known that the board had been run properly and professionally from the time they had joined.

McKillop is a Glaswegian Protestant, but there is no truth in the claims, made in several books, that I goaded him about his support for Rangers in meetings, or that I referred to him as "that Rangers man [who] cannot be trusted". The truth is that I would never dream of making such a sectarian jibe to anyone, and, in fact, I only met him on two occasions: once for five minutes, and the other at the board meeting already referred to. Nor did I refer to the bondholders he represented as "unsecured scum", as has been alleged. I have never used that phrase in my life.

McKillop had been involved in the restructuring of much bigger companies than ours; he had worked with some of the biggest banks and bondholders in the world, and had been involved in very significant corporate deals. According to Gavin Daly and Ian Kehoe, however, he could not deal with me. "He had spent a year trying, without success. Most of the time, Quinn simply would not listen to him. Even when he did listen, he chose to ignore what was being said. In all his years in business, McKillop had never dealt with anyone quite like Seán Quinn." Maybe he had never met anyone like me, but what I can certainly say is that I never met anyone like him, nor do I have any desire to.

It has also been said that McKillop has stated that he couldn't agree anything with my children. In fact, my children never met him at all. How could I or they agree or disagree with him on anything, if they never met him or any of the non-executive directors after April 2010. This all begs questions about where some of these reports came from, and why it was felt necessary to destroy me and my reputation.

Years later, I'm still not sure whether Paddy Murphy, Pat O'Neill and Brendan Tuohy were aware of McKillop's deception at the meeting on 14 April 2010, where he offered to renew the financial arrangements, but if they did know, it beggars belief that they would be part of such a fabrication. If they did not know, it is equally hard to believe that when they found out, they didn't tell the family about the deceit that was being perpetrated on us. A more appropriate course of action might have been to talk to us, and to see if we could make arrangements to get rid of McKillop, knowing that he was out to destroy the company and the family. However, I never met any of Murphy, O'Neill, or Tuohy after my resignation on 14 April 2010. I was very disappointed that they didn't even speak to my brother, Peter, whom I understood they held in high esteem; it was he who invited two of them to join the board.

Shortly after my resignation, Dara O'Reilly and Kevin Lunney were also removed from the board; Kevin on 4 May, and Dara, who was sacked as the Quinn Group's finance director, on 11 May. Dara was replaced by McKillop's appointment, Neil Robson. The new board immediately started attending meetings in A&L Goodbody's and William Fry's offices. Everyone who had ever worked in the Quinn businesses or were from the area – including my brother, Peter, and David Mackey – were excluded from those meetings, which were obviously to plan the takeover of the Group. The only Quinn loyalist left on the senior payroll was Sinead Geoghegan, who became the Quinn Group's interim finance director after Dara left. Liam was left as CEO, and tried to keep all sides happy, as he was now in hot water after causing the administration of Quinn Insurance, as well as taking €500,000 from a Quinn Group company.

Murdoch McKillop did not just remove me and my allies from the Quinn Group board, he quickly put himself in charge of it. As Gavin Daly and Ian Kehoe have put it: "There are certain incontestable truths about people like Murdoch McKillop. If they arrive at your business, your business is in the trouble. The longer they stay, the deeper the trouble." What I would say about that is that the Quinn businesses were never in trouble, but McKillop and the administrators soon changed that.

As soon as I stepped down as the Quinn Group's chairman in April 2010, the board appointed McKillop as its 'interim executive director' – effectively its chief executive. McKillop would spend almost a year in the role. In October 2010, Paddy Murphy invited Paul O'Brien onto the board. We didn't know it at the time, but the intention was obviously to have him take over from McKillop as the Quinn Group's chief executive, which he did after the appointment of a share receiver in April 2011. It goes to show how naïve we were, but at no stage did we ever think that the Irish government would send a receiver into Northern Ireland to take over a company that never borrowed a penny from them, but had grown its profits by more than 30 per cent per annum over the previous 37 years, that had created thousands of jobs, and that was capable of and willing to repay all of the loans, including the loans for share support.

Now that Dara, Kevin and I had left the board, the only Quinns left on it was my brother, Peter, and my old friend David Mackey. From then on Peter and David were ignored, and McKillop added more directors to the board, to tighten his control of it. Later on, McKillop spent two hours at a meeting, at the Kilmore Hotel in Cavan, trying to persuade David Mackey to turn away from the family. To no one's surprise, David was too honourable to even consider that, and he always remained loyal. He told me on a number of occasions that in his lifetime he had never seen men with such excellent reputations as Murphy, O'Neill and Tuohy acting in such an unusual manner. As time went on, it became clear that they were influenced by people and organisations who were blaming and targeting us, and obviously felt that they would rather be in their corner than fight for the Quinn family who had appointed them in the first place.

The very evening that Michael McAteer and Paul McCann were appointed as QIL's administrators, they met with A&L Goodbody, our lawyers, at a hotel at Dublin Airport. I don't know exactly what happened at that meeting. I was convinced at the time that A&L Goodbody were using their best endeavours to first of all avoid the administration, and then to get the company out of administration as quickly as possible.

A&L Goodbody were also legal advisors to the Department of Finance. Ireland, for better and worse, is a small country, with a very small pool of professionals when it comes to sectors such as law and accountancy, so there are inevitable situations where the same names crop up repeatedly acting for different companies and departments. Internal divisions can be created within companies to guard against potential conflicts of interest, but it is difficult to avoid the appearance of conflict in all scenarios, regardless of whether such conflict actually occurs or not.

The guarantees which were found to be illegal had been reviewed by A&L Goodbody in the first place. Between hopping and trotting, A&L Goodbody had allowed contingent guarantees to be put on subsidiary companies of a regulated entity.

Placing QIL in administration meant that the first part of a long-term plan had been implemented. At this stage, they had Dukes, Aynsley, and Woodhouse in the Anglo corner, and Elderfield, Jonathon McMahon, and the recently promoted Pat Brady in the Regulator's corner, and at the same time, Murdoch McKillop was working on removing all of the Quinn Group directors and replacing them with his own. They had the recently promoted Kevin Cardiff and Ann Nolan in the Department of Finance corner, and they had A&L Goodbody, William Fry, McCann Fitzgerald, and MOPs as their legal advisors, and they now had control of the new Quinn Group board. They immediately started to plan the takeover of the Quinn Group, and there wasn't a thing that we could do about it.

* * * *

We did not challenge the administration. I obviously now regret that we didn't challenge it, but at the time we felt that when the paperwork surrounding the guarantees was rectified, matters would resolve themselves consensually. However, when I look back at what was going on behind our backs, with people planning to take over the Group, I feel that they would not have supported a challenge to the administration, as it appears they were going to stop at nothing to get us out of the company.

Later, Michael McAteer and Paul McCann admitted to the *Irish Times* that they knew "nothing about insurance". After they arrived, QIL's turnover quickly fell from €1 billion a year to €180 million, which tells its own story, with sales falling quickly to below what profits had been prior to their arrival.

By now Kevin Lunney and Dara O'Reilly were travelling twice weekly to Dublin to meet John Bowe, a senior manager at Anglo, who was now saying that the deal was going to be done consensually, while in fact, he and McKillop were working in tandem: Bowe with Kevin and Dara, and, by now, McKillop had appointed a new finance director to replace Dara, and they found that the Quinns had retained no money to fight a legal battle. The €800 million of dividends had been spent on assets, and the €40 million of rental income coming from family assets was going into the Quinn Group, and was not retained by the family, so they knew now that they had us where they wanted us.

When Bowe called Dara and Kevin to discuss a deal, whereby QIL would be restored to Quinn family hands, he did not go into much detail. In an interview with RTE's *Prime Time* programme, I outlined that, given QIL's underlying profitability, if I could get the company back I could use its profits to gradually repay everything I owed to Anglo, with interest, but within a month of the administration, the future of Quinn Insurance took a major blow, with the announcement of 900 redundancies, so it became very clear that the company was going to have a very limited future. The fact that they reduced the turnover from over €1 billion to €180 million very quickly proved that point. On 1 May 2010, when the administrators announced the 900 redundancies, it was particularly galling for me, as I had always prided myself on never making employees redundant. The 900 redundancies announced in Cavan were equivalent to 9,000 redundancies in Dublin, as a proportion of the local population. As anyone who has ever created a job knows, having to announce job losses is a terrible moment for any employer. I can still clearly remember the moment it was announced. I knew a lot of the staff, and many of them had worked in Quinn companies their whole working lives. To this day it troubles me, especially knowing that the redundancies were completely unnecessary, and knowing that if the business had been left in our hands, the company would have been increasing its staffing levels considerably, instead of announcing redundancies.

In June 2010 QIL was put up for sale, and I was told that I would have to bid for my old company like anyone else, but it soon became clear that the Liberty Mutual Group, an American insurance company, was the preferred buyer from day one, as Ted Kelly, from County Armagh, had expressed an interest on Liberty's behalf as soon as the company went into administration. Soon afterwards, the family's solicitors, Mason, Hayes and Curran, were taken away from us. Mason, Hayes and Curran summoned my daughter Colette to a meeting. They told her that as they had been asked to work for Liberty, they could no longer act for us. Liberty would be a much bigger client, and they were demanding that Mason, Hayes and Curran could no longer act for the Quinn family, to avoid a conflict of interest. I suspect the real reason was that Mason, Hayes and Curran knew too much about the illegal support that Anglo had given for the CFDs, and could help us cause plenty of problems for the administrators and Anglo. One could be forgiven for asking if they knew from the outset that Liberty would be the new owners of Quinn Insurance.

Since 2010, one of the biggest criticisms levelled at me is that anyone buying insurance in Ireland now has to pay a 2 per cent levy on their policies. But I believe that the destruction of QIL has in fact increased premiums by about 20 per cent on average. QIL sold insurance policies much cheaper than any other company in Ireland or Britain, mainly because of the success of our fast-track model, minimising the use of brokers and solicitors, and the fact that we had a cleaner book than our competitors, due to the fact that our regional claims managers pursued fraudulent claims much more vigorously than our competitors, which resulted in fraudsters moving to other insurance companies. Without us as competitors, other insurers have charged consumers more than they would have done if QIL was still around.

Despite the solvency issues that other insurers had, where they only held a fraction of the €1.56 billion that QIL held for solvency purposes, none were sanctioned by regulators, and unlike QIL they were all allowed to continue trading, while they raised funds to meet their solvency requirements, which some of them had not met for decades.

Why was QIL not allowed to continue? I believe for two reasons. First, I believe that we were too profitable, taking too much of a market share, and causing major issues for other insurers and glass producers in both Ireland and the UK. But the bigger reason was that we had received legal advice that there were multiple illegalities on the part of Anglo concerning the share support scheme, and as the Regulator, the Department of Finance, the Central Bank, and the Attorney General were involved in all stages of the scheme between September 2007 and July 2008, they would have been fully aware that neither I nor my family were involved in the administration of the company. So it was felt that the only way of dealing with the Quinn problem was to get the family completely out of business, and appoint new boards on the condition that they would not sue Anglo for any known or unknown claims, which is exactly what happened. They also knew that getting rid of the people involved in the administration of the company would not affect the profitability of the Group, as it had become stronger and more profitable since 2000, following the family's increased involvement.

Seán's parents, Hugh and Mary Quinn, shortly after they married in 1935

Seán Quinn's father, Hugh Quinn, photographed in Teemore in the early 1950s

The Quinn family photographed in April 1952 (l–r): Hugh, Peter, Seán, Mary, Bernadette, Miriam

Top: The Quinn family pictured in the later 1950s (l–r): Miriam, Bernadette, Mary, Hugh, Peter and Seán

Middle: The Teemore Shamrocks Gaelic football team from County Fermanagh in 1969. Seán is pictured front right

Bottom: Seán and Patricia's wedding day, 12 October 1974. Pictured with the happy couple's mothers, both of whom were called Mary Quinn

Top left: Seán and Patricia Quinn on their wedding day, 1974

Top right: Picture of the sales contract for farm lands in Knockategal dated 28 June 1982 with Pearse Martin for £35,000

Bottom left: Seán fishing in Mullaghmore in 1985

Bottom right: Seán Quinn photographed in his home in 1990

Top: Seán pictured at a golf social event in the Slieve Russell Golf Club. Pictured (l–r): Máirtín McGowan, Seamus Martin, Seán, Jimmy Kelly, Gerry Reilly, Liam Kearns and Brian Early

Bottom: Seán with his brother, Peter Quinn, on the day Peter was elected GAA President in 1990

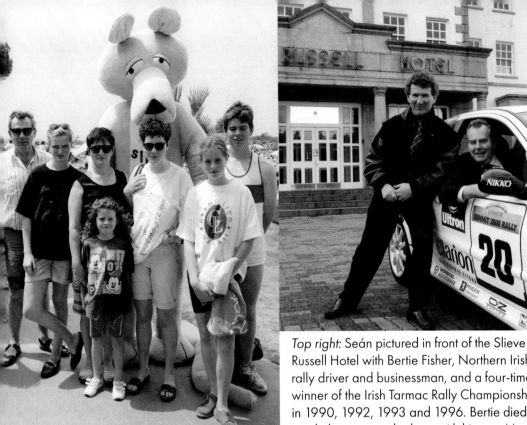

Top left: The Quinn family pictured on a holiday
in Orlando, Florida in 1990. Pictured (l–r): Seán,
Ciara, Patricia, Brenda, Colette, Aoife and Seán Jnr

Top right: Seán pictured in front of the Slieve
Russell Hotel with Bertie Fisher, Northern Irish
rally driver and businessman, and a four-time
winner of the Irish Tarmac Rally Championship
in 1990, 1992, 1993 and 1996. Bertie died
in a helicopter crash along with his son, Mark,
and daughter, Emma, in 2001

Bottom: Seán and Patricia Quinn, pictured
with Gay Byrne in the Slieve Russell Hotel in
1991

Top: Newspaper cutting from the *Anglo Celt*, 13 Feburary 1992, photo taken in the Slieve Russell Hotel of Seán's presentation to former Taoiseach Charles Haughey. Also pictured is Charles' wife, Maureen, ESB chairman Paddy Moriarty, and Eimear Mulhern

Our picture was taken prior to last Friday's lunch in the Slieve Russell when a special presentation was made to form Taoiseach, Charles J. Haughey by Mr. Sean Quinn, Chief Executive Quinn Group (l. to r.) Paddy Moriarity, Chairman of E.S.I Mrs. Maureen Haughey, Charles Haughey, T.D., Sean Quinn and Mrs. Eimear Mulhern pictured with the statue of the lege dary Eimear in the Slieve Russell last Friday.

(Pic.: Brian Mullig

Middle: Seán with his second youngest daughter, Aoife, pictured on the day of her Confirmation in 1992

Bottom: Seán pictured with his family in the Slieve Russell Hotel in 1992 (Back l–r): Aoife, Colette, Seán Jnr and Ciara; (Front l–r): Seán, his mother, Mary Quinn, wife, Patricia, and daughter Brenda

Top left: Seán with Christy O'Connor Snr in the Slieve Russell Golf Club in 1993

Top right: Patricia Quinn pictured with John Kellagher at a function in the Slieve Russell Hotel in April 1993

Bottom: Mary Quinn presented with flowers on her 80th birthday in 1993, (l–r): Bernadette Maguire, Peter Quinn, Mary Quinn, Seán Quinn, Patricia Quinn and Miriam McMahon

Top: Seán & Seán Jnr 1993 Presidents Day, Slieve Russell Golf Club

Middle: Seán at the opening of the Quinn Glass factory in 1996, pictured with Gerry Loughran from the Industrial Development Board

Bottom: 1997 Quinn Direct Pro-Am, Slieve Russell Golf Club – Winners (seated at front) include Seán Quinn Jr and Patricia Quinn. Pictured standing are Kevin Lunney and Seán Quinn

Top left: Seán pictured outside the Slieve Russell Hotel in April 1999 on the day of the official opening of Aghalane Bridge, which had been blown up multiple times during the Troubles. Pictured with then General Manager Sheila Gray and Senator George Mitchell

Top right: The Quinn family pictured in the Slieve Russell Golf Club, for Patricia's Ladies Captain's Day in 1999. Back (l–r): Colette, Ciara, Seán Jnr, Aoife and Brenda. Seated are Patricia and Seán

Bottom: Seán Quinn Jnr and Patricia Quinn at a golfing function with Christy O'Connor Jnr and former Dublin GAA player Keith Barr

Top: Seán on a fishing trip with his daughters Ciara, Colette and Brenda in 1999, "admiring the catch"

Bottom: Seán Quinn Jnr's graduation from Portobello College in 2000, (l–r): Patricia, Seán Jnr, Seán and Brenda

Top left: Seán being presented with his Honorary Doctorate of Laws by Garret FitzGerald in NUI Maynooth, 18 May 1999

Top right: Seán Quinn Jnr playing a golfing competition with then future Taoiseach Enda Kenny on 12 July 2007

Bottom: Receiving an Honorary Economics degree from Queen's University Belfast in 2001. Seán is pictured on the day of the presentation with his family. Back (l–r): Colette, Ciara, Seán Jnr, Aoife, Brenda. Front (l–r): Patricia, Seán and his mother, Mary Quinn

Top: The Quinn family holiday in Cancun, Mexico in 2007.
Pictured (l–r): Seán Jnr, Seán, Patricia, Colette, Aoife, Brenda, Niall McPartland (son-in-law), Ciara and Stephen Kelly (son-in-law)

Bottom: Patricia Quinn, her mother, and her nine siblings on her daughter Aoife's wedding day

Top: Seán pictured with former UK Prime Minister Tony Blair in 2009

Bottom: Seán Quinn with Barack and Michelle Obama, Hilton, Prague, 2009

Top right: The Q Centre, Blanchardstown, Dublin

Top left: Glass bottling factory, Elton, Manchester. Commenced production in 2006 with 1,000 staff

Bottom: Slieve Russell Hotel, Ballyconnell, Co.Cavan

Top: The Belfry Hotel

Bottom: Univermag Shopping Centre, Kyiv, Ukraine

QUINN GROUP LOCATIONS
Local & International

FERMANAGH Fivemiletown
to Belfast
Enniskillen
M4
Maguiresbridge
Lisnaskea

Derrylin

MONAGHAN

Ballyconnell
Belturbet

LEITRIM
Cavan
CAVAN

N
N3

LONGFORD
Virginia
to Navan

Granard
Navan
Williamstown Dublin Manchester
Ireland Newbridge Leigh
Elton Alfreton
Clonmel Warwickshire Nottingham
Newport Cambridge
U.K.
Netherlands
Bel

Denmark
Latvia
Ireland
U.K. Hoofddorp Nischwitz Lithuania Moscow Kazan
Grobbendonk Leipzig Belarus Russia
Diegem Geel Poland
Mainz Prague Krakow Kiev
Moussey Pribram Ukraine
Le Creusot Zilina
France Hungary
Croatia
Barcelona Bosnia Serbia
Sofia
Spain Bulgaria
Turkey
Northern Cyprus

● MANUFACTURING ● GLASS ● HOSPITALITY ● RADIATORS
● PLASTICS / CHEMICALS ● PROPERTY ● FINANCIAL SERVICES ● PACKAGING

Top right: The text message Marianne McCaffrey sent to Patricia Quinn on the day Quinn Industrial Holdings was rebranded as Mannok

Top left: Locations of Quinn Enterprises worldwide

Bottom: John McCartin dismantling the Aventas sign from the former Quinn HQ in Derrylin, December 2014. Photo © Lorraine Teevan, used with permission

The twelve months between March 2010 and April 2011 was a period of uneasy limbo for me, my family, and my companies. Although QIL was in administration, the rest of the Quinn Group was still ours.

I later learned that after failing to take over the Group in April 2010, they made a second attempt, and by October 2010 Kieran Wallace was ringing multiple potential non-executive directors, preparing to go into the Quinn Group. Paul O'Brien joined the Quinn Group board at that time. But the receivership was stopped, and I am still not sure why. The Fianna Fáil politicians who were still running Ireland until the end of February 2011 seemed to stall it. Although Brian Cowen couldn't stop QIL's administration, it seems that he and Brian Lenihan did stop, or at least delay, the receivership of the rest of the Quinn Group in late 2010. Cowen and Lenihan were aware of the underlying strength of the Quinn Group, and they obviously felt that they couldn't go to stage two. At that stage, I believe that Anglo had lost control of the situation, and it was dealt with by various government departments, the administrators, and the new Quinn Group board, supported by their various solicitors and advisors. Anglo had to wait for a full twelve months, until the arrival of a Fine Gael government in the spring of 2011.

Cowen was a solicitor by training, and Lenihan was a barrister. Lenihan was very well-connected with Irish business: his first cousin Fergal O'Rourke was managing partner of PwC's Irish operations, and PwC had been categoric that the contingent guarantees had no effect on the solvency of Quinn

Insurance. By mid-2010 Lenihan and Cowen would have both seen reports from PwC and Moore Stephens, which firmly stated that the administration was wrong, that QIL and my other companies were very profitable, and that in March 2010 we had €1.564 billion of cash and assets. Cowen, whom I had spoken to on the phone and had met in Government Buildings in April, and Lenihan would also have known that until October 2010 Michael McAteer regularly appeared in front of Judge Kearns to tell him that QIL was profitable, and that there was no need to draw on the Insurance Compensation Fund (ICF). The administrators changed their tune seven months later, in October, and announced that there was a sudden need for emergency funds because they had claimed they found deficits once they had "peeled back the onion", but I was never made aware of what these deficits were. It later transpired that these deficits were caused by the administrators, according to the government's own statistics. The timing seemed very strange, as it coincided with the time the administrators were trying to get control of Quinn Group, with Wallace ringing potential non-executive directors that same month.

In the last few months of 2010, Brian Cowen's government entered a major crisis, which soon proved terminal. In November, Ireland received a €78 billion bailout from the International Monetary Fund, EU and European Central Bank. Although the bailout was welcome, it was a humiliating reminder of what dire straits the Irish economy was still in. That same month, Fianna Fáil's coalition partners, the Greens, walked out of the government, which now became a minority one. A general election was called, and Brian Cowen made it clear that he would not be seeking re-election. I always believed, and still believe, that Brian Cowen is a decent man.

At the election Caroline Forde, a longstanding employee of Quinn Insurance, ran as a pro-Quinn independent in the Cavan–Monaghan constituency. She fell well short of gaining a seat in the five-member constituency, but her result showed that there was much support for the Quinn businesses, and the employment and prosperity we had brought, in the border counties.

The main story of the election, however, was the complete meltdown of support for Fianna Fáil. Fine Gael, which had spent the late 1990s and the first decade of the twenty-first century in the doldrums, gained 25 seats and was back in power. Enda Kenny, leader of Fine Gael since 2002, became the new Taoiseach. He headed a coalition government with Labour, which had almost doubled its representation, climbing from 20 to 37 seats.

I had very few political connections. I did not know Enda Kenny very well, and I didn't know the new Finance Minister, Michael Noonan, at all (both of them teachers before they went into politics). Enda Kenny had played golf several times with my son, Seán Jnr, in the 2000s. They had had a few pints together afterwards, and Kenny had jokingly asked Seán Jnr to start supporting Fine Gael, not Fianna Fáil. But when I met him in 2010, after Quinn Insurance had gone into administration, he gave the impression that he was very supportive, and that he felt the administration had been a major mistake. Later, in the months before he became Taoiseach, I became very disappointed in him, when he refused to meet highly respected individuals whom he knew very well, who wanted to meet him to seek his support for me, but, by then, he had done a complete U-turn on what he had stated in 2010. He later denigrated people who were household names who supported me and my family. I didn't think that in his position, as Taoiseach by this point, it was the right thing to do. Some of the people he was ridiculing were more highly respected than any politician on the island, and I would have thought that they should have been entitled to express their view. It begged the question as to why the Irish government wanted to denigrate me and my family if there wasn't an ulterior motive.

Brian Lenihan had at least been re-elected as a Fianna Fáil TD in Dublin West, and for a few months he questioned Noonan in the Dáil about how he was managing the Quinn situation. But Lenihan was now a very ill man, having been diagnosed with pancreatic cancer in December 2009. He died in June 2011, aged only 52.

With the new Fine Gael–Labour government in power, despite the financial strength of the wider Group, whatever was blocking the attempts to put the full Quinn Group into receivership was removed, and three months later the receivers moved in. Around this time, the decision was made to go after our privately held assets, in Ukraine, Russia and India, which would deprive the family of the money to enable them to fight the case we had taken against

Anglo Irish Bank over the share support scheme. After this point, all of the media's focus was on the fight over these assets, and if we had acted illegally by trying to keep them in the family's hands, despite the fact that Anglo had no security over these assets and therefore should not have been trying to claim ownership of them. Our case against Anglo over the illegal share support scheme, on the other hand, was effectively dead in the water.

Matters came to a head with the bondholders in late 2010 and early 2011. At the meeting in London, already referred to, with the banks and bondholders, organised by Shay Bannon, Dara O'Reilly, Kevin Lunney, David Mackey and I sat on one side of the table, while Barry Russell and representatives of the banks and bondholders sat on the other.

Barry Russell was another man who was helping the bondholders. He was described in *Citizen Quinn* as a "charismatic New Yorker ... with bright red braces, fashionable rectangular glasses and [a] larger-than-life persona, like a character from a Tom Wolfe novel." In an interview, Russell once said that he would like Michael Douglas (the star of the 1980s movie *Wall Street*) to play him if a film was ever made about his life, "because he looks good in braces". When I first met Russell he was indeed wearing red braces, and it was very clear to me that he had exactly the same gameplan as Murdoch McKillop, and that they were playing a game they were always going to win and gain financially from, having, of course, the support of the Quinn Group board, who were 100 per cent behind Russell and McKillop, and appeared to be equally determined to get the company out of my hands.

I told Russell that "I have never reneged on a debt in my life", and by the end of the meeting I had promised to come back with a clear repayment plan. Shay Bannon sought to reassure the bondholders that I would be true to my word. He wrote to them in January 2011 to explain that "Local landowners [in the border counties] will often insist on having the final handshake with Seán Quinn himself, or in some cases will only engage in meaningful discussions if he is present. Most have watched and admired as the company has grown and developed from humble beginnings and like to feel part of it by doing a deal directly with Mr Quinn." But I was now dealing with international financiers – who were at this stage playing to the tune of the Irish government – not customers in rural Ireland. Alan Dukes, a non-executive director of Anglo, was by now a determined foe of mine, which he has since demonstrated, and he had once been both Enda Kenny and Michael Noonan's boss, when he was leader of the Fine Gael party. He, or someone else, convinced them that my whole empire had to be dismantled. Indeed, as soon as the political upheaval of the election was over, for the plan that had been devised a year earlier, the long wait was over, and they moved very quickly indeed. Kieran Wallace was appointed share receiver, and Paul O'Brien was appointed CEO. All senior local Quinn directors were replaced by people from further afield. Fine Gael's election victory in 2011 was bad news for me, as it soon put an end to the period of limbo.

* * * *

On 14 April 2011, just weeks after the new government was formed, share receivers were appointed at the Quinn Group. I had not been told about the receivership in advance.

On 13 April Alan Dukes rang me to ask if Dara, Kevin, and I could meet him at Connaught House, IBRC's new head office on Burlington Road in Dublin, at 9.30 a.m. the following morning. Connaught House's lobby contained a statue of Queen Medbh of Connaught, who, according to Irish mythology, invaded Ulster to capture the Great Brown Bull of Cooley. "Quinn, an Ulsterman, would learn at the meeting with Anglo that the bank would be cutting off the head of the Quinn Group, removing him from the businesses that he set up and built over 38 years," says Simon Carswell.

Dukes, Aynsley, and Woodhouse attended the meeting on behalf of Anglo. I had assumed that Kevin, Dara and I had been invited to meet IBRC simply to discuss QIL, which had by now been in administration for a year, and possibly to hear that a new deal was being offered for us to repay what we owed IBRC. I was shocked to be told instead by Alan Dukes that the whole of the Quinn Group was being taken from us. The reason I was shocked was because almost three years earlier, solicitors on our behalf wrote to Anglo stating that the share support was illegal, and that after a number of meetings with Seán FitzPatrick and David Drumm from Anglo, and with Patrick Neary from the Regulator's Office, we had agreed to repay the loans in full. I couldn't understand how they could consider taking all of our businesses on the back of that.

Dukes spelled out the detailed terms of the receivership. IBRC now had a 75 per cent stake in Quinn Group, a company they never loaned a penny to. Some €100 million was being taken out of QIL, to give Anglo a 49 per cent shareholding in the insurance business, and €200 million was being paid to the American bondholders from QIL, with no evidence that they were owed any money. In fact, the only evidence we had sight of was that they were owed no money, and that is still the case twelve years later. It is unbelievable that this €300 million that was taken from Quinn Insurance was never investigated, as it was always as clear as night follows day that it was just money thrown away.

I was told that a KPMG accountant, Kieran Wallace, had been appointed earlier that morning as share receiver of all my companies. "So, you want to take everything?" I asked incredulously. Gavin Daly and Ian Kehoe claim that "I seemed physically shocked" and that I vowed "This will be hard fought." I did not storm out of the meeting after half an hour, as has been claimed. But I certainly did tell Dukes and Aynsley that the takeover was wrong and unjustified, and that we would fight to keep the assets over which they had no control, and that we had financed with dividends from Quinn Insurance – namely our foreign property assets in India, Russia and Ukraine, which the family had bought and paid for with no outside financial help.

Since then, Dukes has stated on national television and local radio that he tried to do a deal with me before he took that drastic action. That is completely untrue, and I can swear my life on that. I never met the man or spoke to the man prior to that morning, apart from taking his telephone call the previous evening to arrange the meeting. What chance did we have when you hear this man stating more than eleven years later that he tried to do a deal with me, when in fact, he had never met me at the time? This is a similar story that was told by Murdoch McKillop, when he stated that I was an extremely difficult man to deal with, and that I wouldn't agree to increase the interest charge, when in fact we had agreed to increase it by more than 400 per cent. Unfortunately, it appears that the current directors in Derrylin now have adopted a similar strategy: they saw with their own eyes what had been done to the company between 2010 and 2014. They now knew for certain that it was the Quinns that they wanted rid of, not the directors who were responsible for the breaches.

There seems to have been an agenda to try to discredit me, by Richard Woodhouse, Murdoch McKillop, Mike Aynsley, and Alan Dukes, all of whom stated that they had met me and tried to do various deals with me, when in fact there is absolutely no truth to any of it, and none of them can give any details of when or where the meetings took place, and who was present, and that is something that it will be impossible for them to come up with.

At no stage, either then or at any time since, did I make any attempt to interfere with assets that any financial institution held mortgages or security over. While I felt that we were entitled to retain the family's own assets, I knew that we would have no claim on the €350 million of remaining dividends that the family had put back into the manufacturing business.

It was always clear to me that the sole motivation for the bank and the grotesque waste of taxpayers' money had nothing whatsoever to do with debt recovery, but was about covering up the bank's illegal activities. Indeed, the very deal made between Anglo and the Quinn Group financiers confirmed that in facilitating the takeover the only self-serving benefits that Anglo derived were two-fold, namely, that Anglo received a €7.5 million transaction fee, and they received a release against all known and unknown claims by the Group against them, now or in the future, which I later pointed out in correspondence to Enda Kenny.

Alan Dukes had stooped very low by inviting Kevin, Dara and me to that meeting at Connaught House on the morning of 14 April. It seems to have been scheduled very carefully, to ensure that we would be nowhere near Derrylin that morning. Just as we were sitting down to be told the news of the share receivership in Dublin at 9.30 a.m., 100 staff organised by KPMG marched into the offices in Derrylin and Ballyconnell to take over our business. And that very same morning, a petition was being delivered to the

Central Bank in Dublin. It carried more than 90,000 signatures, collected by local support groups, and it called on the Central Bank to pull the administrators out of QIL, and to reinstall me at the helm. The Central Bank knew in advance about the petition, as the organisers had called them to let them know they were coming, with TV crews and photographers, early on the morning of 14 April. I believe the arrival of the share receiver was deliberately timed to coincide with this event, and knock it off the front pages.

Soon after that meeting with Dukes, I drove straight to the offices of Eversheds, who were acting as our solicitors. Some of my family were already there, and when I told them what had been said at the meeting, they already knew from news reports. Everyone agreed that we should try to defend the particular assets which Anglo had no legal claim over. This has been evidenced by the fact that from the time these assets had been bought three to five years earlier, Anglo had never even attempted to take out mortgages on the properties, nor could they, as they hadn't provided the finance for them. Despite the fact that we felt they had no claim on these assets, they turned it round in such a way that rather than our claim against them, it was their claim against us that made the headlines, and the court found by their actions that they were innocent until proven guilty, and the Quinns were guilty until proven innocent. With the outgoing Attorney General at the helm for Anglo, they changed the narrative that our foreign assets took precedence over what we considered the illegal takeover of our companies, and the €2.34 billion of illegal loans that were put in my family's name, and the media were happy to make hay of that narrative.

The share receivership was staged with almost military precision, and very tight security. A team of more than one hundred people had met at a hotel at Dublin Airport at 5.30 a.m. on 14 April 2011. They were then driven up to Derrylin, armed with a "Day One Sequencing" memo, which was on its sixteenth draft, and a large security team from Risk Management International (RMI). The hire cars they drove in were deliberately small and inconspicuous to avoid attracting attention, and they were driven by security-trained drivers.

KPMG's local headquarters was the Radisson Hotel on the outskirts of Cavan town, on a country estate once owned by the Lords Farnham.

Their cover story was that they were there for a management conference for a fictional company called Realise. RMI's top priority on day one was to change all the locks to the Quinn Group's buildings' external doors. Contingency plans were made to deal with a staff revolt. If any of the senior management team appeared on site, RMI were supposed to ask us to hand over our company mobile phones and laptops.

On day one, they brought in E&Y, who had been auditors for Anglo before being forced to resign, so they would have known where the bodies were buried. Also on day one, the new Quinn board, none of whom had ever worked a day for the company, had to sign that they would never make a legal claim, for any known or unknown claims against Anglo.

The share receivers gave my family little leeway. We had always kept important personal documents at Quinn Group's head office. It may seem strange, but that was the way it was. My daughter Ciara, who was heavily pregnant, went to the head office to pick up her passport and the deeds to her house, but she was told "We have been told to give the Quinn family nothing." She went home crying. In the end, the documents that she needed had to be smuggled out of the building by Quinn family loyalists. It was clear that they wanted to leave us with nothing, in case we would use it for legal fees against them, but they were happy to give millions to people who hadn't been in the company for the first 25 years of its existence, but who had caused its breakup, by giving Anglo share pledges over the company, signing documents pertaining to the contingent liabilities pertaining to Quinn Insurance, and investing the €398 million from Quinn Insurance in shares without the approval of the board or the Financial Regulator. It has since been disclosed by a journalist that at the time of the takeover of the Quinn Group, Liam McCaffrey's loan of €500,000 had been written off, and the question I'd be asking there is – was it right to write it off if it had been taken without authorisation in the first place?

Wherever the share receiver himself, Kieran Wallace, went, he was accompanied at all times by a security detail. Wallace was a high-profile receiver and liquidator, with much experience of dealing with big companies in financial trouble. I did not meet Wallace face-to-face until 2013.

But I later learned that he didn't just enter this story as the Quinn Group's share receiver in early 2011. Wallace had in fact been actively involved in planning our demise for over a year, something that we were not aware of.

Unknown to the Quinn family, or some members of the Quinn Group board, its receivership had been meticulously planned at secret meetings over a period of more than a year. Gavin Daly and Ian Kehoe claim that in 2010 Wallace (assisted by two KPMG sidekicks, Shane McCarthy and Eamon Richardson) had started meeting regularly with the Quinn Group's non-executive directors and Murdoch McKillop in the A&L Goodbody and William Fry offices, even though MOPs were Anglo's regular solicitors. Michael McAteer and Paul McCann also attended some of those meetings. When Wallace and Richard Woodhouse met for the first time in early 2010, Wallace had advised Woodhouse that there were three parties to the Quinn Group financial arrangements – the Group itself, Anglo, and the bondholders. He advised that any two of the parties could work together to outmanoeuvre the third, and that Anglo needed to be sure that they were one of the two parties. There were many meetings to discuss hypothetical scenarios involving the Quinn Group, and on 14 April 2011, things changed from hypothetical to reality.

****

Disappointingly, it was a man I had counted as a supporter, Pat O'Neill, who I had nominated as chairman of the Quinn Group board a year earlier, on 14 April 2010, who made many of the first public comments on the share receivership, in his capacity as Quinn Group chairman. KPMG's 'Day One' memo contained the following words from O'Neill to be conveyed to staff and the media: "Like you and people throughout the country, I've admired what [Seán Quinn] has built up and what he had achieved, and the employment he has given to so many. It makes it all the more difficult to understand how everything was gambled on one massive stock market bet." Did O'Neill not know that it was Anglo who had illegally provided €2.34 billion, or 78 per cent of the money, and the Quinn family had put €660 million, or 22 per cent of the money, for that "massive stock market bet"? Surely he would have known that he was doing this in support of Anglo, who at that time had been nationalised and was being investigated for criminality. As chairman, did he not feel that he had a fiduciary duty to verify the legality of the proposed receivership that had been planned for twelve months, from April 2010? It beggars belief that he could support this action rather than the family who had appointed him.

As soon as the share receivers arrived, the media and Quinn directors went into overdrive. It was unreal to watch Michael Noonan announce on the evening news that "this is a good day for the border counties". It showed just how little Noonan knew about the border counties, their history, and their people, and that he was unaware (or was he?) that he was ruining one of the best companies in the country, because the Irish government had essentially invested €2.34 billion in supporting the Anglo share price. The company that he was destroying had paid over €1.3 billion in taxes to the Irish government, and he was handing it over to foreign owners, while he was laying out the red carpet at Shannon Airport for a man who paid no taxes in any country. The Noonan legacy lives on, as his right-hand man, John Moran, is currently a director in Mannok.

The public statements soon became a lot more critical of me. A letter was sent to staff, informing them that "as part of the corporate restructuring, Seán Quinn ceases to be director of the Group and of the holding company and will no longer have a role in managing the business." My removal was "a prerequisite of the restructuring for the lenders, due to loss of confidence … in all circumstances the decision to remove Seán Quinn is not reversible", the letter continued. "Among staff, there was shock, disbelief, horror", claim Gavin Daly and Ian Kehoe. Richard Maguire – one of four Maguire brothers working for the company – told reporters that "It's an absolute disgrace, they've hounded that man out." The majority of the staff were of the same view, but, understandably, they couldn't say too much, as they had their jobs to look after. Richard was always a man of great integrity, which he later proved when he refused to sign a credit note for Liam McCaffrey for £30,000, knowing that it would have been a fraud. Liam, however, found someone at a higher level than Richard to sign off the fraudulent credit note.

The only workers to be fired on day one, apart from myself, Dara, and Kevin, were Liam McCaffery and Sinead Geoghegan. I was particularly sorry for Sinead, who had been very loyal and hardworking over the years she worked for me. But many more job losses soon followed. Another 24 jobs were cut at QIL's office in Manchester, and it was announced that QIL's office in Navan, County Meath, would close, with staff forced to relocate to Cavan or Blanchardstown.

Liam McCaffrey was succeeded as chief executive by Paul O'Brien, who been appointed to the board on Paddy Murphy's recommendation six months earlier. There were also big changes to the Quinn Group board – all the company's boards were flooded with new appointees, and all Quinn family members, including my brother, Peter, and existing or previous executive directors, including David Mackey, were removed. Jimmy Menton became the board's new chair. Other new non-execs included Ray Jackson, Timothy Quin (no relation), Frank O'Riordan (a former partner at A&L Goodbody), Rory O'Ferrall (formerly of Deloitte), John Boyd (ex-Ulster Bank), and Robert Dix, who became responsible for the Quinn property portfolio, where he stated at the time that there were 44 properties in 14 countries, and that Seán Quinn had bought all good assets. The board now had no local people on it; most of its directors were now Dubliners. Not one of them had ever worked an hour in the company.

The share receiver got rid of PwC, who had been our auditors for fifteen years, and installed Ernst and Young (EY), who had been Anglo's own auditors until 2008, and had audited their fraudulent accounts. The accountants and bankers were now firmly in control, and EY would have known what the issues were, and what needed to be said or done regarding potential claims, particularly in relation to the illegal share support and the €7.2 billion of false deposits.

On the same day, 14 April 2011, Pat O'Neill announced to management that the banks and bondholders were writing off €550 million, which left a debt of €720 million. Within months, O'Brien and McKillop went back to the financiers to say that the debt of €720 million was still too high, and they asked for it to be reduced to €475 million to make the company viable. This was off the wall, as just a few months earlier, in January, David Mackey, Kevin Lunney, Dara O'Reilly and I had prepared a proposal with Shay Bannon of BDO. We had offered to pay back 100 per cent of the debt – more than €1.2 billion – at an interest rate of 3.5 per cent. We got the feeling that the bondholders were very interested in our proposal, but it appears that the powers that be who wanted to take over the business, but who weren't allowed to at the time – and there were many – decided that Anglo would offer the bondholders €200 million of Quinn Insurance money to refuse our proposal. There was nothing to suggest that €200 million was ever owed. Everyone knew there were rich pickings on the table, and they now got their way with Enda Kenny and Michael Noonan at the wheel. Some are still feasting on the carcass twelve years later.

The reaction of the local community to the share receivership was angry, and immediate. Within days, there was unrest in the area. On 18 April a 70-tonne dumper truck was driven into bollards in front of the head office's entrance, barring all access. Alan Dukes rang me and asked me to get the dumper moved, which I did, and to meet him and Mike Aynsley in Dublin. I went to the meeting with my daughter Aoife. I stupidly thought he might have seen some sense and was going to offer me a deal. I was wrong again. Instead, Dukes gave us a lecture on our obligation to bring peace to the area. In fact, it was they, and they alone, who had brought hostility to our area.

As that meeting was happening, a large number of people occupied the Quinn Group's head office in Derrylin. One of the protestors called me on my mobile and said they wanted to stay in the building on a rota, for the next few weeks, I told him that they had already made their point and I urged them to go home, which they did. I am still reminded by many people locally that my advice was silly, and too trusting. I now realise how right they were.

Within days of the share receiver arriving, Kevin, Dara and I met a number of politicians, from both north and south of the border, in County Monaghan. Both Kevin and I were emotional as we went through the company's latest figures, emphasising its underlying strength and how we had begun to reduce its debts. We asked the politicians to relay our concerns back to Michael Noonan, who either didn't understand, or didn't want to understand, the strength of the company. They were all very supportive, and many of them said they would demand meetings with Noonan, or even with Enda Kenny. A local newspaper reported that I was "upset and felt he had been left high and dry".

But before long Alan Dukes held his own meeting with these same politicians from the border region, on 19 May. He gave them a completely false narrative, telling them that the Quinn Group was in a financial crisis and insisting that the receivership was the only way to reduce its debts. His extraordinary presentation included the fact that he would receive €270 million from Quinn manufacturing businesses, even though Pat O'Neill had advised Quinn Group management five weeks earlier, on 14 April, that the bondholders were in fact writing off €500 million of debt. In a *PrimeTime* interview with Paul O'Brien, CEO of Aventas (the holding company created to dispose of Quinn Group assets), when asked how much Anglo would recover from the manufacturing group, he confirmed unequivocally, "Zero, to be blunt, and it was never going to be anything else only zero."

At the meeting however, Dukes predicted that the receivership could release €600 million from international properties, €400 million from QIL, and €270 million from the Quinn Group's manufacturing business. He knew at the time that QIL had made 900 people redundant, had reduced its turnover by 80 per cent, and was going to need hundreds of millions of euros from the Insurance Compensation Fund thanks to the mismanagement of the administrators. Dukes could not have it both ways, claiming that QIL was bankrupt one moment, and then claiming that it had a net worth of €400 million. While some in attendance knew that the figures made no sense, at the time they didn't want to go on record as the whole transaction was being supported by the Irish government. Of course, none of these figures were ever realised. They were ridiculous predictions, and well he knew it, and, of course, they never received a penny, either from manufacturing or insurance. To my knowledge, this misrepresentation to Dáil Eireann was never discussed by the Public Accounts Committee, and I believe that of the €2.8 billion of debt that we had committed to paying in full, with interest, no money will ever be recovered because of the destruction they have caused over the past twelve years. In reality, this means that 100 per cent of the businesses that were generating between €400 and €500 million per year of profit were given away for nothing, and probably anything up to €1 billion along with it, rather than the €2.8 billion that we had agreed to repay them, plus interest and €100 million per annum in taxes.

It is a fact that during all of the discussions that were had with Anglo and the bondholders during the critical period between 2007 and 2011, nobody ever suggested that we would not be able to repay the money. In fact, the opposite was the case: Seán FitzPatrick, David Drumm, Donal O'Connor, Mike Aynsley and Patrick Neary indicated that they had no doubt we would be able to repay the debt in full.

In total, IBRC forecasted that their strategy would recoup €1.27 billion, rather than the €2.8 billion that we had committed to paying. However, even this proposal was fundamentally flawed, misleading and untrue, and Anglo knew this prior to its implementation, and anyone who knew the history of the Quinn Group would know that repaying the €2.8 billion was no problem.

Each year the Irish Central Bank (formerly the Irish Financial Regulator) produce an insurance statistical review. This report is based on the statuary returns filed by insurers. The Central Bank Insurance Statistical Review for 2009, at table A, page 13 [19], compares the reserves for the 'home' regulated motor insurers (whose head office is based in the republic of Ireland). In 2009, these figures prove that QIL had average reserves of 1.8 times the industry average, and the highest average reserves in Ireland (see Table 1).

It has been reported in the media by Matt Cooper that our solvency margin in 2008 was 25 per cent. When you consider that our average reserve was 80 per cent higher than our competitors, that would amount to 45 per cent, and the same article stated that the solvency in March 2010 was 31 per cent. When you consider our higher reserves, which were 80 per cent higher than competitors, that would have left us with a solvency of 56 per cent. Our household and commercial books were even more conservatively reserved, with an average reserve of more than €90,000 per claim.

There has been very little explanation from the administrators about why the €1.6 billion proposed at the time was required from the Insurance

Table 1: Extract from Central Bank Insurance Statistical Review, 2009, Table A, Page 13

Table A: Extract of Data from 2009 Statutory Insurance Annual Returns in the Motor Claims Settlement Analysis Forms in respect of 2009 Accident Year (Form 8) – (Monetary Values are expressed in 000s)

	Allianz plc	Aviva Insurance (Europe)	AXA Insurance	Charis Insurance Ireland	FBD Insurance	Irish Public Bodies	Quinn Insurance	RSA Insurance Ireland	Zurich Insurance
No. of Claims Outstanding	10,634	12,058	16,905	6,331	8,678	870	17,282	9,658	8,894
Gross Estimated Liability for Outstanding Reported Claims at End of Year (000s Euro)	45,917	129,178	117,835	11,596	68,680	3,824	238,845	41,177	75,033
Gross Estimated Liability of Outstanding IBNR at End of Year (000s Euro)	27,197	18,341	12,693	5,118	5,485	3,174	36,341	1,261	15,577
Gross Estimated Liability Total for all Outstanding Claims at End of Year (000s Euro)	73,114		130,528	16,714	74,165	6,998	275,186	42,438	90,610
Average Liability per claim	6.88	0.00	7.72	2.64	8.55	8.04	15.92	4.39	10.19
Industry Average incl. QIL	9.39			Industry Average excl. QIL			8.83		
Ratio of QIL Reserves to Industry Avg	1.70			Ratio of QIL Reserves to Industry Avg			1.80		

Compensation Fund (ICF). I have seen a copy of Grant Thornton's tenth report, filed in the High Court on 30 July 2012. From examining this, and the annual accounts of QIL signed off by the administrators, it is clear to me that about € 1.023 million of the required ICF funding is down to the mismanagement of the administrators.

Table 2 shows the funding they claimed they required.

Table 2: Extract from Grant Thornton, Tenth Report of the Joint Administrators, 30 July 2012

Requirement	€m's	Notes
Original Funding Requirements	775	
Increase in claims provision	208	Increase in provision for claims.
Adverse Deviation Provision	300	As per the Administrators' report to the Court, this called 'safety net' for the Administrators, it is not assigned to anything in particular, just provided for in the accounts of QIL [12].
Reserve of sterling hedge	215	In the Administrators' report to the Court it states "_we (the administrators) have been unable to implement a hedging instrument to protect against adverse sterling fluctuations, in the absence of a hedging strategy we have based our reserves on a conservative Euro/Sterling exchange rate of .70_" and "_A contingency reserve of €215m against currency fluctuations as it is not possible to put a hedging strategy in place_" **[21]**. This reserve is due to the Administrators' failure to hedge against currency exchange risks. The provision is grossly over esimated, on the basis that the provision assumes a sterling rate at .7 to the euro, while the current rate is .86.
Reduction in asset values and miscellaneous adjustments	152	This is the write down of assets, including the write off of the share capital provided to Anglo for fund their shareholding of €92m, this was originally taken from QIL's reserves to fund their shareholding in the joint venture
Total revision in July 2012	**875**	
Total Requirement	**1650**	

Source: Grant Thornton, Quinn Insurance Limited (Under Administration), Tenth Report of the Joint Administrators, 30 July 2012

It seems unbelievable that the administrators were able to convince the public, and the Minister for Finance, that the massive draw on the ICF was because Quinn Insurance wasn't properly reserved. According to their own figures, only €208 million of the €875 million additional funding they sought in July 2012 was for claims reserves.

Large sums of money were written off and wrongly paid to the bondholders, and I believe that any money required can be better summarised as shown in Table 3.

Table 3: Breakdown of Funding Required for the Insurance Compensation Fund

Requirement	€m's	Notes
Payment to the QIL bondholders	200.0	Payment to secure the release of contingent guarantees
Write off loans due from other Quinn companies	87.1	QIL loan write-offs, €67m due from Barlo Financial Services Limited, €9.36m due from Mantlin Limited & €10.70m due from Quinn Group Limited
QIL's Reserves for Anglo's Shareholding	98.0	Funds taken from QIL's reserves to fund Anglo's 98% shareholding
Subsequent write-off of Anglo's shareholding	92.0	Referenced in Table 2
Adverse Deviation Reserve	300.0	As stated by the Administrators in their 10th Report, dated 30 July 2012
Failure to Hedge the Sterling	208.0	As stated by the Administrators in their 10th Report, dated 30 July 2012
Redundancy	9.9	Redundancy payments in 2010 [figures likely to increase when the Redundancy payments in 2011, 2012 and 2013 are taken into account]
Administration Costs	18.3	€6.8m in 2010 and €11.5m in 2011 [this will increase when the costs for 2012 & beyond are included]
Loss Recognised on the sale of business	10.4	Assets in excess of liabilities transferred to Liberty, plus carrying value adjustments

Source: Grant Thornton, Quinn Insurance Limited (Under Administration), Tenth Report of the Joint Administrators, 30 July 2012

The administrators completely failed to understand or manage the QIL claims model, which was the cornerstone of the company's success. QIL historically employed more staff in its claims department than its competitors, in order to proactively manage claims within hours of them being notified. This saved dramatically on claims costs, and, in particular, on legal fees. The administrators' redundancy scheme removed hundreds of staff from the claims department. This had a detrimental impact on the efficiency of the model, as it did not give the claims handlers adequate time to negotiate with all parties – our insured customers, third parties, garages, our regional claims managers, witnesses, the Gardaí or police, or anybody else who might be able to assist in getting an early settlement.

In order to understand the cost savings in proactively managing claims, it is easier to explain by way of an example. The average 'fast-track' claims handler would settle around 30 claims per month, at an average cost of €2,900 per claim. They would have had an open workload of about 30 claims at any one time. The staff cost for a typical claims handler would be about €35,000 per year.

Once a solicitor comes on record for a claimant, the average claim cost increases to €23,182, an eight-fold increase. In the UK, the comparative figures for fast-track claims were £2,073 and £7,608 once a solicitor comes on record.

After the redundancy programme, workloads increased substantially. The fast-track handlers had workloads in excess of 60 claims each. Even minor inefficiencies would have the most detrimental impact on claim costs. For example, if a fast-track handler let just one more claimant per week obtain a solicitor, over a one-year period that would lead to additional claim costs in excess of €1 million for that handler. This makes it ridiculous to have increased their workload. At the same time, under its new owners, QIL, now renamed as Liberty Insurance, had a policy of avoiding giving cover to young, male drivers – the very opposite of QIL's old approach.

It has frequently been said that "in Seán Quinn's time, the big claims weren't settled". In fact, the direct opposite is the case. As everybody knows, the big claims are normally the old claims. The following figures have been produced by the administrators themselves. Pre-administration, only 6 per cent of claims were over four years old. A year later, this increased to 8.6

per cent, and, two years later, to 15.2 per cent, an increase of 150 per cent in two years. In addition, the management information produced by the administrators show that the average settlement up to March 2010 was €7,071. In March 2011 it was €8,283, and in March 2012 it was €11,765 (see Table 4). This is a 66 per cent increase in two years, and when you consider that they weren't settling the old claims at this time, it is clear that the claims cost, in real terms, increased by more than 100 per cent, and probably closer to 200 per cent. I have two concerns about that: first of all, why were they not settled during those two years, and, secondly, when were they settled?

Table 4: Insurance Settlement Costs, 2010–2012

Average Settlement Cost		
Year	Average Cost	Year-on-Year Increase
2010	€7,071	-
2011	€8,283	17%
2012	€11,765	42%
Increase since Administration		66%

Source: MIS Stats 13 March 2010, MIS Stats 12 March 2011,
MIS Stats 13 March 2012

The increase in claim costs can be put down to the fact that Liberty had absolutely no incentive to settle claims cheaply. Liberty effectively purchased QIL's Irish insurance business with no risk. If they required further funds within three years of buying the business, it was guaranteed to them by QIL, through the Insurance Compensation Fund. Under the contingent liabilities in QIL's annual accounts for 2011, for the "Sale of the Republic of Ireland General Insurance Business", the accounts state "the revised structure included in the final terms of the sales agreement gives LIL [Liberty Insurance Limited] the opportunity to re-visit the completion reserves on a quarterly basis over a 36-month period from completion. Any increase in completion reserves in that period will be funded by QIL with additional cash."

The poor performance of the company in the early Liberty days was exacerbated by the fact that sales staff in the commercial division were informed that any customers looking to renew or place new business with a premium in excess of €50,000 should be directed to Liberty Mutual in the IFSC. This was Liberty's standalone operation. By seeking to move this business to Liberty, this had the effect of showing Quinn Insurance in a worse light, as that was the most profitable business in our book. I suppose the question has to be asked, why it was done?

To ensure the maximum loss to the Irish taxpayer, on 13 September 2011 Finance Minister Michael Noonan brought in the Insurance (Amendment) Act 2011. This was just days before the transaction to transfer QIL's business to the Anglo/Liberty Joint Venture. This legislation confirmed that the liability for UK claims would be met by the Irish Insurance Compensation Fund. Prior to this point, the fund had no obligation to pay these claims.

So, in reality, what Liberty received for a €100 million investment was an insurance company that had made profits of between €200 and €300 million a year between 2002 and 2007, along with dozens of other assets, including windfarms, offices, and hotels, as well as the remaining balance of the €1.1 billion in the company's bank account. They received €738 million of cash from the Insurance Compensation Fund, along with an undertaking to pay any further shortfalls over a three-year period. Where was their incentive to run the business well? If this type of deal had been known about, wouldn't there be hundreds, if not thousands, of individuals and companies that would have offered a much better deal than this, knowing that they were getting all of this value. Why was this offer restricted to Liberty Insurance?

* * * *

Local anger intensified. In late April, Enda Kenny was heckled by Quinn family sympathisers while on a visit to Drumshanbo, Country Leitrim, not far from my home. Later, despite a judgment from Judge Charleton, Kenny talked to the Ukrainian Prime Minister and asked him to help secure the return of our assets in Ukraine. What legal advice did he have in order for him to believe that the government owned these assets while the case hadn't even been heard? Did he check who paid for the assets and who had security on them? Gradually, Quinn Group plants began to be closed down by the receiver, leading to more job losses. Our Williamstown quarrying operations and factories in Galway and a landfill site in Armagh were closed, as was a polyurethane factory site in Cardiff, where we had bought all of the plant and machinery. All further work on our chemical site plant near Leipzig in Germany, which had been mothballed since 2009, was stopped, even though €200 million had already been spent on it. We had other sites in Counties Tipperary, Wicklow, Kildare, Dublin and Louth, along with others in England and Belgium. I don't know to this day what happened to any of them, but I never heard of any money being recouped for the Irish taxpayer from them, as was promised, nor have I seen any income from them recorded in the annual accounts of the company.

As the spring of 2011 turned into summer, there were more acts of sabotage against the new management of the Quinn Group's businesses. On 8 August a car owned by Quinn Group director Paul O'Brien was destroyed by a firebomb at his home in Ratoath, County Meath, though luckily no one was hurt as he was on holiday in Portugal at the time. Later in 2011 threats were made to Quinn Group staff, fibreoptic cables were cut, electric cables torn down, and hundreds of thousands worth of damage was done around various parts of the business. Trevor Birney later stated in his book that Paul O'Brien knew the individuals who were working in the company during the day and causing the sabotage at night.

Pat O'Neill sent me a stupid letter saying what a great guy I was, and urging me to condemn the sabotage. It was breath-taking that a man who was so highly respected in his previous roles could lower himself to that level, as it has always been my belief that if a company is loss-making it deserves very little sympathy, but the company that he was now chairman of had out-performed all its competitors in all of the fields in which it operated. I even remember him saying at one of our early meetings in the insurance office in Cavan that he had never been involved in a company in his life that had such high profit margins and growth.

From Pat O'Neill on 20 May 2011:

Dear Seán,

The Board of Quinn Group Limited, following a discussion yesterday about the number of instances of sabotage and intimidation of staff, requested that I write to you to advise you of the situation and seek your help. That these acts of sabotage and intimidation are as a result of the change of ownership of the Group, is accepted by all. However, the increasing possibility of personal injury, the destabilisation of the business platform and the potential for job losses locally to the disadvantage of everyone concerned if the intimidation and sabotage is to continue, cannot be under-estimated.

As a respected and influential person in the local community, I have no doubt it would be very helpful if you were to issue a statement to the media deploring these acts and calling on the perpetrators to cease such actions immediately.

Yours, etc. ...

His letter made me wonder what world he was living in, and my response on 25 May 2011 was as follows:

Dear Mr O'Neill,

I refer to your letter of 20ᵗʰ May, which, to put it mildly, I found perplexing and, having regard to the manner in which this entire matter was handled by you, nothing short of insulting.

Clearly by asking me to condemn these so-called "acts of sabotage and intimidation" you are insinuating that I am promoting instability in the business, which I find deeply offensive considering I have spent my life building up the business in this area.

First of all, I wish to make it clear that, apart from hearing anecdotal reports, I have absolutely no knowledge of any "acts of sabotage and intimidation", as referred to in your letter.

Secondly, I find it mystifying that you would have the audacity to turn to me for help in any matter whatsoever. Quite frankly, I find this profoundly insulting especially since it was only from media reports, rather than you directly, that I learned of the actions that you undertook, a situation which still pertains six weeks after your actions.

You mention the respect I hold in the local community and the potential destabilisation of the business. By your actions, you showed no respect for me, for my family, for my colleagues or for the local community. Quite the opposite, you showed nothing but total contempt for all of us. No one has done more to destabilise the business than you have.

We operated in this area for almost forty years, with no sabotage, no intimidation, and an exceptional level of community harmony, and all at a time when we were surrounded by a sea of disharmony and ill-feeling. The local community is not accustomed to the type of intimidatory, spineless, and callous actions such as those that you have undertaken.

There is nobody more disappointed than I am at the devastation that you have caused in our area, and if a statement is needed, you should make it.

Yours, etc.

Seán Quinn

* * * *

The family launched legal proceedings against IBRC, on the basis that the bank had breached Section 60 of the Companies Act, as well as the Market Abuse Regulations. These regulations are clearly defined in European legislation, and the Central Bank and the Department of Finance would have been fully aware of the legislation, so this case had to be stopped at all costs.

And so they brought a case against the family to block us from managing our own assets that we had bought and paid for with our own money. That case became the talking point and our case against them was put on the back burner.

IBRC made an application to the High Court to have the market abuse claims heard as a separate and distinct preliminary legal action to the main proceedings. The bank made the argument that a decision regarding a potential breach of the Market Abuse Regulations would streamline the entire proceedings and ultimately lead to a quicker and more cost-effective resolution of the litigation. In order to secure the Court's approval for the preliminary action, the bank undertook not to appeal the High Court ruling. However, when the decision didn't go their way, they changed their minds and appealed. In his judgment of 23 February 2012, Judge Charleton, who was later appointed a Supreme Court judge, stated that "it would be contrary to public policy if the Plaintiffs [the Quinn family] were to be shut out from responding to the flagrant illegality which they now alleged against Anglo and Seán Quinn."

In relation to the manipulation of Anglo's share price, he stated, "It was beyond doubt that false and misleading signals were given to the market-place as to the value of Anglo shares" and that "The illegality claimed in this litigation is the wholesale manipulation of the price of Anglo Irish Bank Corporation Limited shares to the detriment of the Plaintiffs."

Judge Charleton concluded by stating that if the money was used for the unlawful purpose that was pleaded, then the appointment of a share receiver compounded the illegality. At that stage, it was generally accepted that the €2.34 billion that Anglo invested in their own shares in our name was illegal, so if it was, wouldn't that mean that taking security against illegal loans would also be illegal? Anglo didn't have security on the family's privately held assets: firstly, because they never paid a penny towards their purchase; secondly, they never held a mortgage against them; and thirdly, they never even mentioned taking security on them to the family. So, on what basis did they feel they had security against these illegal loans?

Far away from the border counties, the family was making frantic efforts to keep the foreign property assets, which we had bought with our own money, out of the hands of the share receiver. This required very complex planning, and unfortunately, with neither myself nor my family ever having been involved in this type of administration or planning, it is fair to say that we fell well short of implementing the plan properly. Our Group executives, who had been involved in setting up the company structures, had flown the nest, and left us to fend for ourselves. We were out of our depth, and these events did a lot of reputational damage to both me and my family.

On the advice of local solicitors in Russia, we attempted to place assets into the name of companies and individuals that were beyond the reach of Anglo. We had to trust those solicitors to ensure that the assets would be returned to us at some point. The only mechanisms that we could use were weak, and we knew that the ownership of the assets was at risk. At the time however, we were very angry, and felt that we had to take the risk, and I fully supported the plan. The Russian solicitors were happy to safeguard the assets on the family's behalf initially, but when Anglo came in and disputed the ownership of those assets, they couldn't believe their luck. It became very easy for them to take advantage of the situation, and allow two Irish entities to slog it out, while they would keep the assets.

When the problem became apparent, and we could see that the Russians and Ukrainians were going to keep the assets, we approached Anglo, with a view to them and us working together to get the assets back. On 7 September 2011, some five months after the takeover of the Quinn Group, we instructed Mr David O'Beirne, managing partner of Eversheds, to meet with Mr Ronan Maloney, managing partner of McCann Fitzgerald, to advise Anglo of the deteriorating situation abroad, and offered to cooperate with Anglo in securing all the assets involved, to ensure that that assets would remain within Irish control. Anglo, however, categorically refused to work consensually with the family to recover the assets, and to rectify the position. What does it say about our legal system when you have the managing partner of a major legal firm offering, on behalf of his clients, to work with Anglo to secure the return of the assets, that offer was refused out of hand, and then his clients were put in prison for not getting the assets back? Having the top legal brains in the country advising them, they should have known that they had no legal entitlement to these assets, which meant that by recovering them, they would have to go back to the family. Instead, they decided to issue contempt proceedings against us, for trying to protect our own assets and create the narrative that the Quinns were stealing government assets. This would also distract attention away from the real issue, which was the €2.34 billion that Anglo had invested in their own shares.

Subsequently, legal battles were fought in Irish, Ukrainian, Russian, Swedish and Cypriot courtrooms over the fate of these assets. Ironically, Kieran Wallace himself had advised Richard Woodhouse in 2010 that if two parties worked together, they could outmanoeuvre the third one, and I believe he was right. It had been proven when Anglo and the bondholders worked together to oust us, and of course, it would have worked equally well if we and Anglo had worked together against the Russians and Ukrainians, but that is not what they wanted. They wanted to show the Quinns in a bad light and take the assets by hook or by crook.

Later, in spring 2012, Richard Woodhouse approached one of our barristers in a Dublin pub, to say that the bank wanted to discuss a settlement agreement. The family agreed that we would be happy to negotiate, however McCann Fitzgerald brought these proposed negotiations to an abrupt end, stating that Mr Woodhouse did not have the authority to make a settlement approach nor engage in such discussions. Further evidence, in my view, that they didn't want the assets back.

On 2 December 2011, a public meeting was held in the community centre in Ballyconnell, which was attended by a number of politicians, and several people spoke, including Joe O'Reilly, then Fine Gael TD, David Mackey, and Martin Maguire, chief executive of Fermanagh Economic Development Organisation. A letter that had been written by Denis Doogan, the chief executive of the radiator division, who had resigned shortly after the Group had been taken over, was read out, stating:

When the decision was taken to remove Quinn Insurance and Quinn Group from the control of Seán Quinn, the dawn of one of the greatest cover-ups in the history of the Irish Republic had arrived. This cover-up has seen the persecution of Sean Quinn and his family over the last 2–3 years in an attempt to deflect the focus away from a failed banking system and a failed regulatory system. However, the vendetta against Seán Quinn has now become a vendetta against the people of this region, and is gradually impacting upon us all.

Denis's letter was applauded at length. David Mackey also spoke at the meeting, and, agreeing with Doogan, said "What Denis Doogan said was fair and balanced", and he urged the politicians to read the letter again.

****

Towards the end of 2011, it became apparent to me that Anglo were going to bankrupt me, so on 11 November 2011 I filed for bankruptcy in Belfast. I had to tell the court many humiliating details about my personal finances, and how they had been severely curtailed by the share receivership. I said that my outgoings were quite modest: £2,380 a month, including £850 on housekeeping, £1,200 on utility bills, £100 on clothing, £80 on travel and £150 on 'miscellaneous expenses'. I had no income, and my home at Greaghrahan was now owned by my children, not by me. My only personal assets were €11,169 in three bank accounts, a C-Class Mercedes W204 valued at €4,670, a £35,000 interest in forestry, and two pension funds, worth €160,000 and €40,000.

Patricia also had court proceedings to contend with in a Dublin court. A €3 million 'home improvement' loan from Anglo, made to Patricia in 2006, had in fact gone to Quinn Manufacturing, and not a cent of it had been spent on our house in Greaghrahan, nor did she receive a cent of it. Patricia was forced to argue that while she was officially the director of many Quinn companies, in practice her only occupation during our 36-year marriage had been as a 'home-maker'. She admitted that this was "embarrassing

... but it is the truth". The judge, Peter Kelly, ruled that Patricia was making a "cat's paw" argument, and he found that she was liable to repay the €3 million 'home improvement' loan. But the truth is that for many years Patricia, like me and our children, had simply signed everything that was placed in front of her without asking any questions. To this day I do not know why the €3 million loan was taken out in Patricia's name or where it went to.

Ultimately, my bid to be declared bankrupt in Belfast failed. Bizarrely, IBRC appealed my application for bankruptcy there, claiming that I was taking advantage of the more lenient bankruptcy regime in the United Kingdom, under which I could emerge from bankruptcy in one year, as opposed to twelve years in Ireland. IBRC argued that because almost all my business dealings were south of the border, not north of it, I should be declared bankrupt by a Dublin court, not a Belfast one. But I believe that there was another reason why my bankruptcy in Belfast was opposed. The Financial Regulator, the Central Bank, the Department of Finance, and the Domestic Standing Group would have known that we had been advised by the White and Case legal team in the UK that the transactions relating to share support were illegal. Anglo's legal team made a successful case to Judge Kelly that I couldn't give evidence as I was bankrupt. They knew that if I was declared bankrupt in Northern Ireland, after one year I would be in a position to give evidence of all of my dealings with Anglo to the court.

My British bankruptcy was annulled in Belfast in December 2011, after an appeal by IBRC, on the grounds that my links to Northern Ireland were too tenuous. Incredibly, I even had to pay for the costs of Anglo's appeal. Outside court, I told the media, "What Anglo has done to the Quinn Group is like somebody taking a sledgehammer to a child's toy – they've destroyed it."

In truth, if there was one man in Ireland who was entitled to declare himself bankrupt in the North, it was me. I had been born at home in Derrylin, County Fermanagh, only 50 metres from where the Quinn Group's head office now stood. I had gone to school in Teemore, also in County Fermanagh, and played Gaelic football, at both club and county level, in Fermanagh. My first two children had been born in Derrylin, Co. Fermanagh, before Patricia and I moved south of the border in 1977. Although my main residence had been in Ballyconnell since then, the only desk I ever worked at was in the North, which, in a typical week, I drove to six days a week. I told the court that "I have never done a day's work from southern Ireland in my life." Many Irish people seek bankruptcy in courts in Northern Ireland, England, Scotland or Wales even if they don't have any links to the UK, and while I am in no way envious of their success I think it proves, if proof is needed, that when the system works as a unit, it can turn even the most blatant injustices into law. More importantly, it begs the fundamental questions of why did Anglo's legal team not want me giving evidence in a Dublin court? I can only conclude that they didn't want my evidence being heard, as it would have proven that the government and its agents, as well as Anglo and Quinn executives, were responsible for the illegal loans, and, furthermore, that these loans were provided for the benefit of Anglo Irish Bank, and not for the Quinn family. The farcical nature of this decision was borne out by the fact that the Irish government later refused to pay my pension, and directed me to Northern Ireland, where they refused to allow me to be bankrupt a year earlier! Differences in the UK and Irish bankruptcy legislation meant that my private pensions were seized by the Irish state.

I should have realised that I was banging my head against a brick wall after my bankruptcy in Belfast was rescinded. Paul Gallagher, who had been Attorney General from 2007 to 2011 (and who later became Attorney General again in June 2020), was now acting as IBRC's barrister. Gallagher has always been a very successful lawyer who rarely seems to lose a case. One of the few cases he did lose involved NAMA, which wanted to place the Irish hotelier Paddy McKillen's companies into receivership. In February 2011 McKillen had won a landmark Supreme Court case, which blocked NAMA, represented in court by Gallagher, from seizing his €3 billion property portfolio. But I did not share McKillen's good luck, nor did I have the access to finance that he did.

Paul Gallagher had no known association with Fianna Fáil before Bertie Ahern appointed him as Attorney General in 2007, but now, as IBRC was under government control, it was being represented by a lawyer who, as

Attorney General in the Fianna Fáil-led government that had nationalised Anglo Irish three years earlier, was familiar with the Quinn CFD position since 2007. This begs the question: was he conflicted? Gallagher was a tough adversary, and he fought me tooth and nail. He was now determined to see me declared bankrupt in Dublin and put me in prison.

But personal bankruptcy was only one of my problems. IBRC began proceedings to prosecute me, Seán Jnr and my nephew Petey for contempt of court. These proceedings were brought by Anglo Irish Bank to prevent us from managing a business that we had bought and paid for with our own money. Surely it doesn't make sense that somebody can claims rights over someone else's property, resulting in the owner of the property being unable to manage that business? How can this happen without the new claimant proving that they had a legitimate claim on it. If that was accepted in law, does it mean that a new claimant over a business is innocent until proven guilty, and the original owner of the business is guilty until proven innocent? Contempt proceedings were scheduled to start in Dublin on 13 February 2012, with a full trial due to start in the High Court on 21 March, just one month after Judge Charleton's judgment, which indicated that if the share support money was illegal, taking Quinn assets compounded the illegality.

By mid-2011 Ireland had 15 per cent unemployment. Tax revenues were plummeting. Anglo Irish Bank, Seán Quinn, and, to a lesser degree, the other banks and builders made convenient scapegoats for these disasters.

Somewhere, a decision had been made to 'get rid of Quinn'. I had already suffered the loss of my companies, and I was now bankrupt. My enemies were trying to starve me out, by making me run out of money, and, as it turned out, trying to have me imprisoned, and they succeeded in both.

9

On 16 January 2012 I was finally declared bankrupt, at the High Court in Dublin. IBRC had spent tens of thousands bringing over British barristers to overturn my Belfast bankruptcy in 2011. Many media commentators felt that the process of bankrupting me in the South was the right thing to do, something that I could never understand, and, at the time, not a word was spoken about the €2.34 billion of illegal loans.

Anglo bankrupted me for €3 billion. The question is, was this done just to make me look bad and give the media headlines? It made a great headline that Ireland's richest man was now Ireland's biggest ever bankrupt – even though I hadn't owned assets for over ten years, had borrowed no money for over ten years, and wasn't even a director of the companies involved – and it was used to the full, but it did serve its purpose, in that Judge Kelly ruled that I was unable to give evidence as a bankrupt.

After my bankruptcy, Chris Lehane, a senior official in Ireland's insolvency service, became my assignee. Chris was a complete gentleman and I have no complaint about the way he treated me; indeed, he gave me the impression that he thought I'd been the victim of rough justice. To this day, I am still receiving my pension from Northern Ireland, a jurisdiction in which they would not allow me to go bankrupt, and I would very much doubt if there's any other resident living in the south of Ireland who declared bankruptcy in Northern Ireland and is receiving their pension from Northern Ireland.

Throughout my working life, despite what Judge Dunne has stated, I have never knowingly taken a penny that didn't belong to me from anyone, nor do I believe that the family I was born into, or the family I helped to create, did either.

On top of the humiliation of bankruptcy, I still faced the contempt of court prosecution. When my trial began, back at the High Court in Dublin in March 2012, IBRC was represented by McCann Fitzgerald, one of Ireland's top law firms. At various other times the bank was supported by Arthur Cox, William Fry and MOPs, all at the expense of Irish taxpayers. Irish taxpayers' funds seemed to be unlimited for IBRC. Conflicts of interest appeared to be rife throughout these transactions. For example, McCann Fitzgerald solicitors were appointed as the Financial Regulator's solicitors to oversee the administration of QIL; McCann Fitzgerald were also appointed solicitors to the joint administrator of QIL, as well as being appointed solicitors for Anglo as purchasers of QIL. Thereafter, McCann Fitzgerald were the appointed solicitors on behalf of Anglo to litigate against my family. It appeared that they had it all tied up.

As in my bankruptcy proceedings, IBRC's barrister was once again Paul Gallagher, who had been Attorney General during the period that Anglo invested €2.34 billion in our family's name to support their own shares. As Attorney General, he had been happy to allow that to happen, as well as allowing the Maple Ten transactions to happen. How can he have it both ways? Anglo was prosecuted for advancing the money in full knowledge of various government departments, and yet, he was claiming that we owed it. I don't believe any other democratic country in the world would have found those share support loans to be legal, nor would they have found that the agents of the state were not responsible for, and in fact encouraged, many of the actions that others have been found guilty of. This was confirmed by both Judge Charleton and Judge Nolan.

When we were prevented from using the rental income from our own assets to pay legal fees, we were unable to afford to have Eversheds represent us. We were fortunate that Eugene Grant QC was instructed by the Belfast firm Kevin R. Winters, which specialised in human rights, to represent us.

Eugene was only brought in at the last minute. He did a fantastic job, and he could not have tried harder for us, but in reality it could never have made any difference as the Irish state was determined to make an example of the Quinns and send them to prison.

Once IBRC became aware that we had been getting some of the rental income from the foreign properties, they succeeded in having personal receivers appointed over my children's personal finances. They had to account for every penny of expenditure before the court; everything from family home mortgages to payments of medical bills and household food expenditure, right down to children's nappies, was laid bare for the public. It was humiliating for any family to be put through, and the bank and the court knew that, but they were determined to humiliate us as much as possible. The media were happy to lap it up.

The trial took place in the High Court, sitting in the Four Courts, the enormous domed building on Inns Quay in the centre of Dublin, designed by Thomas Cooley and James Gandon, and built between 1776 and 1802. On the bench was Mrs Justice Elizabeth Dunne, described by Gavin Daly and Ian Kehoe as a "middle-aged lady with thin-framed glasses and a sharp turn of phrase".

Despite all that has been said and written about moving these assets, neither myself nor any of the family ever denied the fact that we moved these assets, nor sold them cheaply, and I even told Alan Dukes, Mike Aynsley and Richard Woodhouse, the day they said they were taking over the Group, that we would be defending those assets vigorously. At a meeting more than a year later, Richard Woodhouse admitted I had said that on the day the share receiver was appointed. Furthermore, *Citizen Quinn* states very clearly that on Richard Woodhouse's desk he had two separate bundles of Quinn properties: one bundle he had security over, and the other he had no security over. It is obvious that these journalists had significant access to Richard Woodhouse and Anglo's internal files. It is very difficult for me to understand how the court system can allow a bank to take assets that they had no security over, and at this stage it was a well-known fact publicly that Anglo had loaned money to support its own share price, which was in breach of Section 60 of the Companies Act, as well as other misdemeanours, including market manipulation, and had been nationalised because of those misdemeanours. I believe this has been the kernel of the criticism levelled at us for over a decade – that we had taken assets from Irish citizens, which we have always vehemently denied. I certainly accept now that we didn't do a good job of properly securing our assets. Of course in hindsight, we should have allowed the legal process to take its course, but at the time we felt backed into a corner, and believed they were taking assets that didn't belong to them. Naturally, if someone is taking the last cow out of your byre, you will try to defend it.

I knew very little about exactly what had been done in Russia and Ukraine. My last visit to either country was in 2007, more than five years before the trial began. I can unequivocally say that I never met or spoke to a solicitor, accountant, company or anyone who was involved in moving any of our assets. But I fully supported those who were endeavouring to move assets that we felt were being unjustly taken from us.

In court I made many diatribes against Anglo/IBRC, arguing that our movement of assets was "Mickey Mouse stuff" compared to Anglo's "destruction of the Quinn Group". I argued that the receivership had been engineered to distract attention away from the real scandal: the bank's investment into Quinn Group to cover the CFD losses, which was in breach of Section 60: "I think the cover-up should be opened up", I declared, but I was wasting my time and energy, as the Court was showing no interest in my argument.

In the middle of the trial, proceedings were adjourned for some time so that Seán Jnr could attend his own wedding. On Friday 11 May 2012 we celebrated his marriage to Karen Woods at St Mochta's Church in Porterstown, a western suburb of Dublin. The ceremony was followed by a reception at the Ritz-Carlton Powerscourt Hotel in Enniskerry, County Wicklow, one of Ireland's grandest hotels. We all had a very enjoyable day, and we temporarily forgot about all the negativity surrounding us. Seán Jnr ended up with a wonderful, supportive and loyal wife, who is now an excellent mother to their three young sons.

Later, it was implied by the media that Seán and Karen's honeymoon itinerary allowed them to progress the movement of assets. Indeed, IBRC engaged Kroll, an international investigative company, which sent people to the countries Seán and Karen visited on their honeymoon. In fact, to this day, neither of them have ever visited the countries that they were said to have visited to facilitate the movement of assets. As money was no obstacle to IBRC, it didn't appear to matter how many rabbit holes they went down at the time.

Back at the Four Courts, our case against IBRC was still ongoing, in parallel with the contempt of court case. Paul Gallagher, who was acting for IBRC in that case as well, argued that I should not be allowed to give evidence on the grounds that I had now been declared bankrupt. I wrote to Judge Kelly, who was presiding over the case, to explain that since I had founded the Quinn companies, it was only fair for me to be allowed to address the court. Judge Kelly called me to the front of the court for a short conversation, but he still held with Gallagher's argument, for reasons that are unclear.

Another senior counsel, Brian Cregan (who is now a High Court judge), who happened to be in court that day, awaiting a case he was acting in, over-heard the proceedings; he later represented me in an appeal against Judge Kelly's ruling. Cregan felt that for justice to be served, all evidence should be made available to the court. As I had been the main player in the Quinn Group from its inception, it was wrong that I couldn't give my perspective on all matters. Cregan showed that there are still many respectable, decent people within the legal profession. He mounted a very effective appeal on my behalf, *pro bono*, but to no avail. He offered to take the appeal to the Supreme Court, but, while I was grateful for his offer, I felt it would be futile. When a barrister of his calibre had been unable to win the appeal, I knew we were banging our heads against a brick wall. Ironically, Gallagher and the court were happy to allow me to give evidence in the case they were taking against us, but they wouldn't allow me to give evidence in the case where Anglo invested €2.34 billion in supporting shares in their bank in our name. The Court was happy to allow me to give evidence in what was called the 'conspiracy case', in which Anglo alleged we were taking their assets. However, I wasn't allowed to give evidence in the case brought by my children against Anglo regarding the breaches of the Section 60 regulations and Market Abuse regulations for the period of my bankruptcy.

Fighting the Irish state – whose emblem is the harp – is always an uphill struggle. As Frank Harrington, a longstanding cement customer and a good friend of mine, once warned me, "You'll never beat the harp. If the harp really wants to bring you down, there is no way of stopping them." I should have taken Frank's advice.

26 June 2012 was judgement day in the contempt of court trial. In courtroom six of the Four Courts, Richard Woodhouse and Mike Aynsley were surrounded by well-dressed men with earpieces – bodyguards. The media were also out in force.

Mrs Justice Dunne delivered her judgment at 10.32 a.m. She said that all three of us – Petey, Seán Jnr and I – had taken part in a "blatant, dishonest and deceitful" scheme to place our assets beyond the reach of IBRC, in contravention of injunctions. It is difficult for me to see how it was deceitful when we had always admitted that we had done it and when Anglo had never proven that they had rights to these assets. I had been "evasive and uncooperative". Judge Dunne didn't believe my argument that I had played no part in the scheme beyond April 2011. She spoke of how I had said that the Quinn Group had strived to be honourable and respectable, but she added, "I wish I could say the same about the manner in which the respondents have dealt with the adverse circumstances in which they now find themselves." She went on to say that there was no dispute regarding the €450 million of legitimate money that we owed the bank, and she was right in that, but what she failed to say was that none of the assets moved were related to the €450 million; the bank had undisputed charges over the assets relating to the €450 million, and we never attempted to move any of those assets. She concluded, damningly, that "The behaviour of the respondents outlined in evidence before me is as far removed from the concept of honour and respectability as it is possible to be." She also failed to comment on whether a bank could make a claim on an asset as security for illegal lending.

Straight after Judge Dunne's verdict the court was adjourned for three days. Although Seán Jnr, Petey and I had been found guilty of contempt of court, none of us were sentenced immediately, and we were still free men, for now. We were given three weeks in which to 'purge' our contempt by revealing our assets, or else we could face jail. An RTE journalist asked me if I was going to apologise to the court, and I asked her what she felt I should apologise for. As I was driven away from court, I said only a few words to the media, describing the judgment as "interesting, very interesting", before adding "I am not dishonest."

The family now made determined efforts to avoid our imprisonment. Seán Jnr and my son-in-law Stephen Kelly went out to Dubai and Moscow again, to try to recover assets, but they found that most of them were irretrievable. A&B, the Russian law firm we had engaged, were unwilling to give the assets back, and neither was Yaroslav Gurnyak, the part-time railway worker who was now the owner of the Kutuzoff Tower. It was a similar story in Dubai, where Senat Legal, a law firm that had masterminded the creation of our companies in Belize and the British Virgin Islands, also said it was unable to help. Seán Jnr and Stephen did not go to Ukraine, having been threatened by the new owners of the family's assets there. Gavin Daly and Ian Kehoe allege that "Puga had teamed up with some unsavoury locals to retain control of the shopping centre" in Kyiv. We had been double-crossed by the foreign agents we had relied on to shelter our assets.

I was always convinced that if the family, IBRC and the share receiver had worked together, as we had suggested almost two years earlier, when Eversheds, on our behalf, approached McCann Fitzgerald to offer our full cooperation, we would have got 100 per cent of the assets back, and reached a deal on what should happen to them. But as we were all competing with each other, the Russians and Ukrainians who now owned the assets became more and more unwilling to cooperate with any of us, and soon they became actively hostile. At this stage, while continuing to refuse any assistance from the Quinn family, IBRC engaged the services of the A1 Group, a controversial asset recovery company owned by three of Russia's richest men (one of whom, German Khan, was said to have once

told BP executives that he regarded *The Godfather* as "a manual for life").
A1 would receive about a quarter of any assets they helped to recover, but
in the end they had very little to show for it, despite being engaged for over
€100 million.

The family sent an affidavit to the court stating that we had returned from
Dubai and Moscow empty-handed, and outlining that we were happy to
take any further direction from the bank, and asked for a meeting to see if
any further action was required, but IBRC refused to meet us. The bank still
seemed to be more determined to see us in prison than to get the assets
back. We signed dozens of documents, at their request, and Petey sent them
75 notarised documents. I personally signed anything that was put in front
of me, as I had done for the previous 40 years.

At a further hearing, Judge Dunne sentenced Seán Jnr and my nephew
Petey to three months' imprisonment. Seán Jnr was taken straight from court
to Mountjoy Prison, in the north Dublin suburb of Phibsborough. A challenge
against Seán Jnr's sentence, to get him released from jail early, failed: only
one judge on the Supreme Court panel, the late Justice Adrian Hardiman,
gave a dissenting judgment, stating that there was only circumstantial
evidence against Seán. Seán Jnr wasn't released until 19 October 2012.

On the day of sentencing, Petey headed home to Northern Ireland, and
didn't face the court. He felt that he had done everything he could to satisfy
the bank, and once they refused to meet him, he felt that the return of the
assets wasn't their priority; their priority was to sink the Quinns. I agree whole-
heartedly with my brother, Peter's, comment at the time that Petey "wouldn't
get a fair hearing in the Dublin court". My daughter Ciara summed things up
well at the time when she said that "when you are ordered by a court to do
something that you physically can't do, it leaves you in a very difficult and
frightening place." I wouldn't dispute either of those statements.

I wasn't jailed for the time being, because IBRC wanted me to stay out of
jail to assist their efforts to recover our assets, which made no sense, as it was
on record that fourteen months earlier we had offered to get the assets back
and they had refused, and they had refused every day since. I was given a
stay of execution before my own jail sentence. In court, our senior counsel,

Brian O'Moore, criticised what he called, "This almost medieval approach of holding the son to see what the chieftain father will do in terms of freeing the son's liberty", but Mrs Justice Dunne saw nothing wrong with it.

The proceedings were managed in such a way that IBRC's case against us took place before our case against the bank could be heard, although, of course, our proceedings had been initiated first and was still described as the main case.

By coincidence, the trial of Anglo's former chairman, Seán FitzPatrick, along with former director of finance Willie McAteer and former head of Irish lending Pat Whelan, on sixteen charges relating to the 'Maple Ten' deal, began four days after Seán Jnr entered jail. Some of the charges related to "unlawful financial assistance" that had been given to the Quinn family, and the 'Maple Ten', in contravention of Section 60 of the Companies Act. How can the Irish state stand over this, when executives of the bank were being prosecuted for regulatory breaches regarding these very transactions, and at the same time, claiming ownership of our personally held assets, which we had bought and paid for with our own money?

The prevailing view was that this lending was in clear breach of two principal pieces of legislation: Section 60 of the Companies Act 1963, which prohibits a company from lending money to support its own share price, and the EU Market Abuse Regulations, which essentially prohibits insider dealing, unlawful disclosure of inside information, and market manipulation.

Judge Martin Nolan heard the trial, and in his judgment, he stated:

[B]oth men [Whelan and McAteer] were directors of the bank, executive directors. They had an obligation to make sure that the bank behaved in a lawful manner. This they signally failed to do ... both of the defendants knew of the situation and ... they had a duty to stop the scheme. The scheme ... in my view was an affront to section 60 and it seems to me it should have been stopped. ...

I find it incredible that red lights didn't go off some place in the Regulator's office and the appropriate legal advice was not sought. But it seems that Mr Horan and Mr Neary were more anxious to solve the *problem than comply with the technicalities of the law, but nonetheless the law. I think the Regulator felt that their overarching purpose was to save this bank and save the financial system. ...*

I'm totally surprised that the Regulator did not give some warning to Anglo Irish Bank. That it became apparent that there was going to be huge lending to the Quinn family to buy shares of Anglo Irish Bank in March. ... But again the Regulator ... knew that there was going to be some lending in relation to this scheme, overall scheme. ... The principle was there and it seems that the Regulator didn't realise that it was a breach of section 60 or chose to disregard it. I cannot be sure which was the case. ...

[T]here has been a serious crime committed because ... the market in shares depends on transparency and it depends on people's belief that there's an open and fair market. ... [T]here was not an open and fair market in Anglo shares. Anglo Irish Bank had intruded on the market for their own purposes and therefore people who bought Anglo Irish shares around that time I think were misled and could have lost as a result of that. So, therefore it's not a victimless crime.

Surely at that stage, after the judgments and comments from Judges Nolan and Charleton, it was clear that there was potentially a fraud committed by government agencies, and it's hard to believe that those responsible were never even prosecuted, never mind convicted on those charges. Despite all these legal setbacks, local people in the border counties were unstintingly loyal to our family. Prayers were said at Masses, and Fermanagh District Council voted unanimously to send us a letter of support. On 29 July 2012, 10,000 people gathered for a rally on the streets of Ballyconnell, where Patricia and I were flanked by several leading GAA figures, including Colm O'Rourke, Paddy O'Rourke and Mickey Harte. Father Brian D'Arcy, a well-known priest and broadcaster, said that the banks and Regulator should have been convicted, not the Quinn family. Joe Kernan, a former manager of Armagh's GAA team, called for Ireland to "let Seán Quinn build another empire", while Seán Boylan, a former manager of Meath's football team, said that the Quinns were "not thieves, not vagabonds", but "Irish people who have the guts and ingenuity to create a better life for thousands of people in this country ... we owe them a massive favour of thanks and gratitude." I would like to officially record my appreciation, and that of my family, to all the people who supported us, and to those who spoke on our behalf. I can fully understand, with all of the criticism that we have received over the past ten years, why people would have found it impossible to continue to publicly support us.

Coincidentally, two days after the rally, QIL's administrators revealed that they needed even more money from the Insurance Compensation Fund, further damaging the Quinn family's reputation. Some supporters in the GAA now started to be criticised. Seán Kelly, who had been president of the GAA in 2003–2006 and is now a Fine Gael MEP, had expressed support for us, but Enda Kenny forced him to withdraw his support. Other politicians and the majority of the media also ridiculed anybody who supported us, and the banks were much less flexible about the debts of Quinn supporters, and in some cases bankers asked their clients why they had attended, or made speeches, at, pro-Quinn rallies.

Many of the speeches at the rallies hinted at the existence of two Irelands: Dublin, where a financial and political elite had broken up our business empire, and the rural Ireland "that Quinn seemed to embody", as Gavin Daly and Ian Kehoe put it. Anger about my treatment, and resentment over proposals to close Gardaí stations and Bank of Ireland branches in many small towns in and around County Cavan, became a very potent mixture. Apart from the gypsum deposit in Glangevlin and Quinn Healthcare having to subsidise the VHI, I never felt that we were badly treated, until this point.

In July 2012, a meeting was arranged and attended by myself and my daughter Colette, supported by David O'Beirne from Eversheds, representing the family, and Richard Woodhouse, who attended with Karyn Harty from McCann Fitzgerald. The meeting was chaired by Lesley Buckley, who was Denis O'Brien's right-hand man. Mr Woodhouse explained at the meeting that Mr Dukes and Mr Aynsley had been mandated at the time of the takeover to make an offer to the family of an eight-figure sum to avoid litigation, but that the offer was never communicated to the family or their legal advisers, despite various members of the family attending several meetings shortly after the takeover. Would this indicate that Dukes, Aynsley, and their advisors always wanted a confrontation with the family to deflect attention away from Anglo? Lesley Buckley was surprised and disappointed that the proposed offer had never been made to us.

A second demonstration on 14 October 2012, shortly before my own jailing, attracted another 10,000 people. In a speech to the crowd, my daughter Ciara claimed that "In 2007 and 2008 Anglo Irish Bank pumped €2.3 billion into our companies without asking us, telling us or ever meeting us – this was illegal." Another of my daughters, Colette, told the crowd that we would like to create further employment in the area. Placards denouncing banks and receivers as "the new Oliver Cromwell of Ireland", and proclaiming "Quinn for Taoiseach", were seen. My brother, Peter's, speech was very combative and elicited great applause, but behind the scenes I knew that it was only a matter of time before I went to prison, despite doing everything that I could possibly do to appease the bank. I knew that they would get what they wanted.

My daughter Aoife and her husband Stephen Kelly were invited onto Vincent Browne's programme on TV3 (Vincent had attended one of the rallies in Ballyconnell). They said that they now feared that I would have to go to jail, as "We do not have any of these assets so we can't give them back." Richard Woodhouse had been pursuing me and my family, quite literally, "to the ends of the earth" to recover assets, as Gavin Daly and Ian Kehoe have put it. But by the end of October 2012 none of them had been recovered, despite the fact that we had offered to work with the bank to get the assets returned more than a year earlier, on 7 September 2011, and at all times since then, but our offers had been repeatedly refused.

On 1 November I was back in courtroom six of the Four Courts to find out whether I would be following Seán Jnr into Mountjoy prison. Many friends and colleagues were in court that day. One former employee was in tears, and he told the Irish Times that I'd once given him €100,000 for a

GAA youth development project, and told him to "spend it well". He added that he owed it to me to be in court to see me being jailed.

Surrounded by my supporters, and the media, IBRC's lawyers and Eugene Grant put forward their cases. Grant claimed that "I stood tall as a leading light of the Celtic Tiger", and that I had cooperated as best I could to try to 'purge' my contempt. I should not face jail, Grant argued, as stents had been installed in my coronary arteries in 2003 and 2005, I still suffered from high cholesterol, and I'd had a small skin cancer removed from my back in August 2012. Regardless, Mrs Justice Dunne did exactly what Anglo asked her to do: jail me.

When the court was readjourned at 11 a.m. the following day, 2 November, Judge Dunne told me that I was going to jail, just as my son had. While I maintained that I had signed every document put in front of me, and that I had not been to Moscow since 2007, Judge Dunne still felt that I hadn't purged my contempt. It is hard to believe that I hadn't purged my contempt, when, as already referred to, it was on record that David O'Beirne, the managing partner of Eversheds, had offered on our behalf fourteen months earlier to assist with getting the assets back, and had looked for various meetings since then to arrange how that might be done. Anglo had refused even to meet us to discuss it. I think that this proves that if the state wants to bring you down, it is very hard to stop them. Judge Dunne gave me a nine-week sentence, which meant that I would be in jail until early January.

Judge Dunne did offer to 'stay' the sentence, pending an appeal, but by now I just wanted my jail sentence over and done with. The threat of jail had been hanging over my head for months – I just wanted it over. After a final meal in the Four Courts' cafeteria – curry and chips, with a pint of lager – I returned to court. Grant told Judge Dunne that I had no intention of appealing. Interestingly, Mike Aynsley and Richard Woodhouse were sitting opposite me in the cafeteria earlier that day, and I wondered, then and since, if they hadn't anything better to do than sit all day every day in a court room, considering Mike Aynsley never provided a word of verbal evidence.

As Garda officers gathered to escort me to a prison van, I gave a tearful statement to the press in the courtroom. I told them that while I regretted investing in Anglo Irish CFDs, Anglo's new owners, and the administrators they had appointed, "hadn't proven a thing." Any mistakes I had made were "small fry compared to the overall assault that has been launched on us, on our companies, and destroyed them", I protested. I felt that it was unconscionable for the Irish government to take our companies and wreck them when we were willing to pay all of the money back, including the illegal loans. Just as I was taken to Mountjoy, Seán Jnr was in another court-room in the Four Courts, where IBRC was pursuing a different legal action to get more information on the family finances.

Arriving in prison almost felt like a release, after such a long wait for the inevitable. Although I had been a billionaire, I had never forgotten my humble beginnings and I was well-equipped to spend a few weeks without home comforts.

Like Seán Jnr, I served my sentence in Mountjoy. I never encountered any hostility from its inmates, or its warders. Seán Jnr had been a model prisoner there a few weeks earlier, working in the kitchens, learning first aid and playing football, which had helped to dispel any notion that he was a millionaire prisoner who thought he was above everyone else. One of the inmates had told Seán Jnr that he had stolen Seán's Mercedes from the streets of Dublin a few years earlier, which they both had a laugh about.

Seán Jnr's positive attitude made my own spell in Mountjoy a lot easier. I spent most of my time reading, playing cards, exercising in the gym, and replying to the many letters I received. The governor tried to get me to sign up for work duties, but I said, "With respect, having worked hard for 40 years I don't want to do any work here." In my first few days in jail, I received hundreds of letters, all of them friendly. The community in the border counties still showed its support for me while I was in jail. In the 'Children's Rights' referendum on 10 November, many ballot papers in Cavan and Monaghan were spoilt, with the words "Free Seán Quinn" written on them. Ominously, plans emerged to merge Quinn Group's cement operations with its old rival Lagan Cement, and yet more redundancies at Quinn Insurance were announced, reducing staff numbers to half of what they had been under my ownership.

Although I had regular visits from the family, I still faced Christmas 2012 in jail. I had been told that I couldn't go to the baptism of my granddaughter Orna (Ciara's newborn daughter) on 22 December. I was then told that I'd be released from dawn on Christmas Eve until the evening of 27 December. Thanks to our local priest, Fr Comiskey, obliging Ciara by moving the date at a busy time of year for him, the baptism was shifted from 22 December to St Stephen's Day, so I could attend it after all. I then spent an enjoyable Christmas with all my family and grandchildren; they had come for Orna's Christening and stayed until I returned to jail for a final week.

I was released for good on 3 January 2013. On my way home, as I passed through Virginia, I noticed a JCB digger with a large sign on it – "Welcome Home Seán Quinn" – which made me smile. After I left Mountjoy I did a short interview with Julian Fowler, in which I said that I'd had a "very positive" response from its inmates. Prison had been a "learning experience", which had made me "feel happy that I have a good wife and a good family". But I added that IBRC and the current government seemed determined to destroy me, and I wasn't sure that it wouldn't be my last spell in jail. I honestly did not know what they would do next.

My overall experience in prison was that I met all sorts of individuals, who were there for all sorts of reasons. One person in particular, I felt, was given rough justice. A successful businessman had described garlic as apples for customs purposes, and received a six-year sentence, which seemed outrageous, as he and his family had been big employers, and up to then he and his family had been model citizens, and they still are. Thankfully, on appeal, he had his sentence substantially reduced.

10

I'd now like to say a bit more about the most important people of all: my wife, Patricia, our five children, and everyone who helped to make me a success, and who helped to guide me through the ordeal of the destruction of everything we had built up together.

Patricia and I were blessed with five children. Our eldest daughters, Colette and Ciara, were both born in Enniskillen hospital, in 1975 and 1976 respectively. Patricia and I lived with my mother at Gortmullen until 1977, when we moved to Greaghrahan, near Ballyconnell. While Greaghrahan was only five miles from my mother's house, it was south of the border. We bought a vacant plot of land and I had a house built from scratch on it. Our three younger children were born at Cavan Hospital: our son, Seán, in 1979, and our daughters Aoife in 1981, and Brenda in 1987.

I should be ashamed to say it, but Patricia took on most of the burden of rearing our five children. I am regularly reminded of the time when Patricia was bathing Colette in a plastic basin on a chair, in the kitchen of my mother's house. I was watching *Match of the Day* on television, and when Patricia went to find something in the back kitchen, she asked me to keep my hand on the basin. When baby Colette jumped my hand was absent, and the basin, water and child all landed on the floor. Colette had a lump on her head and we probably should have taken her to the doctor. Thankfully she made a quick recovery, but it dented Patricia's (and everyone else's) confidence in my baby-minding abilities.

After we moved to Ballyconnell, my mother rented her bedsit out to a local young couple, John and Marian Mulligan, and she moved back to the house's main living quarters. It gave us all peace of mind that she had some company, and she was very happy living with the couple until one night when John tragically suffered a brain haemorrhage and died. John had previously lived next door to us with his mother, brother, uncle, and granny for years, and we all loved him. We had protected and encouraged him in his boyhood. One day, many years earlier, John was helping me to put in cattle for a formidable farmer, and one animal escaped. "You little bastard, why didn't you stop it?", the farmer shouted. I was incensed by the use of the term bastard, which at the time was a term of abuse for children born to single mothers, and I crossed the fence and told her never to speak to John like that again. In fairness to the woman, she obviously respected my intervention, because she later became a great friend who sold me any land I needed to develop my business.

John Mulligan's sudden death shocked us all. Mammy was as devastated as John's young wife and mother were, and so was I. While I can be tough in many ways, I can also be a very emotional man. Premature deaths and tragedies have always hit me hard, and I can become emotional when praised in public. They are not 'crocodile tears', as some like to call them. I am totally the opposite when lied to, or falsely accused; I get very angry, and tears are the last thing you will see.

I always found it very difficult to say goodbye to the children, be it dropping off a thirteen-year-old Colette at a Gaeltacht (a summer Irish speaking course) in Connemara, or dropping Ciara off at her new digs in Dublin when she was starting her nursing career. I was so bad at saying goodbye to my children that I started to say my goodbyes at home in Ballyconnell, and leave Patricia to bring the kids to the airport or to their first digs away from home. (I was a bit of a chicken when it came to that!)

From the late 1970s onwards, we had a standard Sunday routine as a family. After going to morning Mass in Ballyconnell we would collect a number of newspapers in Paul Reilly's shop. This tradition has now changed.

Over the past twelve years we have stopped buying newspapers, as I don't trust much of their content.

After Mass on Sundays, I would head down to the office of my quarry business in Teemore with the children. This was two miles away from Bally-connell, in Northern Ireland. There were never any workers in the office on a Sunday, and the children would play, ringing each other from one office to the other, and stocking up on stationary – pens, pencils, rubbers, and rulers for school, while I got on with some work. When we'd visit the quarries and factories themselves, the children often got up to devilment, which would probably be considered dangerous nowadays, such as climbing up hills of sand and stacks of blocks and rooftiles. For a few hours every week, the business was their playground, and the weekly visit, often with a stop in the sweet shop on the way home, was something they looked forward to.

When I was ready to go home, I would take the children up the road to visit their Nana (my mother) for some juice and buns. When the four oldest children outgrew these Sunday excursions, my youngest daughter, Brenda, used to accompany me on her own. As Brenda had no one to play with she stayed with me as I worked, and she surprised me one day by reciting to Patricia the components, and the correct percentages, of all the raw materials used in making cement. I was stunned to discover that she had absorbed so much complex information. On other days we took the Range Rover up the mountain and rambled round the quarries with our two dogs, Jack and Scholes. They were an integral part of our family, and many tears were shed when they died of old age. Mannok (as the former Quinn Group is now known) has since barred me from travelling this road.

At one stage we decided to dig a swimming pool in the back garden in Ballyconnell. We had it tiled and ready for use, but Patricia insisted that the children weren't to use it until I came home from work. That day I left work early, and as soon as I got home I went upstairs to change into swimming trunks. I then rushed out of the back door and jumped straight into the pool. It caused great excitement, and we all had a very enjoyable evening. The novelty of the pool soon wore off, especially for me as I wasn't keen on swimming, and could barely keep myself afloat, but the children enjoyed it as a special luxury. One sunny day the children were in the pool with their cousins (my sister Miriam's children), and one of them came in to tell Patricia and Miriam that there was a big, strange black cat outside. On investigation it turned out to be a mink, so swimming had to be suspended for the day.

I was always very busy with work. On Sunday afternoons we sometimes had to abandon plans to go out as a family when someone called round to talk to me about business or to pay a bill. While I loved people dropping in, and always welcomed bills being paid, the children were often very disappointed, so I resorted to hiding the car at the back of the house when we wanted no interruptions. Patricia and I sometimes played football with all five of the children, and I often took them out to buy ice cream in Ballyconnell, where I had long jovial chats with James Pat McKenna in the corner shop. James Pat always kept an eye out for the Customs men who were frequent visitors to the area, as it was an unapproved route for commercial use. James Pat was a very popular shop owner and was known as a bit of a character. But I didn't see enough of the children and I was never very active as a father. I got away with it because Patricia was such a wonderful mother.

Patricia was always much stricter with the children than I was, but they always took Patricia's side if we had an argument, because, deep down, they knew who looked after them on a daily basis. Patricia took it in turns to drive them to Greaghrahan primary school with the McGovern family, wonderful neighbours of ours in Ballyconnell. The McGoverns had seven children of their own, and sometimes Teresa McGovern or Patricia had as many as nine Quinn and McGovern children crammed into one car, with no seatbelts, and if they were present they weren't used!

After Greaghrahan primary school, all five of my children went to non-fee-paying Catholic secondary schools in Cavan town: the girls to Loreto, and Seán to St Patrick's College. By a strange coincidence, Gavin Daly, who was very critical of me and my family as co-author of *Citizen Quinn*, was at St Patrick's College with my son, Seán Jnr.

Going to state schools was what I was brought up to do, and I didn't want anything different for my children, much as I could have afforded to pay fees at a private school. I always thought that common sense and respect for others, irrespective of their background, were more important than education. I liked a phrase that one of our footballers, John McCaffrey (RIP), used to say: "smart boys wanted; not too smart." I wanted my children to get some education, but not too much. Neither Patricia nor I had much formal education, but both of my sisters, and my brother, Peter, went on to higher education – Bernadette and Miriam to study teaching, and Peter to study accountancy. All our children progressed to higher education as well, without being put under any parental pressure to do so, as we were more interested in them being businesspeople than academics.

As the children became adults, I planned two new roads across the mountain; one was 12 kilometres down to Kinawley, and the second was a similar distance across the mountain to Swanlinbar. As no vehicle ever travelled this land, because it was full of bog holes and drains, often on a Saturday or a Sunday I would walk the route to see where the best location would be for a new road; I would prearrange with Patricia or one of the kids to collect me at the far side – a 24-kilometre return journey would have been too much for me at that time, and particularly in that terrain. During that period, I spoke to dozens of farmers to negotiate the purchase of their land to build the road. Many of them told me that I would never be able to construct a road capable of bringing stone across the mountain in the location I was proposing. One day, when two of my daughters, Ciara and Aoife, came to collect me outside Swanlinbar, I pointed out what I was planning, and they seemed interested. We walked across the fields and I showed them the route I was planning for the road. As we walked along the route, we pulled twigs and branches from the trees, and used them to plot out around 2 miles of the road. They thought this was great fun initially, but after a while they got fed up, and said "Dad, are you mad, you'll never build a road through here!" When they went back around a year later, they met dozens of lorries drawing stone over the road.

None of our children have lived with us fulltime for the last sixteen years, as they mostly moved out in their late teens, but were regular visitors at weekends and holidays. To this day, Santa appears in Ballyconnell more often than any other home in our family! By the time our eldest daughter,

Colette, left school we had already entered the hotel business. She did a hotel management course at Shannon College, followed by a commerce degree at University College Galway, near where Patricia had grown up. Colette had a car by then and would often drive the three hours home at weekends. She then spent a year or so in Lausanne, Switzerland, working at a hotel (I once visited her there amidst continuous thunder and lightning, the likes of which I never experienced in Ireland). She later returned to manage the Quinn Group's hotel and pub division, which had become our highest growth area. I believe that if the Group had been left in our hands, hotels and property would easily have been the largest part of our business today by a long stretch.

Ciara always wanted to be a nurse, since early childhood. After leaving school she trained at the Mater Hospital in Dublin. In the summer of 1998 she went to Romania, to work in an orphanage. I can still remember saying goodbye to her in our kitchen, and watching her walk out the door with Patricia, a red rucksack on her back. While I was proud of what she was doing I was apprehensive about her wellbeing and safety. The communist regime of Ceaușescu had only fallen a few years earlier, and I knew that once she was in Romania we could only communicate by letter. Over the following months her letters contained horrific descriptions of what the children had to endure, in a rat-infested building, chained to their beds. I made a large donation to the orphanage she was working in. Proper toilets were installed to replace the holes in the floor, mattresses were bought to replace hard wooden boards, and proper windows were put in. Until then bed sheets, not glass, had protected the children from sub-zero winter temperatures.

Ciara arrived back safely from Romania, and over the next few years she took several more voluntary positions in Albania and Kosovo. After returning from eastern Europe for good she worked at the Mater Hospital for a year or two, before deciding to leave nursing. In the early 2000s she joined Quinn Insurance, and by the time the company was taken over, she had become an integral part of the claims department. Throughout our decade-long fight with Anglo Irish Bank she continued to do voluntary work, but always in Ireland, as she now has five children. After our businesses were taken away she returned to nursing to pay the bills, and she still enjoys working in the nursing profession.

Ciara has always been full of compassion. One Monday I received a telephone call from a lady in the Midlands explaining that her daughter, a teacher, was dying from kidney failure and needed a new kidney. She seemed like a lovely lady on the telephone, and was heartbroken about her daughter. She said that a saint had advised her at Mass the previous day that I might be able to help her. She told me that her other daughter was a suitable donor, and was promised that the operation would be done by the Irish health authorities, as the operation was urgent and her daughter was on dialysis, but months had gone by and the operation had not taken place, and she would need to go to America to have it done. As it turned out at the time, my daughters were aware of this lady, as they had seen her a few weeks earlier on television. I asked Ciara and Aoife to meet the family at their home. They felt so sorry for her, and felt that the case was so compelling, that they rang me back to tell me that she needed the operation urgently, but it was going to be very expensive to send her to America for the operation. I said that I had never been asked to save someone's life before, and that we would be more than happy to pay for it. Together with this lady's family, they organised for the daughter's trip to an American hospital, where she had a kidney transplant. The daughter recovered good health within a few weeks of returning, and we took the family for a weekend at the Slieve Russell, where the daughter threw her arms round me and said, "You saved my life." It made me emotional, and I felt that I now had five daughters and two mothers-in-law! Sadly, once things went wrong and I started receiving a bashing in the media, communications with her went quiet. I am not angry with her, but disappointed. I am angry that our own government and their civil servants, who we as taxpayers pay to represent us, destroyed our reputation to such an extent that this lady, who was a government employee, felt that she couldn't be associated with us.

After leaving St Patrick's in Cavan, our son Seán Jnr took a year out to play golf in Florida with his friend Eoghan O'Connell, whom he'd met at the Slieve Russell and who had married an American lady. Back in Ireland,

Seán went to Portobello College in Dublin to study business and finance, before joining QIL. After a year or two in the claims department, he and I had a number of discussions on how slowly our claims were being settled, and the legal costs associated with those claims. Following that, he and a couple of lads he worked closely with started the fast-track claims model, which turned QIL into the most successful company that I ever owned. Seán played football for Teemore and Fermanagh at minor and senior level, and won the senior championship with Teemore in 2005. He had an unfortunate incident playing for the Fermanagh senior team against Kildare in Newbridge in 2000, when he was approaching his twenty-first birthday, where he suffered a bad break to his leg. I remember Patricia and I listening to it on the radio, and the commentator saying that Seán Quinn was being stretchered off with what looked like a broken leg. Patricia jumped up off the sofa, saying "What did he say?" Seán had never been blessed with speed, and he never recovered full fitness after that accident, and so his Fermanagh career was cut short.

A few months before our companies were taken from us, Seán Jnr spent more time in the UK seeking new business opportunities and forming strong relationships with Irish businesspeople there. These new relationships were becoming very effective, and one of them translated into our biggest premium ever, with a policy of more than STG£10 million.

After school Aoife went to a technical college in Tralee, County Kerry, where she qualified in sports and leisure, following her childhood success in sporting activities. She then did a law degree in Dublin and qualified as a solicitor, but she never practised. Like Ciara and Seán, she also became a claims manager at QIL, where she dealt with large complex cases, which hadn't received the attention they deserved in the early years, and immediately the percentage of old outstanding claims started to reduce.

Our youngest, Brenda, left school in 2005 and did a business degree at GMIT in Galway. She also worked in the claims division of QIL and later spent a year in Australia, where she worked for Allianz Insurance. Brenda was only 25 and not long finished college when the businesses were taken over, but she had started working in QIL by the time it was placed in administration.

Patricia and I always made money freely available to all our children, but thankfully none of them ever took advantage of it; they all worked long hours, sometimes up to 60 hours a week. They seemed to enjoy their work, and the impact they were having on the various areas they were concentrating on. By 2010, the four of my children who were working in QIL lived in Dublin, and Colette, in the hotel and pub division, lived in Cavan, but travelled frequently to visit the various hotels we had throughout Europe.

Ciara was the first of our children to marry, in 2007, when she married Niall McPartland, a solicitor. It was a wonderful wedding at the Slieve Russell; however, since then, there have been many false stories about the expense of the wedding. Ciara was followed by her three sisters and her brother over the next eleven years. We are now the proud grandparents of fourteen strong, healthy and often boisterous grandchildren, for whom we are very grateful, and they all appear to have great lungs, particularly if you are trying to doze off in the corner!

Our children are now leading as ordinary lives as they can, despite all the adverse media attention of the last fifteen years. In 2017 they started QuinnBet, an online betting business.

QuinnBet has proved to be a successful business, although it is still small compared to more established competitors. It is still growing on an annual basis, with more than two-thirds of its business in the UK, and the remainder in Ireland.

My family and in-laws continue to work at QuinnBet; however, I have no formal involvement. As a keen sports fan I give advice from time to time, but it is rarely followed. It had never crossed my mind to go into the gambling business, and I am very proud of what my children have achieved in a relatively short time, which convinces me that they would have continued the success we had enjoyed from 1973 until 2007 – particularly considering the input they had from 2000 onwards. It hurts me every day to think that it was I who gave the power to those who gave away our businesses in 2008, rather than giving it to my own family. While failing in a number of start-up businesses of their own, those same people blew their chance for a second time in 2014 when an opportunity arose to acquire our manufacturing business. Instead of trying to remedy the situation they had left us in years earlier, they put us out, and kept the business for themselves. They even went to such an extent that executive directors' families are still using a farm in Co. Meath that I paid €2.8 million for around twenty years ago. Even after doing what they did so blatantly, these same men present themselves as leaders of society and pillars of their communities, which is still believed by many. I, being the eternal optimist, still live in hope that the Slieve Russell Hotel, which I look at out my window 365 days a year, will, someday, return to Quinn ownership.

11

After I left prison in January 2013, I was of pension age, but there was no respite from the government.

In the first few weeks of 2013 IBRC carried on dragging the family through the courts to try to track down our assets, but still steadfastly refusing assistance from the family. But in February IBRC was itself liquidated. Mike Aynsley and Richard Woodhouse left IBRC's offices immediately. In due course, all of IBRC's remaining staff were made redundant, on bare minimum terms.

In April 2013 Matthew Elderfield left the Irish Central Bank and returned to the UK. Unfortunately, in my opinion and that of many others, during his time here I feel he did huge damage to ourselves, the Irish banks, and the nation as a whole.

Ironically, Kieran Wallace of KPMG, who had been appointed as the Quinn Group's share receiver in 2011, was now the liquidator of IBRC. He inherited Richard Woodhouse's job of pursuing the Quinn assets. Wallace, and those who were appointed to manage the assets, are still earning fees on some of them twelve years later.

I did not meet Wallace until 2013. As soon as he was appointed as IBRC's liquidator, I asked to meet him. To my surprise, he agreed, even though some of my children were still trying to sue IBRC. I arrived at the Nuremore Hotel in County Monaghan at the appointed time, but Wallace did not show up. I called his office and they told me he was in America and there had been a mix-up with his diary. I made an appointment to meet him at the same place on a later date, and this time he did show up. I wanted to meet him to see if we could agree a way forward for the litigation, and to tell him that the offer we had made two years earlier to assist in any way we could with the return of assets was still open. It was a warm and friendly meeting, and I met him a number of times afterwards, twice in the Castleknock Hotel, where we discussed a potential settlement, whereby he would return the Slieve Russell Hotel and some other Irish properties to the family in return for us dropping our legal cases. However, as the court cases continued, and the prevailing narrative was that we were stealing government assets, he had less motivation to strike a deal.

By then I had given up hope of returning to any of my former companies and the executives on whom I had relied for the previous eleven years had gone their separate ways. Kevin Lunney had stayed loyal after 2011, and he, along with a local woman, Patricia Gilheany, founded Concerned Irish Citizens (the local group that campaigned against my companies' administration and receivership). But Liam McCaffrey and Dara O'Reilly deserted the Quinn family in 2011.

Although I never received a penny of redundancy when we lost our companies, the executive directors – Liam, Kevin, and Dara – received very significant financial settlements. At least one of them received over £1 million. In 2012, Liam, Dara and Kevin started a consultancy company together. Dara and Kevin also managed a start-up insurance company called Quick-Sure, on behalf of local entrepreneurs, but both companies failed. Liam McCaffrey had started a new concrete company, Nu-Span, in England, where he lost £1.3 million in the first two years, prior to his return to the former Quinn companies as chief executive.

Although the former Quinn manufacturing companies in the border counties and eight other countries had a turnover of more than €1 billion a year, it proved difficult for the financiers to sell any of the assets between 2011 and 2014, because of constant sabotage in the area. In 2013 the company finally abandoned the half-built chemical factory near Leipzig in Germany. The unease locally made it more difficult for Paul O'Brien to manage the business – a lot of staff were not particularly committed to it, and many customers had withdrawn their support.

The family carried on pursuing its legal actions against IBRC and the Irish government. On 27 May 2013 my daughter Aoife filed an affidavit with the High Court, arguing that the Financial Regulator had been aware of the Quinn Group's CFD stake in Anglo as early as September 2007, and that the Department of Finance had later tried to cover up exactly how much they had known about it.

In June 2013, Seán Jnr sold a penthouse flat that he shared with his wife, Karen Woods, with half the proceeds going to 'purge' his contempt of court. In the High Court, Judge Dunne told him that she was, "In the nicest possible way … delighted to see the back of him." In July 2013, recordings and transcripts of a number of phone calls between Anglo and the Financial Regulator's office, known as the 'Anglo Tapes', were then serialised in the Irish media.

A new pro-Quinn community support group had been set up on Easter Monday 2011 by two local businessmen, and was running alongside Concerned Irish Citizens, which had been established in 2010. The new group was called CFL (after the three border counties of Cavan, Fermanagh and Leitrim, in which most of the Quinn Group's operations had been based). As well as representing the interests of employees and customers, CFL actively sought a takeover of our old companies, with a view to recovering their former glory, rather than just laying people off and shutting things down.

We felt confident in CFL – their integrity, and the people involved. Since 2010, their representatives had had a number of meetings with the Taoiseach, Enda Kenny; the Financial Regulator, Matthew Elderfield; Alan Dukes, the then chairman of Anglo, and an ex-Minister for Finance; and a number of senior ministers and politicians. They and Concerned Irish Citizens had also gathered 90,000 signatures on a petition calling for the return of Quinn Insurance to the family, and they organised demonstrations in Ballyconnell attended by tens of thousands of people.

At this stage, while Kevin Lunney had been advising Patricia Gilheaney from Concerned Irish Citizens since 2011, now in spring 2014, John McCartin entered the fray, and began advising her on what to say. John Mooney of the *Sunday Times* was able to reveal that McCartin was happy to criticise Arlene Foster, the then leader of the DUP. When Patricia expressed concern that perhaps he wouldn't want to criticise Foster, he replied "Probably no harm Patricia. She deserved a slap on the wrist. She let O'Brien make a cat's paw of her, so she can suffer the consequences". QIH would later sue Patricia for making defamatory comments when she saw that they had turned their backs on the community. Up until then, McCartin had appeared to be saying all of the right things. He even went as far as to do an interview with the *Leitrim Observer*.

In a statement to the *Leitrim Observer* in 2013, he stated that "the government is in danger of sleepwalking into a fiasco, as the legality of Anglo's loans to Quinn is clearly untenable. It is now abundantly clear that Quinn was hoodwinked into taking the loans in an effort to support the share value of the bank." He also said that the management of Anglo set about "conspiring with the institutions of the state to draw Quinn into a massive drive to shore up the share price." He added that if the €2.3 billion loan to us was found to be illegal, we would have to be compensated for our loss from the appointment of a receiver over the family's shares in Quinn Group. Around that same time, he was telling me and my family that he felt he could get the manufacturing business back, as well as getting our legal case settled.

In early 2014 there arrived an opportunity to recover at least some of my former business empire. At that stage, John McCartin and the former executives in Derrylin knew that the government agencies didn't want the Quinns back in business, and I knew that they, the executives themselves, didn't want the Quinns back in business. Both the government agencies which facilitated the illegal loans in 2007–2008 and the executives themselves, who during the same period were responsible for the Quinn Insurance guarantees and the removal of €398 million from Quinn Insurance to support the CFDs, could have had a major problem if the Quinns were back in control of the business and wanted to pursue legal avenues against either party. John was a Fine Gael councillor in Leitrim, and was a regular visitor to our home. As is known, he was very close to and had the ear of the Fine Gael government, and was very prominent in the media regarding the Quinn businesses. He used to talk about Leo Varadkar sleeping in his home in Newtowngore, and later, when Varadkar became Taoiseach, he attended a Quinn management meeting in the packaging factory in Ballyconnell. McCartin would often leave the room to take a call from the then Taoiseach, Enda Kenny, and he told me that if a deal could be done for the manufacturing business, he felt confident he would get the support of the Irish government. I informed him that I would be delighted with that, and, at the time, there were a number of discussions between himself, myself, and CFL, where it was recognised by all that the previous senior executives couldn't be trustees of the new company, as they had been responsible for the administration of Quinn Insurance, and that appointing them as shareholders could collapse any potential deal. At the time, I also said that involving either myself or my family would be unwise, as we were in the throes of litigation with the Irish government. I advised all concerned that neither I nor any of my family would be attending meetings and that we would be kept up to date by CFL. I nominated John McCartin himself, Ernie Fisher, and John Bosco O'Hagan to act as the three trustees on behalf of CFL, the support group that had been formed three years earlier. There was 100 per cent consensus on that arrangement.

John Bosco and Ernie had been close friends and supporters of the Quinn family for over 20 years, and I trusted them implicitly. Ernie was the chairman of Fisher Engineering and the brother of my old friend Bertie, who had died in a helicopter accident in 2001; John Bosco O'Hagan owned a joinery company in County Derry and had done much joinery work on the Slieve Russell Hotel, several of our pubs, and our new house, while working closely with my daughter Colette. He was also at the forefront of the group that raised funds for our legal fees when Anglo closed down our access to the rental income.

Although Aventas (the Quinn Group's new name) had borrowings reduced from €1.2 billion to €475 million, a write-down of more than €700 million, to reduce the debt to levels that McKillop and O'Brien felt they could service within the environment in which they were working, it still couldn't be sold because of the regular acts of sabotage – of offices, factories, and plant and machinery being burnt out.

The new company that was meant to buy the assets was named QBRC (Quinn Business Retention Company). They offered to pay me €500,000 a year to work as a consultant for it. For the time being I would be QBRC's employee, but the local community was reassured by my involvement, as they believed that I would be managing the business, and it would become successful again.

While I didn't trust Liam and Dara to be trustees, I felt that they would be an important part of the team that negotiated with the bondholders, as they were the only people who really knew them, having often flown over in the company jet to meet them in America, and were on first-name terms with them.

The proposed new company's financial advisor was Michael McAllister, a former senior manager at our auditors PwC, who was now a financial consultant in Magherafelt, County Derry. Some core principles were agreed: above all that the business would not be broken up, which was at the forefront of all correspondence coming from Liam McCaffrey and Michael McAllister. In an email on 2 March 2014, Liam stated "As you will see from our mission statement ... the sole motivation driving this initiative is to protect the economic wellbeing of this local area, ensuring that the former Quinn Group business is locally managed and controlled for the benefit of this community and, most importantly, kept whole and not disposed of piecemeal."

At that time, a CFL executive accompanied Liam to Dublin to meet a potential financier of the business.

Michael McAllister helped to keep CFL up to date, reassuring them that there would be no break-up of the remaining Quinn businesses. CFL contacted hundreds of organisations, politicians and sporting bodies, sending them letters that Michael McAllister had drafted, and urging them to support the deal. Everyone they approached offered their full support.

Liam was in daily discussion with representatives of CFL, and provided wide-ranging assistance, including drafting correspondence for them. He drafted a letter, on their behalf, to a potential investor in the packaging factory, stating:

> All local politicians, community leaders, workers, business, social and sporting clubs, everybody, are in agreement that the Quinn Group of companies should be retained as a whole. Therefore all the local community are supporting the current QBRC bid recently lodged. The QBRC Group consists of all the previous local successful management team who build the Group in the first instance and are going to keep the Group in its entirety. We would not be in support of any deal which involves the break-up of the Group and the area cannot tolerate the unrest we have experienced over the last few years.
>
> As your bid ultimately means the break-up of the Quinn Group we cannot see this is being the best solution for our area and therefore ask you to reconsider your bid.
>
> There are several community groups in this area, with a combined membership of 90,000, all lobbying for the same cause and we are happy to meet with you at any time to discuss our concerns.

Everything seemed to be going according to plan, until one day one of the trustees, John Bosco O'Hagan, rang and asked to meet me. I travelled to Maghera, County Derry, to meet John, and he surprised me by saying that having met with Liam McCaffrey on a number of occasions, he didn't have faith in him. He was just as surprised to hear that neither did I. When I asked John Bosco why he felt this way, he said that he just had a bad feeling about him, but it appeared that his main concern was that Liam was giving the impression that it was he, rather than me, who would be calling the shots at the new company. John Bosco wanted an assurance from me that it would be me who would be running the company. Of course, I gave him that assurance, believing that to be the case. We agreed that in my role, while only described as a consultant, I would be in control of the business. We both knew that the executives wouldn't have any shares or ownership rights in the business, these would sit with the trustees. With Michael McAllister as the business's auditor, we felt that there wasn't much damage that Liam could do. How wrong could we have been? I believe, rightly or wrongly, that Michael McAllister, Ernie Fisher and John Bosco O'Hagan wouldn't have been aware that there was any conspiracy taking place. They are honourable men, but I still can't get my head around how they didn't see within a few months what was happening.

Around the same time, Liam McCaffrey and John McCartin met Val Flynn to line up potential lenders. At first Val wouldn't entertain them, until he was reassured that I was involved in the new venture. As Val had raised the finance for the first cement factory, before Liam McCaffrey had even started working for the company, he was a bit uneasy about Liam and John McCartin's motives. At that stage I had also started to become a bit concerned about McCartin, as he was in our house practically on a daily basis and never mentioned that they had a meeting planned with Val. When Val filled me in on the meeting, it increased my concern.

Everything changed on 30 July, just four months after Liam's email and Michael McAllister's correspondence to CFL stating that the purpose of the exercise was to protect the economic wellbeing of the area, and, most importantly, not disposing of the company in a piecemeal fashion. I received a six-page document which showed that the American bondholders, the three executives, and John McCartin were working together, and that nobody, including Paul O'Brien, then-CEO of the Quinn Group, could see the document they had prepared together. The document showed that by getting rid of the Quinns, and getting rid of CFL, and ignoring the local community, the directors could benefit to the tune of €46.2 million over a five-year period if a certain plan could be implemented, as well as getting large salaries and bonuses along the way. That plan was that there would be no assets bought, 85 to 90 per cent of the business would be sold to foreign investors, and current management would manage the remaining part of the business, which shocked me. It also said that if targets to reduce sabotage (or 'community interference' as the Americans put it) were met, the directors would be given a bonus of more than €5.5 million and a 22 per cent share in QBRC, which could rise to 26 per cent if other targets were met. As Trevor Birney would later say, "... the deal also, on the face of it, linked QBRC directly with the violence. The violence was being addressed head on." The upshot of the deal meant that there were zero assets being bought, and 100 per cent of profits were leaving the country.

Unaware of what was happening behind my back, I had been hiring seven managers of my old companies, who had a huge input into its growth but had left when Aventas was running the company. I knew that with their help, we'd be able to return the company to its previous glory. These seven included my sales director of the Group, Paddy Mohan, and its technical and quality director, Denis Doogan, and all of them were delighted to renew old acquaintances, as most of them had worked for me for more than twenty years before the share receiver was appointed.

The new plan from QBRC and the three bondholders, who participated in this arrangement, detailed on the 30 July 2014 document, was totally contrary to what had been planned and agreed. They weren't going to be buying any assets, as evidenced by discussions they had and documents they produced, and the glass business would be sold as soon as possible to a third party, as well as plastics and radiators. This information came as a major shock to me, as the glass division, which had been rebranded as Encirc in May 2014, was a particularly important part of the Group, and employed more than 1,000 people. I now felt that I had been used, and brought in under false pretences, not to help revive the Quinn Group, but to asset-strip it. This was devastating news for me, because myself and my youngest daughter, Brenda, had been introduced by Val Flynn to two different groups that were very keen to assist in the purchase of the glass business.

When I studied the new plan, I immediately invited Liam McCaffrey and John McCartin to my house. They brought Kevin Lunney along with them. When I expressed the level of my concern that no attempt was being made to purchase the glass business in particular, the meeting became very subdued. I said that I would have to meet a number of other people to discuss the matter further. At that stage I was thinking of meeting Ernie Fisher, John Bosco O'Hagan, and members of CFL, as well as renewing my business relationship with Val Flynn. They obviously realised that this was going to become a problem, and after about an hour they left in two separate cars: Liam and Kevin in one, and John in the other. Within two minutes, McCartin was back at my gate. He told me that there was no need for me to talk to other people, as he was acting as spokesperson for Ernie and Bosco. He then reassured Patricia and I that all would be well. Putting his hand on Patricia's shoulder, he complimented her on how I had handled the meeting. He finished with the words, "Patricia, I won't allow those boys to fuck you over again." As he said it with such sincerity, we both believed him.

The deal between management and the financiers was due to go live on 1 January 2015. Shortly before Christmas 2014 there was a gathering at my former head office in Derrylin to celebrate the taking down of the Aventas signage, and the unofficial installation of the QBRC team. The new company would be called Quinn Industrial Holdings (QIH). I am still haunted by John McCartin's hypocrisy in removing the old Aventas signage on the outside of the building with a sledgehammer, with great excitement, to reveal the old Quinn Group signage underneath. It was seen as symbolic moment.

When my sister Bernie rang me to see if I was going to the gathering, she was disheartened when I told her that I had not been invited. After the sign came down, a group gathered in the head office, where some of the staff had prepared tea. Paddy Mohan, the new venture's sales director, put one of the supportive administrative staff, Melania Kerr, on the phone and she persuaded me to go down, as all gathered wanted me there. I was pleased to hear this, so I decided to turn up with a bottle of whisky, so that everyone could toast what we hoped at the time would be our success. The blue-collar staff on the shop floor seemed very pleased to see me, but the senior executives, who were gathered separately in an upstairs office, looked much less pleased. But John McCartin came down to join us and he appeared happy as we served drinks to the assembled supporters. It was only around this time that I began to fully realise what McCartin was all about. Unfortunately, it was too late, and he had been working for months with Kevin, Dara, and Liam in particular, to overthrow me, the family, CFL, and the local community.

After the gathering was over, the three trustees invited me and Seán Jnr for a meal at the Slieve Russell, which was paid for by McCartin, but something felt very wrong with the atmosphere at that dinner. Everyone seemed wary as they watched each other, and Ernie and John Bosco were advising me to stand back and let the executives run the business – the very opposite of what had been agreed some months earlier. It soon became very obvious that Ernie and John Bosco had been influenced by John McCartin and the three senior executives, as for the twenty years prior to that it was always Quinn family members who dealt with both John Bosco and Ernie. It came as a surprise to me that they felt it would be best for the executives to run the business, as this had never been mentioned up to this point. I had hired seven senior managers, who had previously left the business, to support me in managing it.

I soon discovered that in the run-up to Christmas John McCartin and Liam had met the new would-be owners of the glass business at the Slieve Russell Hotel. Paddy Mohan had approached me during the Christmas holidays, to tell me he had been asked to sign a 141-page legal document, which had been prepared by solicitors on behalf of the bondholders and Quinn management. The document outlined that shares of the business were to be distributed to senior and junior directors of the company, contrary to what had been agreed, which was that the shares would be held for CFL by the three trustees. This change was made without any agreement from or the knowledge of CFL or myself, who had proposed the three trustees. Paddy was so concerned that he discussed it with QBRC's technical director, Denis Doogan, and sales director, Seamus McMahon, and they agreed to meet in the Watermill restaurant in Lisnaskea later that evening to discuss it. They said that they had only agreed to sign it when Liam McCaffrey assured them that I had agreed to the terms of the document. When I told Denis that this was the first that I had heard of it, he was very angry, after all the difficulties he had encountered with Liam for the previous two or three years.

The document was a secret agreement, which had been developed over a number of months, and it was accompanied by a side letter from John McCartin giving certain assurances to the financiers. We haven't seen this letter to date, and I don't know if Ernie or Bosco ever had sight of it, but I have a feeling that it may well have given an assurance that he would be able to do what he ultimately did – dispose of the assets and me, and make sure that the Irish government's position, where they could not be sued, would be maintained.

There was growing concern in the area that glass hadn't been part of the takeover deal. On 12 January 2015, CFL organised a big public meeting in Ballyconnell Community Centre, to which 800 people turned up. QBRC's directors were asked to go along to reassure the community that the glass factories would be acquired by QBRC and that the jobs were safe. Attendees at the meeting immediately raised their concerns about why none of the senior directors attended – they were beginning to smell a rat, that there was something wrong. There were very strong contributions made from the floor by a number of speakers, and John McCartin sent a letter to the meeting, supporting the retention of the glass business. However, he didn't attend the meeting, but asked me to join him for a drink in the Angler's Rest, my local in Ballyconnell, assuring me that the glass businesses would eventually be retained. I now realise that this drink was a ruse, to ensure that I stayed away from the public meeting, as McCartin and the executives were worried that my attendance would further galvanise the community's concerns.

It was only when I read the 141-page document that I fully realised what they had done. There was no doubt that between January and April, it had been accepted by all that the executives couldn't be involved as shareholders, and that Ernie Fisher and John Bosco O'Hagan were going to be trustees of 66 per cent of the business. As they were friends of the Quinns, and nominated as trustees by the Quinns, they could support us by turning their shares over to CFL or the Quinns, who in turn, could issue proceedings against the bank or the Quinn executives, who had been responsible for the administration of Quinn Insurance. So, as far as I was concerned, what they had done was crystal clear: they had bought nothing, had taken control away from John Bosco and Ernie, and had us completely tied up, just as we had been during the previous three years, when Anglo took control of our Group and formed new boards on the condition that they could never be sued. So we were right back there again. I find it difficult to understand how Ernie and John Bosco didn't see that there was something badly wrong. They were invited by myself and CFL to hold 66 per cent of Quinn manufacturing assets in trust on our behalf, but then agreed to halve their shareholding and buy no assets without ever mentioning it to those on whose behalf they were holding the shares.

In hindsight, even though it never crossed my mind that they would give away half of their shareholding, I should have met Ernie and Bosco following the meeting in our house when McCartin had given myself and Patricia the assurance that he wouldn't allow the executives to fuck us over again. But surely they must see now the disastrous consequences of giving control to current management, which has led to the business being run into the ground, and, according to their own audited accounts, has lost money every year since they took it over, while there have been tens of millions of euros of cash or assets reported stolen, and the belief in the area that myself, my family, the staff, CFL, and the local communities have all been betrayed, and that justice hasn't been or isn't being served. That feeling is as strong today as it was the day the receivers came in on 14 April 2011, but the anger is even greater, as it is now known that it was those who caused the downfall of the company who have betrayed the community since 2014.

Things soon went sour for me in my new role as a consultant to QBRC. I had been walked into a trap, believing that I was going to control the businesses, as I had for over thirty years. So, when the first meeting of the executives took place in January 2015, I knew I had been hung out to dry. I told the executive directors that they were "grabbers". When I was told later by Paddy Mohan that some of the junior directors felt hurt by this accusation, he and I called a second meeting with the junior directors, and I also invited Donal O'Rourke, who had been a director in my time. They told me that they had known nothing about the 141-page document, and just signed it without being advised of what it was about. They had never expected to benefit as shareholders of the company; they had only expected their salary and whatever bonus they were entitled to, and would not be keeping the shares for themselves. I accepted their bona fides, and apologised for the misunderstanding, as I never felt that they had been involved in the deception. We all left the meeting on friendly terms.

On 14 January 2015, just two days after the community meeting that QBRC had shunned, it was announced that Encirc had been sold to Vidrala, a Spanish company, and Vidrala executives arrived onsite. They were taking over the only glass factory in Ireland, as well as the most modern factory in Europe, which we had built in Elton, outside Manchester. These factories had cost €800 million to build, including start-up costs, stock and debtors, and now they were being sold for roughly half of that. The Derrylin factory that I built is still the only glass factory in Ireland, and it takes all of the glass to be recycled in Ireland, from every household, hotel, and public house in the 32 counties. This is what these men had given away behind our back, and to make matters worse, it turned out that the deal they denied had been done in January 2015 had actually been done in October 2014, and the Vidrala shares, traded on the Spanish stock market, had increased by 20 per cent at that time.

In late January, Paddy and I organised a well-attended meeting with the company's salespeople. Most of the attendees were long-serving Quinn Group staff who were delighted to see me back. I ran the meeting, just as I had run sales meetings at the old Quinn Group for over 30 years. We all agreed that we should go back to what Quinn Group had always done: treat small customers as well as we treat large ones, and offer large and small customers the same discounts. Small customers had complained that since 2011 they had been treated less generously than before, so this made good business sense. We all agreed that it would be useful to meet monthly, but from January onwards all the meetings were cancelled by the executive, without my knowledge or agreement, and with no reasons given.

Although I was still employed as a senior consultant, all my initiatives were thwarted by the executives. In early 2015 I started to build a new road, to shorten the distance between the quarries and the gravel plant. But the executives put a stop to the project, and took the machines off it. The executives started legal proceedings on very minor matters, which traditionally the company would never have got involved in. For example, they issued legal proceedings against an 84-year-old farmer, Pa Treacy, to prevent him from grazing his cattle on their land – something he had been doing for nearly 30 years. Liam later signed an affidavit for a court in Omagh, stating that Pa's cattle hadn't been on Quinn roads or land. I don't believe that there's anyone living or working in the locality that didn't know that Treacy's cattle grazed full-time on Quinn land even before Liam McCaffrey ever came to work for the Group. The cattle could be clearly seen by anyone travelling the adjoining roads. The executives also issued legal proceedings against a number of parties, including me. Very recently, they gave instructions to the Enforcement of Judges Office in Northern Ireland to withdraw in excess of £20,000 from Pa's account, without his consent.

The proceedings against me were to prevent me from accessing roads that I had built and travelled on for decades. I can only assume that they didn't want me to see the company's factories and quarries in such a depressed state. All this increased anger in the area, as it became more and more obvious that they weren't going to be touched, regardless of what they did.

When I received my consultancy contract, I discovered that it gave me no control over any part of the business, and there wasn't even one person reporting to me, not even the seven people I had rehired just a few months earlier. It even carried a condition stating that I had to obtain written approval from one of the three senior directors before I could buy a meal for a customer. I knew, and other staff warned me, that they were doing this to annoy me to such an extent that I would throw my toys out of the pram, and give them an opportunity to sack me, so I decided that I would keep my head down, and not give them that opportunity. When Peter Cosgrove from Grange Builders from Dublin, an important customer, rang Paddy to arrange a meeting with me, Paddy booked the boardroom on my behalf, two weeks in advance. On the day of the meeting, I discovered the booking had been cancelled by Dara O'Reilly so I could not use the boardroom after all.

A major point of tension in the local area was Mantlin, the windfarm I had built in 2008. Mantlin had been sold by QIL's administrators to a French company, but local farmers had never granted a right of way to the new owners, and a number of them wrote to QBRC complaining that it was allowing the new owners of the windfarm to trespass over their land, and asking them to stop. Up until that time, March 2015, it was felt in the community that it was John McCartin and Liam McCaffrey who had planned the betrayal of the family and the community. However, it later transpired that Kevin Lunney wrote to Coillte (Ireland's forestry division, which owned much woodland in the area) on 30 March 2015 asking them if the windfarm owners had permission to drive over Coillte land, which was on the same stretch of road. Coillte's response to Kevin, from their solicitor, was an unequivocal no, advising that there "are no Rights of Way registered over that part of our land ... and therefore it is the position of Coillte Teoranta that there are no Rights of Ways over The Lands that are capable of being assigned to any party ... Please note that the obstruction on The Lands will be removed by Coillte Teoranta as they see fit. Clear-ance of obstructions on lands belonging to Coillte Teoranta are dealt with on an as needs basis." At the time, the Lunneys, Kevin and his brothers, had built a windfarm, and the only access they had to it for heavy vehicles was through this same road, through which they had no right of way. When the 40 local farmers who owned the land the road was built on realised that the Lunneys were allowing a French company to trespass on their land because it also benefited them, the Lunney family, they were outraged, as it became clear that if the French company had no right of way, then neither did the Lunneys. Up until then, the Lunneys had been very much a part of the community, and had been born and reared on the side of the mountain. It was felt that they were now helping to sell their neighbours down the river, for their own financial gain, and they immediately lost all respect in the area. Shortly afterwards, a nasty incident occurred when a pig's head was left at the entrance to Kevin Lunney's house. The animosity towards the Lunneys continued to such an extent that the local community has been very much against the new Quinn/Mannok team, and pledged at the time that they wouldn't accommodate them with any raw materials as long as their lands were being trespassed on. Nine years later, they have stuck to their guns, which means that now the company has to import their raw material from the Tyrone border, from Co. Antrim, and from Co. Roscommon, as well as using some sub-grade material which had been considered unsuitable for producing a quality product fifteen years earlier.

At the time, this left me in an awkward position, as I had always worked in close harmony with the farming community, so David Mackey and I attended several meetings with the farmers to try to put an end to the trespassing over their land by the windfarm's new owners. We agreed with them that Mantlin had no right of way over their land. However, we were overruled by the executives, and the anger of all the local farmers intensified. In April 2015, John McCartin even informed the local Gardaí that the local farmers, Quinn staff, and Seán Quinn were blocking rights of way – a complete untruth, as the rights of way did not exist, as indicated in writing by the local farmers and Coillte. However, the Gardaí believed McCartin, and apparently accepted his word that there was a right of way in place, as he was a councillor at the time. The Gardaí even went as far as, probably unknown to themselves, supervising sabotage perpetrated by strangers, who broke down gates and barriers and pushed limestone boulders into drains, which flooded the local area. The reason for employing strangers was because Quinn staff wouldn't carry out the sabotage, as they knew that both David Mackey and I were in support of the local farmers who claimed that there was no right of way over their land, and in fact some of them confronted these thugs who were carrying out these acts of sabotage. QIH's health and safety manager, Gerry Glancy, provided a comprehensive health and safety report of the incident to the Gardaí at the time, and they promised to investigate the matter, but to date, no response has been received. It is interesting that in December 2019, in an interview that McCartin did with John Mooney of the *Sunday Times*, he gave the impression that what he had done was right, despite the legal fact that there was no right of way, and that tremendous damage had been done by forcing the illegal right of way.

Worse was to follow: I was formally asked to take the French company's side in the right of way dispute. Carson McDowell, a solicitors' firm in Belfast that represented the French windfarm owners, was invited by Liam McCaffrey to attend a meeting with me and Liam in head office. They told me that I would be "well looked after" if I persuaded local farmers that their client did indeed have a right of way over their land. I replied that I simply could not lie to these farmers with whom I had done business for many years, and tell them that a French company had a right of way over their land, as it did not exist.

Within weeks, I had a similar meeting with John McCartin and Vidrala, the Spanish company that had acquired Quinn Group's glass operations. It turned out that John McCartin's father, Joe, knew the Spanish company's chairman's uncle, who had served as an MEP at the same time as Joe McCartin. McCartin invited two other well-respected community leaders – Father Gerry Comiskey (a local priest) and Freddie Walsh (a local hotelier) – to the meeting. I was never sure why they had been invited, apart from the fact that they were both Fine Gael supporters, but I think it was to encourage me to play ball. It is ironic that since then, McCartin has reported Freddie Walsh and two other businessmen to the Gardaí, saying that they threatened him. This claim was investigated by the Gardaí, but there seems to have been no evidence to support it.

When the contingent with the two Spanish businessmen arrived, it would be an understatement to say that I wasn't very pleasant to them. I told them frankly that the community had been treated very badly, as they had been assured that the glass factories would end up in local hands, just as a secret plan to sell it off to them had been agreed, behind everyone's back. Again, I was told that I would be "looked after" if I persuaded the local community that Spanish ownership was in everyone's best interests, and that the sale had been "above board" and done with my agreement. Of course, after starting these businesses over 40 years earlier, there was no way I could agree to that. The Quinns had lived and worked in the community for generations, and there was no way I was going to mislead them. It has since been stated in a book that the Spaniards came to meet me before the deal was done, and that I requested a 25 per cent shareholding, a statement that makes no sense, as I didn't meet them until February/March 2015, while in fact the deal was done in October 2014, some three or four months before they arrived to take the company over in January 2015, and five or six months before I met them. If the author of the book was gullible enough to believe that, it is little wonder that the book is full of extracts and comments that make no sense.

No specific financial offer was made to me at those meetings; I was simply informed that if I cooperated, I would be well looked after. But some time later, John Bosco O'Hagan, one of the company's trustees, handed a letter to my brother, Peter, to forward on to me, which said that if I had played ball with the French, Spanish, and Belfast companies I would have earned between €1.25 million and €2 million per annum as a reward. If I had taken that bribe, management could have stolen whatever they wanted, as I had taken a bribe to mislead the local community. I still do not know if any others have benefitted from that bribe.

* * * *

In May 2015 I wrote to the three bondholders who still ultimately owned the remains of the company – Brigade Capital Management, Contrarian and Silverpoint – to say that I wanted to meet them to discuss my concerns about the way QIH was being run. They replied that they would be in Ireland in August, and that I could meet them then.

In August Mike Gatto (from Silverpoint), Matt Hartnett (from Brigade Capital Management) and Bill Raine (from Contrarian) came to Derrylin, and I met them for the first time. I advised the Americans – in the presence of Liam, Kevin, and Dara – that the company's management was not working out, and that raw material was running out, as has since been proved to be the case.

The bondholders asked for my view on what the company needed most. I explained that three things were needed. Firstly, the business needed to be properly managed. Secondly, more raw materials were critical for the company's future, and €45 million needed to be spent within three years. Finally, QBRC's poor relations with the local community, and its staff, had to be repaired. The meeting finished amicably, but afterwards the bondholders and the executives went for dinner in the Slieve Russell, and I wasn't invited.

At Christmas 2015, Liam and Kevin came into my room in head office, and as it was Christmas week, we had a drink together. They asked me if I would agree to having a meeting in early January to resolve some of our problems, and I agreed to do so. As the blatant lies that had been told in 2015 were being believed by a lot of people, I decided to invite two neutral people to the meeting, and to make sure that the meeting was balanced, and not just seen to be attended by Quinn supporters, I invited Freddie Walsh, whom John McCartin had invited to a glass meeting some months earlier. I also invited Martin Maguire, who had spoken at the glass meeting in Ballyconnell the previous January, and was a man I didn't know very well, but who had a lot of respect in the local area. Some of my family attended. At the beginning of the meeting, Liam asked Freddie to chair the meeting, and he agreed to do so. Freddie opened the meeting by asking what the position was regarding the long-term ownership of the company. This was a difficult question for both the trustees and the executives, which was emphasised by the fact that John Bosco, who had told a meeting of around twenty managers about three weeks earlier that it was "always, always, always" being done for the Quinns, wasn't in attendance, as I presume he couldn't retract what he had said three weeks earlier. The executives, McCartin, and Ernie waffled on about the community, and when questioned about why they bought no assets, they tried to say that they did buy assets, which, of course, we knew was untrue. Ernie and McCartin gave no explanation as to why they gave away half of their shares.

Different members of the family raised various concerns about the lies that were being told about me, in particular the lies about my mental health – the family took exception to that. When my daughter Brenda exposed one of John McCartin's lies in relation to settling the case, pointing out to him that one of his accusations couldn't possibly have happened, he became incensed and shouted, "I had no fucking solicitor with me at the meeting."

The meeting was a bit of a waste of time, but near the end of the meeting, Seán Jnr, who was working in a junior capacity for the company, and knew that I had concerns about how the business was managed, asked Liam how the business was performing. Liam's reply was that anybody with 'half a head' could run this business. I didn't comment, but just smiled to myself, knowing that the business was being mismanaged, and having never heard the expression 'half a head' before.

It was clear at the end of the meeting that a lot of lies had been told that couldn't be stood over. After the meeting, Ernie Fisher accepted that he was surprised at some of the facts that came out of the meeting, particularly regarding the windfarm.

In the meantime, there were a number of incidents of fraud reported to Paddy Mohan and Denis Doogan that gave rise to concern. These incidents amounted to a potential loss to QIH of hundreds of thousands of euros. Paddy, Denis, and I wanted them investigated, and I wrote to the bondholders to ask for a meeting to discuss the issues. We met in Dublin in May 2016 – Seán Jnr, Ronan Barrett, and I with the bondholders – and I expressed my concern that the potential fraud wasn't being investigated, wondering why this was. Ronan is a financial consultant who acted on the family's behalf and had travelled to Connecticut to meet the bondholders.

The three of us met the bondholders in Dublin and I expressed my concern that the reported fraud wasn't being investigated. They claimed that they had done a forensic investigation into the matter, and that no fraud had taken place. Of course, I knew straight away that there was a cover-up, as there had been at least four areas where fraud could easily be established; one of €500,000; one of €97,000; one of €30,000, and a load of steel, and that nobody who had been familiar with these acts of fraud had been interviewed. The bondholders had no answer to my queries as to why the witnesses weren't interviewed, but just stuck to the position that there was no fraud. They said that if I wasn't prepared to withdraw the accusations, they would have to reconsider my consultancy contract. They then flew back to America, and just a few days later, on 16 May, I received a letter from Liam McCaffrey stating that I was being sacked for making false allegations of theft and fraud, which, after a forensic investigation, had been found to be baseless. Paddy Mohan, who had been the first to inform me of the fraud, was totally convinced it had taken place after Liam had told him that there had been a misunderstanding regarding steel as the driver was Russian, which caused a language problem, when, in fact, the driver was from Ireland. Paddy escaped censure. However, the more outspoken Denis Doogan, who, like me, wanted the reported fraud investigated, and who was also very angry with Liam, later outlined in a letter to the bondholders a number of other frauds that Liam had been involved in, including the fact that Liam had caused a warrant to be put out for his (Denis's) arrest because Liam had not honoured his financial commitments on a different transaction. Denis went on to state in his letter that Liam still owed him and a number of others a lot of money. All of Denis's assertions were, like mine, dismissed, and he was also sacked. The infuriating fact is that at the time, in 2014, when a deal was being arranged, it was being done on behalf of myself, CFL, Concerned Irish Citizens, the local communities, and the staff, and there was a feeling of betrayal when they used the proceeds of the company to hire the best legal teams in the country to sue all of us, knowing that none of us could afford to take them on.

While I had my doubts about the integrity of the bondholders for almost two years at this stage, I had now become fully convinced that the bondholders were front and centre in the whole fraud, with their six-page document in July 2014 and their 141-page document in December 2014, which included John McCartin's side letter. I have copies of both of those documents.

I was told that I could still use my office for as long as I wanted, and that my consultancy fee of €500,000 would continue to be paid if I agreed to leave by mutual consent, which I did. But I chose to make no further use of my office, and the deal was immediately reneged upon and the money from my consultancy contract soon dried up. This was a continuation of what had been done to the family from 2010 onwards – there was an unwritten rule to give the Quinns nothing. This was obviously to starve us out. When my sister Bernie and daughter Colette asked Liam why my fee had been stopped, he told them that he, Dara and Kevin were willing to carry on paying me, but the bondholders had changed their minds. None of us accepted their excuse.

As I had once regarded Liam, Kevin and Dara as good friends, I felt badly betrayed by them. I felt that the guarantees they had given to the bondholders between 2005 and 2008 was done by carelessness – there was no malice involved, but I was very annoyed with them when I later found out that they used my name and tried to drag me into the Central Bank Inquiry into suspected breaches related to the soundness and adequacy of QIL's administrative and accounting procedures and internal control mechanisms relating to the management and monitoring of the assets of QIL's subsidiaries (Regulation 10(3) of the European Communities (Non-Life Insurance) Framework Regulations 1994 (S.I. 359/1994)), saying that I attended meetings that never took place. At this stage however, I had zero confidence in them; not only had they betrayed me, they were either involved in fraud, or were covering up fraud. However, I was pleased that they were no longer able to buy my silence. I believe that the bondholders simply could not fire Liam, Dara or Kevin because they were compromised by the 2014 agreements in which they offered, in writing, rewards of millions of euros for stopping the sabotage and selling most of the businesses and getting rid of me, and this is the reason they didn't investigate the fraud alle-gations. This was done behind everyone's back, including that of their own CEO at the time, Paul O'Brien, the junior directors, staff, CFL, and myself.

I still had confidence in John Bosco O'Hagan and Ernie Fisher, but my confidence in John McCartin was completely blown at this point. When he was reminded of the promises he had made to Patricia, he, who had visited our house on so many occasions, and had reassured her repeatedly that he was doing all he could to get our companies back, dismissed these out of hand.

When I began raising concerns about these acts of fraud, the first reaction of some of the directors was to question my credibility and sanity. They had seen how well this had worked for the government, the judiciary, the admin-istrators, and the receivers, and how the media were happy to spread their gospel. They had come to the conclusion that the only way to overcome my support was by giving me a bad name, and telling lies about me. Liam told my son, Seán Jnr, that he felt that I was "mental". When Seán Jnr asked him about this at a later meeting, he said he stood over what he said. He told my daughter Colette and my sister Bernie the same thing. The only thing I can say about that is that I was no more mental in 2015 than I was in the other 75 years I have lived on this earth, and well Liam knows it. At the time, there seemed to be a deliberate campaign to question my sanity. John McCartin started telling the local community, and far beyond the local community, that he had loaned me €500,000, even though he never lent me a cent. When asked about my lack of involvement in the business, he would say that I had had a hard few years, and that they had taken their toll on me. He would say that they were running the business to give me an opportunity to recover. He was also saying publicly that he had settled our case with the bank, but that I wouldn't agree to the settlement. He added that I had fallen out with both Judge Finnegan (retired Justice Joseph Finnegan, who was mediating between the family and IBRC in 2015) and Kieran Wallace, when in fact, I had got on very well with both of these men.

In late December 2015, a management meeting, with around 20 attendees, was held in the Quinn packaging factory in Ballyconnell, to intro-duce the three trustees, John McCartin, John O'Hagan, and Ernie Fisher, to the management team. At that meeting, in my absence, I was accused of being disruptive. This meeting was recorded by an attendee and later tran-scribed. During the meeting, John McCartin stated:

> Now I would still feel the programme that we signed up for is very much a live programme and that the programme is get control of the business, run them well, invest in them, make sure that you have Rolls Royce staff and Rolls Royce everything around here ready for reinvestment. Be cute, don't flow the profits off the books, don't make the thing too dear for yourselves but make sure you are credible and investible ....

So if you don't push your profits too high, you talk about your raw materials problem, you make sure that they trust you and talk well about you and help you to refine it but they are not looking to a big long bright future for themselves here. But we can have a big long bright future ... I see no harm in that at all. I see no harm in profits petering out and coming back to the steady level, none at all, and I would love to work on a strategy that says let me see how we might massage and retain the profits for the next three, four, or five years and make sure that this can be bought.

How do you sell that to everybody else? And have you been reading the newspapers by the way and seeing what is going on? The business cannot be sold to anybody only us .... We make sure that we manage their expectations and make sure that we don't let them think that they can get too much out of here but they think that they can just get themselves paid for and get out the door. That is what we need them to think and now they are going to give us a reference and say those lads are bankable lads ... let them at it. That is what we need. That is what our plan was.

At the meeting, McCartin also said:

As far as I am concerned, I have from, you know, from the very beginning said that I got involved with this to make sure that these businesses stayed here, stayed in local ownership and didn't get broken up.

You have to remember that there is a wider community here whose views have to be respected, wider community here who also built these businesses and these are very important men and we have to respect what they want.

Some attendees at the meeting felt that McCartin had had a brain freeze, as a year earlier, he had been one of the chief architects of the breakup of the company, selling its most valuable assets, and buying none. As it was the first time that the majority of the attendees had ever met McCartin, he left them very confused as to what type of guy he was, as they could make neither head nor tail of what he was attempting to do.

His hypocrisy was breathtaking, as on the 24 September 2019, almost four years later, he would make the following statement to the Gardaí:

> *From the outset, it was clear that Seán Quinn Snr wanted us to run the company in a fashion that would devalue it so that he could purchase the shares for bottom dollar. We were not willing to commit the fraud necessary to do this or to risk the jobs in the business. Seán Quinn Snr immediately instigated a campaign of slander, defamations and intimidation against the executives of QIH, namely Liam McCaffrey, Kevin Lunney, myself, Dara O'Reilly, and Tony Lunney.*

So he was accusing me of doing exactly what he had proposed to do at the management meeting almost four years earlier!

His attempts to manipulate everyone and everything was almost limitless. Later, he would say to Joey Smith, a businessman from Ballinamore, who had been a very loyal supporter of the McCartin family when they had got into financial trouble in the 1970s, and spoke publicly on their behalf at the time, that "... the only solution would be for Seán Quinn to buy the whole lot back himself."

Joey would later detail the conversation in an affidavit to a Belfast court:

> *I asked John McCartin 'well what do you want out of it?' John McCartin said that number one the 'boys' will want a golden bridge to leave because after all they have put an awful lot of work into this. I then said 'well, what about yourself?' and John McCartin said, 'I do not want anything', but he followed this up by saying 'I don't want to be seen to be getting anything.' He continued by saying that 'there was a possible way of doing this, there was land on the mountain', although I was not aware of what land he was talking about at the time, but John McCartin had told me that Seán Quinn had walked the land with him at one time and it turned out to be land at Ballyheady Mountain. John McCartin said that*

this was his family land but once Seán Quinn reacquired his companies that he, John McCartin, would be able to sell this land to Seán Quinn but he would want it to be agreed at a bumped-up price. He said, 'that is how I would get my money back and I would be seen to be doing it legitimately.' John McCartin said that he wanted to be seen to be in it for the local community and not for any personal gain and/or for political gain. He said with regards to the money 'for the boys' that that could be put into an escrow account. The reason I particularly remember that phrase is that I did not know what an escrow account was. I replied by saying that if they worked with Seán Quinn that he always promised that he would be fair with anybody who helped him.

Knowing that fraud had taken place, CFL continued to try to have dialogue with the executives, to try to find out why I was sacked, why QIH was performing so badly and what the long-term plan for the company was. But after a number of meetings with Liam and Kevin, CFL were getting no satisfaction, and the executives began to refuse to meet them. CFL and the community became more concerned when manufacturing machines worth around €16 million began to go missing from the sites, on top of worries about why CRH was buying so much cement from Quinns, while they had spare capacity in their own factories, and the fact that Liam had now moved his business to a CRH factory that was twice the size of the one that he had been using up until then. In 2018, CFL called a public meeting at the Tiler-Made factory in Ballyconnell, and invited QBRC's directors to come and explain what was going on within the company. Patricia, our children and I were there, with about 800 others – many of them stood outside as there was no room in the hall. Once again, the directors did not even show up, despite being invited with ample notice, which created a lot of ill-feeling.

Questions that the meeting wanted answers to include the following:

1. Liam McCaffrey had said repeatedly that he advised Seán Quinn to sell the Anglo shares, yet he borrowed millions of euros from the Quinn Group and Anglo Irish Bank to meet his CFD commitment on his own personal Anglo shares. Why?

2. Would a guilty finding in the inquiry into Quinn Insurance stop the executives from acting as directors of Quinn Building Products? If so, is that the reason you looked for a delay in the hearing?

3. Why, after receiving so much support from the Quinns, staff, and community, have the directors failed to buy any assets, despite saying they would do so?

4. When did you give the bondholders the first assurances that you would facilitate the new glass owners with cheap sand, and the use of the company's garage, weighbridge, and diesel pumps?

5. What were the contents of the 'Regulatory Side Letter' signed by John McCartin in favour of the company as described on Page 11 of the contract signed on 16 December 2014?

6. Why did this document, which was 141 pages long, not outline what the implementation plan was in any way?

7. How much money did John McCartin's companies earn from Quinn Building Products over the last 12 months?

8. Why was there no attempt made to raise equity to purchase the assets?

9. If there were no assets being purchased, what was the purpose of Quinn Business Retention Company (QBRC)?

10. Why did the senior executives feel it necessary for Seán Quinn to have to seek written permission from them to buy a meal for a customer?

11. How come the people who reported fraud within the company were never interviewed?

12. Who made the decision not to investigate the allegations of fraud within the company?

13. If the executives were working on behalf of the Quinns, why did the chief executive sack Seán in writing?

14. At that time, was Seán offered a new consultancy contract which was later reneged on?
15. Did the Quinn directors entertain the Vidrala executives in the Slieve Russell prior to them announcing their takeover of glass?
16. Was the entire QBRC project a sham from day one?

These questions were put up on local Facebook pages, but the executives immediately pursued legal proceedings to get them removed, which they were. They then issued legal proceedings, which are still ongoing, against the organisers of the meeting. Right through all of this process, QIH tried to create the impression that the business was very successful. I believe that this may be a good time to outline some of the main points in their 2021 audited accounts.

- From the time they took possession of the company, in December 2014, to January 2015, less than one month, they increased the value of the business they were managing by €39 million.
- Between 2015 and 2021, they have classified €28 million of that €39 million as a trading profit.
- At 31 December 2021, the company had total assets less current liabilities of €102 million and it had creditors' amounts falling due after more than one year of €187 million, which, as the accounts described, left a shareholders' funds' deficit of €85 million.
- 2021 itself appears to have been the worst year from they took over the management of the business, with a net debt increase of €15.2 million, creditors falling due within one year increasing by €25 million, cash available at bank reducing by €6 million, and interest due but unpaid of €6 million.

These accounts were signed by Liam McCaffrey and Dara O'Reilly on 24 August 2022, and by the auditors Ernst & Young on 30 August 2022. It is difficult to believe these figures when both CRH and Kingspan are producing record profit figures on an annual basis since these boys took over in 2014.

What you might not be able to find is what they describe as 'additions to tangible assets', as there aren't any, even though they claimed recently that they have spent €90 million on capital investment. The facts are, however, that there has been a significant reduction in plant, machinery, and lorries as the company is subcontracting a lot of the business to third parties. How can you have additions to tangible assets if more assets are either scrapped, sold, or, as is the case here, tens of millions go missing and are reported to the Gardaí. I am not in a position to say how much they have spent on replacing or maintaining equipment and machinery of the business over the period, but what I can say is that it would take capital investment of tens of millions of euros to bring it back up to the standard it was at in 2014. What is also missing from the audited accounts is depreciation of limestone, shale, sand, and gravel. Surely if you were using a raw material that has to be replaced by a similar material that has to be transported ten times further, at a huge additional cost, in terms of both money and carbon emissions, it would be absolutely necessary to use a depreciation figure. There doesn't appear to be any reason given for why depreciation is not accounted for.

Traditionally, the company did not depreciate raw materials, as they were always replaced from the same area, and in fact, in 2010, the company had reserves of raw materials more than ten times greater than what it started with in 1973.

* * * *

Six months before my sacking, on 6 November 2015, the Central Bank of Ireland informed me that they had "decided to discontinue the investigation into your involvement in the matters ... pertaining to regulation 10(3) of the European Communities (non-Life Insurance)." In effect, I was being told that I faced no further action, as the bank knew that I hadn't been involved in the placing of guarantees on the Quinn Insurance assets. I believe that it was unfortunate that, as these guarantees were given ten years earlier, and had come to the notice of the Central Bank five-and-a-half years earlier, the Central Bank hadn't cleared my name earlier, because if they had, the current senior directors would never have been allowed to be in the position they are in today.

See below an extract from *Village* magazine, November/December 2022:

On 18 February 2013, the Central Bank reprimanded QIL again and fined it a further €5 million. This enforcement action satisfied the crucial "participation link" criterion by which individuals can be subject to Central Bank enforcement actions only after a contravention of financial regulations or legislation by a relevant Regulated Financial Services Provider has been established.

As a consequence of this 2013 action, in 2015 the Central Bank launched a separate investigation into the conduct of McCaffrey and Lunney. Initially they co-operated with the Central Bank's Inquiry and engaged with it in a positive manner over a number of months.

Ultimately, though McCaffrey sought to frustrate the Central Bank's investigation by challenging the inquiry in the High Court. In his judgment delivered on 3 October 2017, High Court Judge Seamus Noonan was scathing in dismissing the arguments advanced on behalf of McCaffrey and Lunney in their last-ditch, kitchen-sink challenge.

"It seems to me that this can only be viewed as an impermissible attempt to collaterally attack the decision of the [Inquiry Members] and must therefore constitute an abuse of process. Moreover, it also represents a similarly impermissible attempt to impugn the relevant provisions of the Guidelines which have obtained for many years and of which the applicants must have been well aware. As I have already noted, the applicants abandoned an attempt to directly challenge the guidelines in their amendment motion but now seek to do so by the back door as it were."

On 28 May 2019, almost four years after inquiry members had first been appointed, they finally held their first full hearings in public.

Opening statements and evidence were heard, including the startling admission about the signed minutes of meetings that had not taken place.

The inquiry was adjourned on 6 June 2019, as had been scheduled, with the intention of resuming its proceedings a month later. However, the inquiry would not convene to hear any further evidence because McCaffrey and Lunney indicated that they wished to avail of the Central Bank's settlement process. Section 4.24 of the Central Bank's Inquiry Guidelines allow the work of an inquiry to be suspended in order to facilitate the conclusion of a settlement agreement which the Central Bank regards as the optimum conclusion.

When Liam McCaffrey and Kevin Lunney were issued with proceedings by the Central Bank, they mounted a High Court challenge. But the Central Bank successfully defended itself, and on 3 October 2017 costs were awarded to the bank. Eventually, the Central Bank found that Liam McCaffrey and Kevin Lunney were responsible for a number of breaches: no adequate procedures to manage assets, a failure to maintain an adequate solvency margin, using subsidiaries to guarantee borrowings without consultation with the board, and holding board meetings on three occasions without a sufficient quorum.

Bizarrely, Liam and Kevin claimed that the guarantees had been agreed at a meeting that all three of us had attended, with Liam in the chair. But in twenty years of knowing Liam I had never gone to a meeting he chaired. This was never disputed by either Liam or Kevin. After I spent fifteen minutes in the witness box at a hearing in Dublin, explaining that I did not recognise the documents that were being shown to me, Liam, Kevin and their lawyers were given the opportunity to cross-examine me, but they chose not to. At that stage the game was up, and Liam had changed his position from blaming me to blaming A&L Goodbody, and Kevin told the inquiry that he would have to live with what he had been responsible for, for the rest of his life.

I have never been told exactly what sanctions, if any, Liam McCaffrey and Kevin Lunney faced for their breaches of the rules. On 3 September 2020 the Central Bank announced that it had reached a settlement agreement with McCaffrey in December 2019, and with Lunney in July 2020. But the statement added that "given the circumstances arising for the individuals at the time these settlements were concluded", the bank would be giving no further details.

The 'circumstances' behind this unprecedented secrecy were some very unexpected events in September 2019: Kevin Lunney was abducted and badly beaten. It is still unclear why this prevented the Central Bank from completing its job. I don't believe it was ever about Kevin's abduction, as they were two totally different matters that would be dealt with by two totally different law enforcement agencies, but which may have meant that if the investigations were carried through, the individuals concerned wouldn't be allowed to continue as chartered accountants or company directors.

Much has been written about Kevin Lunney's abduction. There is no denying that he was treated savagely. On 17 September 2019, on his way home from work, Kevin drove into the lane leading to his home and noticed a white car ahead of him. It quickly reversed into his own car. He locked his doors but two men smashed the windows and dragged him out. A third man threatened him with a Stanley knife, and he was put into the boot of a black Audi.

Kevin was driven across the border into County Cavan, to a farmyard. In a horsebox he was badly beaten, and then dumped on the side of a country road. He feared he was going to die as he was cold, in excruciating pain and losing blood, but at about 9 p.m. he was found by a man driving a tractor, who called the Gardaí. Kevin had been badly cut up, and one leg broken in two places. It was three weeks before he was back at work, on crutches.

The first I heard of Kevin Lunney's abduction was a phone call from a local radio presenter, Joe Finnegan of Northern Sound. Finnegan assumed that I had already heard about the abduction. I hadn't, as I had been playing cards that night, as I do every Tuesday night, so my reaction to him was very 'off the cuff'. Based on what he told me, I condemned it as a barbaric act – a statement that I stand by to this day. I was shocked to hear about it. I had known Kevin and his wife, Bronagh, for a long time, and had attended their wedding. I had tremendous sympathy for them and their family, which I expressed to Joe Finnegan.

I also remember telling Joe that I would be blamed, just as I had been blamed for everything that was happening in the area up to that point. It was an easy sell for them, as I had been blamed for everything that had gone wrong for the previous eleven years, without a scintilla of evidence to support it, but these guys were professionals. Within an hour, my children heard the news of Kevin's abduction, and some of them rang me to ask, "Are you going to be blamed for this?" I visited my daughter Aoife and her family at Center Parcs in Longford the next day: a day trip that had been long planned. I remember seeing my name on all of the news programmes. Of course, local people who knew me, and people who had done business with me over many years, felt initially that I had nothing to do with this despicable incident, but as the clamour to blame me grew from a local priest, the media, and some politicians, even my family and my biggest supporters started to wonder. Within a short time, the abduction had disturbing consequences for me, and my family.

Father Oliver O'Reilly, Ballyconnell's parish priest, invited the television cameras into the church during Mass, indicating to them the previous day what the sermon was going to be about. Part of his sermon was in the print media before he even delivered his homily from the pulpit. It was subsequently widely reported that he said a Mafia-style campaign had shrouded the community in fear, and that an unnamed "paymaster" was behind it all. Although Fr O'Reilly had not named me, many people, including myself, felt that it was me he was talking about. The "paymaster" term soon appeared in the media, and on people's lips, and it is still being used today. In fact, the judge in Kevin Lunney's criminal trial, when he was imposing sentences, stated that he was leaving the maximum sentence for the paymaster.

I called in to see Fr O'Reilly shortly afterwards. I told him he was "wrong, wrong, wrong", and that what he had done to me, and my family, would have devastating consequences. I asked him to clarify whether it was or wasn't me he was talking about as the "paymaster". In the days following this meeting, my son, Seán Jnr, rang Fr O'Reilly from Dublin, to express the same concerns. In neither case did we get any satisfaction. While I never considered myself to be very religious, my respect for the clergy has not diminished, as I believe that the vast majority of them provide an excellent service and comfort to millions of families throughout the world. I believe that Fr O'Reilly should have read the commandment "Thou shalt not bear false witness against thy neighbour" before delivering his sermon. After that, I never stood inside Ballyconnell church for three years, until Fr O'Reilly was moved to a different parish. I am still disappointed, but not surprised, that Fr O'Reilly would allow this matter to continue indefinitely, considering there was never a scintilla of evidence to support his accusation. The question remains, does the hierarchy of the Catholic Church believe that I should carry this injustice to my grave? People who know me would know that hurting someone physically was not something that I would do. I played competitive football for 20 years and was never sent off the playing pitch.

I believe that the Gardaí, Kevin Lunney, and all of the other directors are well aware that I had no hand, act, or part in Kevin's abduction, and in fact I was never interviewed by the Gardaí regarding it. Even when they raided my home in April 2022, it was never mentioned, and I still don't know what they came here for, but while they said it was for intimidation and coercion, I believe it was a fishing expedition. As regards intimidation or coercion, does anybody seriously consider that if I am aware of sabotage and fraud in the company that I founded fifty years earlier, before some of these directors were even born, am I not entitled to talk about it, and, in any event, is it not those who are controlling a false narrative who are guilty of intimidation and coercion? There is an overwhelming belief in the community that justice has not been served evenly.

What happened next was very curious. One of the main suspects in Kevin Lunney's abduction was Cyril (Jimmy) McGuinness, a local godfather in the Cavan and Fermanagh area, who was known as 'Dublin Jimmy', after the city of his birth. On 8 November 2019, Dublin Jimmy died of a heart attack during a police raid on a house in Buxton, Derbyshire. Jimmy was in his early sixties and in poor health, so there may be nothing suspicious about his death. The house he died at was owned by a Polish man, a sidekick of Dublin Jimmy, who worked at a tyre factory in Belturbet ironically owned by Tony Lunney, Kevin's brother. This connection was reported on in a full-page article in the *Sunday World* in December 2019. Dublin Jimmy had been suspected of many acts of sabotage against Quinn companies between 2010 and 2015.

Some have speculated that I knew Dublin Jimmy well. The truth is that I only knew him by reputation and by sight, having seen him a couple of times in local pubs. Acts of sabotage on the company were frequent, and probably the most costly to the business was the burning of the electrical substation that ran the windfarm – very close to the homes of two of the Lunney brothers – in November 2012. It was notable that Dublin Jimmy, who has been accused of being involved with acts of sabotage and criminality relating to the company, had a rock-solid alibi for the substation burning: he was serving a jail sentence in a Belgian prison at that time, and I was in Mountjoy prison. I have since made statements to the Gardaí, informing them of who I believe was responsible, and whose house the saboteurs left from and returned to following the crime. I also gave them names of eight people who may be able to assist them in their investigations regarding sabotage and fraud within the company in July 2020. Later, a solicitor on behalf of CFL added another six names to the list of people who would be able to help the investigation, but, unfortunately, these people have never been interviewed by the Gardaí.

Kevin Lunney gave an extended interview to the BBC shortly after his abduction, in which he appeared to tell all about what had happened that night. He said that he had been told to resign from Quinn Industrial Holdings, along with his co-directors, and that the abductors had even carved the letters 'QIH' on his chest. It is notable that he did not say publicly at the time that he was also told to withdraw all legal cases against individuals both north and south of the border. This came out two years later in the trial of those convicted of his abduction. Had this been known at the time imme-diately after the abduction, it would have perhaps widened the discussion regarding the motivation for the attack, and the people who could poten-tially benefit from it. The implication is that I was the only one who could potentially gain, but this was patently untrue. Surely anyone with an active cell in their brain would have known that I was going to be blamed for this, as I had been blamed for everything that had gone wrong over the previous eleven years, which was believed by many without a trace of evidence. It beggars belief how anybody could believe that this act was going to serve my interests. Why did Kevin keep quiet about this added warning about legal actions for two years? Possibly because he wanted to keep the spotlight on me. Revealing this detail could have shown that there were others with a grudge against him, and deflected blame away from me.

It is interesting that Trevor Birney, the presenter of the RTE documentary *Quinn Country*, rang me on his way home from Dublin on the opening day of the Kevin Lunney trial to tell me that there was a major breakthrough that day in the court – that Kevin Lunney had told Gardaí at the time of the abduction that he had been told to withdraw all legal cases, both north and south of the border. Trevor felt that this was of major significance, as it meant that there were another six to eight people who might feel hard done by, by Kevin.

Soon after Kevin's abduction, the directors met with the Taoiseach, Leo Varadkar, and the Garda Commissioner. The executives in Derrylin now felt that they could say or do what they liked about me, as my name had been linked to the abduction, and they used the airwaves and the print media to the maximum.

To this day, I still feel very annoyed that neither the Gardaí nor Kevin Lunney gave any public indication that the abductors had demanded that Kevin arrange the withdrawal of all legal cases against all individuals both north and south of the border at any stage when detailing his abduction and physical injuries. There seems to be a continued desire to imply that I have been responsible for everything that has gone wrong over the past fifteen years, while in fact at the Central Bank Inquiry I was fully cleared of any wrongdoing, and during the trial of Kevin's abductors, my name was not even mentioned. I have been told by a friendly journalist that his profession don't really want to tell my story. In fact, I have brought some journalists to my home and gave them clear evidence of criminality, and they told me they wouldn't print it. I have always believed, and still believe, that Kevin Lunney and his co-directors have known all along that I had no involvement whatsoever in Kevin's abduction, but it suits them to portray this as justification for betraying me and my family. The directors know that they left a lot of the dirty work regarding suing and sacking people to Kevin. This may have led to a lot of bad will towards Kevin in particular in this area, and there were of course many grudges regarding the betrayal of the farmers on the windfarm road.

I do not suggest that any of Kevin's fellow directors were involved in his abduction, but it is certainly true that the incident insulated all of the directors from unfavourable comment – they were the darlings of the media, and boy did they milk it! The attack on Kevin in 2019, the threats made to executives and McCartin since, as reported by journalists, and the perceived danger to their lives, appear to be the only reasons why the Central Bank never revealed what sanctions they imposed on them, even though they were found to have breached multiple rules, but I believe there may be a much greater reason.

An investigation into Liam and Dara's conduct by Chartered Accountants Ireland – the professional institute – seems to have been started, but then it was discontinued, which allowed these men to continue to serve as company directors. They are still seen by many nationally as the golden boys of Irish business, even though the company has been loss-making since they took it over, but in local counties they are much less popular, where their level of betrayal and the destruction of the company is well-known.

It was felt that the name change to Mannok was the final insult to the Quinn family, and it annoyed the staff and the local community immensely. I, and some of my family and friends, have received many letters, texts, emails and phone calls from people all over the world who are totally disgusted with what has happened. On the evening that the name change to Mannok was publicly announced, Liam McCaffrey's wife, Marianne, sent a gloating photograph by text message to my wife, Patricia, showing her husband with his arms folded and other directors standing proudly in front of a re-branded Mannok lorry. While I knew Marianne, and had attended her wedding to Liam, I never dreamt that she would stoop so low.

The current state of the company is worrying, and long-serving staff believe that the breakdowns in plant are running at three times what they used to be, but they are past worrying about it, and just take it for granted, as they believe the necessary investment is not going to take place. As I have said in the weeks following Kevin Lunney's abduction in 2019, I never want to own the company again. However, as I also said at the time, I would love to see the company becoming successful again, and if someone with the ability to buy it and run it successfully again takes over, I will be willing and able to assist them in many ways.

The current position, as I write this book, is that following a number of accusations made against me and a number of other businessmen in the area by John McCartin to the Gardaí, I met the Gardaí and explained to them that what he had told them was complete and utter nonsense. How could it be anything else, as he had reported me for criminality in 2018, 2019, and 2020, stating that I had told him I had been involved in this criminality in 2013 and 2014, at the time we were on friendly terms? If that was the case, was John McCartin, as a member of Leitrim County Council, not bound to inform the Gardaí that I had told him that I was involved in criminality, rather than waiting five or six years to tell them? I decided at the time that between those accusations and the fact that I was suspected of being involved in Kevin Lunney's abduction, I felt compelled to inform the Gardaí of wrongdoing within the former Quinn Group, something that I never thought I would do, and had resisted doing for five years. However, as the lies and innuendo continued unrestrained, so when the Gardaí wanted to meet me regarding John McCartin's complaints, I felt that I should give them some detail of real complaints and criminality. Following that meeting with the Gardaí, which took place in Carrick-on-Shannon, the Cavan Gardaí visited my home on three days, where I reported in detail my knowledge of who was involved in the fraud and sabotage that had occurred in recent years, and I gave them the same details I had given to the bondholders four years earlier, namely fraud of €500,000, €97,000, €30,000 and the load of steel. In addition, I gave them details of additional acts of fraud, which had occurred since I met the bondholders, regarding €16 million of production plant that had gone missing and suspected fraud in the cement business. I gave them a number of credit notes that had been issued by Quinn Cement for amounts up to as much as €167,000, as well as the names and telephone numbers of eight individuals who would be able to assist them in their enquiries. Later, a local renowned solicitor, from a practice that has been in existence for more than 100 years, reported similar and other incidences of fraud and sabotage, and gave them a further six names of people who would be able to assist them. He has written many letters to the Gardaí, including the Commissioner, and also the ODCE, the Central Bank, and Chartered Accountants Ireland, and, to date, there doesn't appear to be any investigation into any of the matters.

Approximately one year later, when I had received no satisfactory response from the Gardaí, I contacted a local TD, who had previously visited our home. He returned, and we discussed all of the reported fraud that had taken place; I gave him a file, which included a credit note to a cement company for €167,000. I still have a copy of that credit note. I informed him that after I had reported this to the Gardaí, a director of the company that received the credit note took early retirement two months later. He said that there were no ifs or buts, but that allegations like this must be investigated. I have since written to him and rang him a number of times, and I have received no response, nor has he returned the file that I gave him at the time. I believe the reader will be able to make up their own mind on what the agenda is. It is interesting to observe, just recently, the time and energy that has been used at government level to investigate those who are responsible for misusing RTE money, while in the Quinn case, which has cost the Irish taxpayer more than €1,000 for every €1 the current RTE investigation is costing, they have done nothing about it. In the case of the Quinn executives, it is even more blatant, where the Central Bank has found two of them guilty, and a third one admitted his guilt in both the Swedish and Irish courts. Rather than them being investigated, they are being supported by the Irish government.

12

While I understand and appreciate not everyone might have understood what exactly happened my companies, and the associated cost to the state, most people will be aware of what happened the economy, and what *that* cost the state.

It has been said for the past fifteen years that the government saved the banks, and while I have no love for the banks, I can't understand how that can be the case. It was the government that gave tax relief to wealthy home-owners to purchase a second, or third or more, home; it was the Central Bank that allowed 100 per cent mortgages of €300,000 to marginal inves-tors in 2006, and, four years later, wouldn't loan €240,000 for the same house to a high-quality investor. It was well known that up until the crash, the government had built a rainy day fund of €17.5 billion, but when the rainy day came, the government didn't use that money to bring Ireland's banks up to a level that would have left them equal to the highest solvency margin of any bank in the world, which would have made it much easier to attract deposits. What they did instead was practically close down the banks, and borrow €20 billion a year to keep the lights on. It wasn't until November 2010 that they used the €17.5 billion as part of the bailout, rather than using it as an investment in 2007/2008. By then, tax revenue was reducing from €47 billion to less than €32 billion. Unemployment was heading for 450,000; 250,000 people were emigrating to countries that had the same financial crisis that Ireland had, but dealt with it differently;

70,000 builders emigrated; housebuilding reduced from more than 80,000 per annum to 7,000 at a time when there were 90,000 families waiting for social housing, and less than 300 were provided in 2013. New mortgages reduced from €40 billion to €2.4 billion. Families renting went from 145,000 up to 300,000. Home ownership reduced from 82 per cent in 2006 to 68 per cent today, while a poor country where we had a factory, Slovakia, has increased home ownership to 92 per cent today.

The United Nations wrote to the Irish government in 2013, advising them of their obligations in terms of housing provision, and I believe that it is vitally important that any forward-thinking government would do whatever needed to be done, within reason, to maximise home ownership – let it be by means of relief on stamp duty, mortgage interest relief, or any other means – as, financially, it has to be in the long-term interest of the country, because during a person's lifetime, those who own their own home will have more cash available to spend in the economy than those who are paying rent. Why is this not happening?

It was the government who blew the financial crisis through the roof when they took control of the banks. AIB, for example, was partly nationalised and made sell off very profitable businesses. As well as that, tens of billions of euros of loans were taken from that bank by NAMA, a state agency, and sold at half-price. Furthermore, AIB was made to provide billions of extra solvency, which meant that its loan book reduced from €180 billion to less than €90 billion.

Mike Aynsley, according to his interview in 2013 with Tom Lyons, reduced IBRC's loan book by €95 billion, including the Irish Nationwide loans, and when you consider the loan reduction in the other banks, there was no option but for the country to go bust. New loans almost became something of the past, and management were forced to resign. Based on this, how could AIB, or indeed Anglo, avoid going bankrupt? However, any banks that were left standing have since either repaid the government all of their loans, or are in the process of repaying the government all of their loans, plus interest. If this is the case, how can it be said that the banks busted the country? Surely, it has to be said that the government busted the banks and the country, but the banks and the country are bailing out the government.

In my opinion, there doesn't appear to be any doubt but that the government makes a mess of most projects it gets involved in. It felt it could manage the banks better than the banks could manage themselves, and from when the government took them over during the financial crisis and practically closed them down, they cost hundreds of thousands of businesses and homeowners throughout the island of Ireland their life savings. Now, when the banks are allowed to run their own businesses again, they have returned to profit. In the Quinn case, the state felt that it could run the business better than I could; a business that prior to the crash was making between €450 and €500 million a year of profit and was paying €1 million a day in wages. They have turned that into a loss-making business, and if further evidence is needed of their ability to manage businesses, one only needs to look at the children's hospital, the planning and construction of which took three times longer and cost three times more than it should have. I feel that the worst has yet to come on the children's hospital, and it may well take another ten years to settle all the legal arguments caused by the mismanagement of that project.

As anyone who ever worked in a business (let alone owned a business) knows, if you let it run down too far, it is very difficult, and sometimes impossible, to rebuild it, and that is what happened the Irish economy, proven by the fact that even after the bailout in November 2010, the government had to borrow an extra €100 billion in the years that followed to rebuild the economy to its pre-crash levels. That was the extent of the destruction.

It has been asked frequently why there are not more houses being built, but it seems very clear to me that for eleven successive years, our government has sold houses to vulture funds at half the price it would cost to replace them, so how or why would anyone build houses while that was happening? These vulture funds are getting approximately a 20 per cent return on their investment, as well as an asset that has multiplied in value since they bought it. I am just amazed at how that was allowed to happen for eleven successive years: selling assets at less than the replacement cost, knowing that a significant number of houses will become uninhabitable on an annual basis. On the figures available, it appears that they have sold 110,000 houses to these vulture funds, including 12,000 as recently as 2020. To make matters worse, many of the people these houses have been taken from are now renting their homes, and paying more than what a mortgage would be costing them if they had been allowed to stay in their home and allowed to pay their interest only for a few years, until the country recovered and they got their jobs back. The government is now subsidising rents by a billion euros per annum; if they had used that billion euros per annum to assist first-time homeowners from 2008 to 2015, we wouldn't have the crisis that we have today. During those same years thousands of good businesses were also affected, and many were put out of business.

Because of the banks being essentially closed between 2008 and 2012, house prices reduced by 55 per cent – not because they were only worth 45 per cent of their cost, but, because the Irish banks couldn't lend, this was all that the vulture funds would pay for them. If the banks had been open to finance distressed mortgages in the period 2008–2012, they would have had a queue out the door of credible borrowers if they were able to purchase a house at 20 per cent less than it would have cost to build a new one. That would also have been of huge assistance to the banks, who could have charged slightly more for their loans to credible borrowers and increased their profits accordingly.

In fairness to the government, it was a very difficult period. However, I fear that the same people who advised them on the banking crisis also advised them to wind up the Quinn Group, and the government have learned from it. In the most recent crisis, the Covid epidemic, they provided the necessary supports to help businesses and individuals over a two-year period. I don't believe that the government should ever have allowed new builds to reduce to fewer than 25,000 per annum, and that should have been a minimum – which would have created a floor in the market – if the government wanted to make a serious attempt to eat into the 90,000 social housing waiting list, and to have some private housing come on stream. It would also have meant much shorter dole queues and would have meant the number of people in negative equity would probably have been reduced by 70 or 80 per cent.

There were conflicting reports at the time: Davy's Stockbrokers said that there was still a shortage of 300,000 houses required to bring the Irish housing stock up to the European average, while others argued that there was a surplus of houses during the crisis, which was never the case, as there were hundreds of highly populated areas, particularly near the colleges and universities, that always had a shortage of houses.

As regards where we are now, I don't believe that building 50,000 houses per annum between now and the end of the decade will improve the current situation by one iota, considering the increase in population and the number of houses that will become uninhabitable. This will most likely lead to an increase in what's already happening: people who are currently abroad won't be able to come home; more people will emigrate; and, thirdly, couples will decide against starting a family when they don't have a home.

I believe that the fundamental error that was made over the past fifteen years was for the government to allow a situation to develop where houses were being sold for less than it cost to build them. Obviously, that never made any economic sense, which I believe the government themselves have proven since, by allowing house prices in Ireland to reduce by twice that of the rest of the world, and, in the last ten years, they have increased by twice that of the rest of the world during the financial crisis, and I believe that the housing crisis is going to get worse before it gets better. After being involved in supplying the building industry for most of my lifetime, I think that the cost of building houses in the future is only going to go one way, and that's upwards, and no government is going to change that.

I have been very impressed by the work of the citizens' assemblies over the past number of years, and I feel that they might well be appropriate to consider some of the issues that may arise in the years ahead, for example, we have one of the lowest housing densities in western Europe. Could we manage another 2 million inhabitants? With climate change already happening, how could we deal with an increase in water levels of one metre, particularly if it were to bring a corresponding increase in the strength of tidal waves? As the average life expectancy has increased by more than two years per decade over the last one hundred years, does the pension age need to be reviewed every decade? Do the recent advances in IT, and AI specifically, mean that the four-day working week should be looked at sooner rather than later?

Where Are We Now?

While there have been thousands of articles written and millions of words spoken, in simple man's terms, what happened was that after we bought the CFDs in Anglo Irish Bank, the bank invested €2.34 billion of their own money in their own bank shares in my children's names, which the Financial Regulator, the Central Bank, and the Department of Finance were fully aware of. Nobody ever mentioned it to my children, in whose names the money was invested. When the investment went wrong, they put the full blame on me, and took all of our businesses, putting new boards in place, and making it a condition that the board could not sue Anglo Irish Bank, which was now owned by the Irish government.

At that time, the Quinn executives and John McCartin were very critical of the government and its agencies, but in less than three years, the investors realised what they had been hoodwinked into, and wanted out. This suddenly could become a major problem; if I was in collaboration with a new owner, we would have the financial resources to fight the legality of the takeover. That had to be stopped at all costs. At the time, John McCartin had one foot in the Fine Gael camp, and the other in the Quinn camp; by August, the executives had heads of agreement on their desk (which I have a copy of) agreeing to sell between 85 and 90 per cent of the manufacturing business to third parties. It also outlined how they would receive huge salaries, as well as bonuses of between €5 and €9 million, depending on the price achieved for assets sold, and a potential €46.2 million after five years if all targets were met. By year end, there was a 141-page legal document prepared between them and the bondholders, which stated that the Quinns could never own any part of the business again. Since then, the executives have been able to do what they like, and despite the fact that the company has borne huge losses, and tens of millions of euros of reported fraud, nobody appears to care and it is still unclear who is picking up the tab for these losses.

To this day, Liam McCaffrey, Kevin Lunney and Dara O'Reilly are still running 15 per cent of the Quinn Group.

The close relationship between Fine Gael and Mannok continues, as Michael Noonan's right-hand man, John Moran, has recently been appointed to the Mannok board.

Regrettably, David Mackey, Seán FitzPatrick, and Brian Lenihan are since deceased. Brian Cowen has retired from politics. Matthew Elderfield and Jonathon McMahon have moved back to the UK. Mike Aynsley and Richard Woodhouse have also left Ireland. Alan Dukes still pops his head up from time to time.

The future of many of Robert Dix's 44 properties seems uncertain, considering what is happening in Ukraine and Russia.

Huge payments have been made needlessly to the Insurance Compensation Fund, while only a fraction of the income that was promised from asset sales has materialised.

Some of the businesses are still run to a high standard and are performing well, but many of them have been destroyed and are currently closed down or loss-making.

PwC has settled their action in relation to the Quinn Insurance guarantees. There doesn't appear to have been any similar payment or even sanction against A&L Goodbody, who signed off on the guarantees. Nor have we seen the sanctions that were taken against Liam McCaffrey and Kevin Lunney for giving the guarantees.

It appears that even after taking all of the assets, including the windfarms and Quinn Insurance, worth billions of euros, the taxpayer will have to meet the shortfall caused by the destruction of the companies.

It all begs the question that, considering after the administration of Quinn Insurance I was a witness on behalf of the ODCE against Anglo Irish Bank, and I was a witness for the Central Bank in their investigation into Quinn executives, and at no stage during those investigations was I ever accused of being involved in any wrong-doing, so I do wonder why I, and I alone, have been blamed for everything over the last fifteen years, while it is as plain as the nose on my face that those who have been found guilty have been protected by the state, and have not been investigated regarding reported fraud. It has always been the case that those who hold the keys control the narrative, and everyone made sure that I held no keys.

I believe that the way the whole fiasco has been managed has cost the Irish taxpayer more than €5 billion, and if the Public Accounts Committee felt this warranted an investigation, I would be happy to assist in any way I could.

Appendix

P.J. FLANAGAN & CO.

INCORPORATING MAGUIRE & HERBERT

SOLICITORS

A MEMBER OF THE HOME CHARTER SCHEME

DX 3551 NR

ENNISKILLEN

date:

your ref:

STRICTLY PRIVATE AND CONFIDENTIAL

SENT BY EMAIL –

27 April 2023   CMCG/0005500125/MH

Mr Sean Quinn

Dear Sean

Re: Your case

We refer to our recent discussions and now provide you with an update in terms of where some of your key matters are at.   In respect of the information provided by you and our ongoing investigations it does appear to us that there exists a *prima facie* argument that the reacquisition of the Quinn Group from the Receivers was subject to potential criminal fraud and corporate wrong doing.   We are still following other lines of enquiry but can advise you that we wrote to the Garda Siochanna on 27 occasions, our Mr Christopher McGettigan met with the Garda Superintendent for Cavan on the 13 January 2022 and there were two subsequent meetings with Garda at Ballyconnell Garda Station.

We provided supporting evidence and as you are aware multiple documents together with an extensive list of witnesses who could assist to the Garda.   The Garda in our view were remiss in their investigation glossing over the information provided, not making contact with any of the relevant witnesses provided to them by us and in our view their investigation fell way below the standard we would have expected from them.   We, in fact, were astonished by their inadequate and deficient approach to investigating your complaints given the multitude of evidence available to them.   Your complaint was also backed by a significant community organisation being the Cavan Fermanagh Leitrim Community Group.

As a result we found ourselves in a position where the matter needed to be referred to the Garda Commissioner who in turn referred the matter back to the Garda Superintendent for Cavan.   They now also seem to have washed their hands of the matter altogether.

CHRISTOPHER McGETTIGAN B.A. (HONS)
TONY McGETTIGAN LL.B.

MICHELLE McVEIGH LL.B.
GRAINNE MULLIGAN LL.B.

We as you know reported your complaints to the Office of the Director of Corporate Enforcement (ODCE), now the Corporate Enforcement Authority (CEA). The complaints to the ODCE were sent on the 18 February 2022 and at this stage their lack of response again is somewhat alarming. Despite requests for updates from us on your behalf they are unwilling to provide us with any relevant information with regards to any investigation being undertaken by them although you can take some comfort from the fact that they have not queried or challenged the evidence produced by us to them. We are however concerned that they have not spoken to any of the significant number of witnesses put forward by us to them.

We feel that our efforts on your behalf are not being treated with the seriousness that they deserve and warrant and believe there may be political influences blocking any detailed or credible investigations but nonetheless we shall keep pressing your matter forward as in our view and given the information available to us that there has been very serious criminality and corporate fraud committed at a level we believe never seen before in Ireland. The evidence in our experience is overwhelming. We shall keep pressing the relevant authorities in all jurisdictions until such times as we receive a satisfactory response on your behalf.

Finally we have also, on a number of occasions, raised the issue with you that a number of individuals and organisations have attempted to pervert the course of justice at your expense and our investigations have confirmed to us that this is the case. There is one particular matter that is still being investigated in respect of perverting the course of justice by a third party which is subject to an ongoing investigation by the Garda which we will chase up on your behalf as this investigation has been going on for almost 12 months and as far as we are aware at the time of writing this letter the perpetrator of the actions has not yet been interviewed by the Garda.

If you have any further queries in the meantime please contact us and we shall of course endeavour to keep you advised as and when matters develop.

Yours faithfully,

P.J. Flanagan & Co